MARTIN LINDSTROM

CLICKS, BRICKS & BRANDS

KOGAN PAGE

First published in Australia in 2001
By Hardie Grant Books
12 Claremont Street
South Yarra Victoria Australia 3141
www.hardiegrant.com.au

First published in Great Britain in 2001 by Kogan Page Limited

Kogan Page Limited
120 Pentonville Road
London N1 9JN
UK
www.kogan-page.co.uk

Kogan Page (US) Limited
163 Central Ave, Suite 2
Dover NH 03820
USA
www.koganpage.com

British Library Cataloguing in Publication Data
A CIP record for this book is available from the British Library.

ISBN 0 7494 3490 2

Cover Design, Text Design, DualBook™ website design and construction by Squib
Typesetting by J & M Typesetting, Australia
Printed and bound by Griffin Press, Adelaide, Australia

DualBook is a Trademark™ of MartinLindstrom.com
1-to-1 is a Trademark™ of the Peppers and Rogers group.

Translation Rights
For information on permission to translate all or parts of *Clicks, Bricks & Brands*, contact Kogan Page Limited

International content syndication
MartinLindstrom.com produces a weekly article about interactive Brand Building for syndication purposes. For permission to syndicate these articles apply inwriting to brand@lindstrom.com

Any further information about Martin Lindstrom, *Clicks, Bricks & Brands* or *Br　ıd Building on the Internet* can be found at MartinLindstrom.com

For Dorit, Tore & Allan

Acknowledgements

Writing this book was both a project and a realisation. It required not only inspiration, but also a systematic collection and structuring of knowledge captured from all over the world – a project that in many ways managed to put the Internet into a totally new perspective for me.

A small group provided immense support by managing demanding schedules to allow me to stay reasonably productive. First of all, a warm thanks to my editor-in-chief, Clare Watson, who at this stage is probably capable of writing the second edition of this book without my involvement. Clare you don't know how thankful I have been for your help. Also a warm thanks to editor Lynne Segal who gave birth to all the case studies in the book, and managing editor Amanda Finnis, of Hardie Grant who, in the end, managed to tie everything nicely together and finally make a vision become reality.

Don Peppers and Martha Rogers have in the past year been a big source of inspiration for me – and having them contribute to *Clicks, Bricks & Brands* has not only been an honour for me but has also added something very special to this book. Thanks for your vision.

DualBook.com and MartinLindstrom.com didn't create themselves. Behind the concepts is Squib, a small and practically unknown digital agency in Melbourne, who are the brains behind the execution of this outstanding concept. Thanks to the whole team and in particular the founders Heath Rudduck and Dean Joel.

I also owe a special thanks to Lynne Ankrah from Nokia in London, David Fox from Astrology.com in San Francisco, Terry Hunt from EHSrealtime in London, Bernadette & Glenn Williams, Melbourne and Tiffany & Frank Foster in Sydney, who in all sorts of ways have contributed to this project.

Last but not least, thanks to Tim Pethick, a dear friend of mine who patiently over the last year has listened to a lot of talk about *Clicks, Bricks & Brands* and still managed to smile.

Martin Lindstrom
Sydney, Australia, February 2001

The effectiveness of the DualBook™ concept has required more than a dual effort.

The main aim in the development of the online component of DualBook™ has always been to provide a compelling relationship between printed book and website. It has required detailed research and planning by key members of the digital agency Squib in partnership with Martin Lindstrom and Hardie Grant Publishing.

Those members of the Squib team involved with the DualBook™ project have been uncompromising in developing an interface that is useful, intuitive and importantly adds strength to the DualBook™ brand. Through the duration of the project, Squib's focus has been to develop a clear understanding of how people's online and offline encounters with DualBook™ could be tied together to create a truly valuable experience.

Squib is a new form of digital agency focused on the development of appropriate design, usability and technology to help add value to organizations' brands and achieve their business objectives. The relationship between online and offline marketing is a key consideration in every project undertaken by Squib.

squib™

www.squib.com.au
info@squib.com.au

Contents

WWW: What, Who and Why

Clicks-&-mortar: what does it mean?

The term "clicks-&-mortar" was coined by Charles Schwab in 1999 to describe the partnership between an Internet-based business and an offline business. In 1996 Charles Schwab was operating eschwab.com, later renamed schwab.com, a website which integrated the company's off- and online enterprises. While Schwab was forging a new online/offline business model, drugstore.com surfaced in February 1999 as the world's first partnership between an independent offline and an independent online entity. This pioneering manifestation of the clicks-&-mortar approach inspired Schwab's invention of the term.

In a clicks-&-mortar business, the on- and offline partners bring their mutually exclusive assets to each other, creating a harmonious business union. "Clicks" represents the online world: dotcom companies and e-tailers characterized by innovation, fast turnover, the potential for developing 1to1 marketing (see Chapters 12 and 14), and a capacity for eliminating the high infrastructural and personnel costs traditionally borne by bricks-&-mortar business. "Mortar" represents the offline world: old-world companies characterized by consumer brand recognition, customer loyalty, high running costs (compared with online running costs) and established distribution networks, infrastructure (like stores and distribution centres) and customer-handling processes. Each partner brings strengths and weaknesses to the marriage. The idea behind the clicks-&-mortar partnership is that it has the capacity to shortcut the weaknesses of each partner while promoting their combined strengths.

So, who's this book for?

My aim with this book is to demystify the clicks-&-mortar concept. The term is one which used with facility but which is often misunderstood, or hardly understood at all. I want to clarify the term, make clicks-&-mortar a tangible reality for you rather than a nebulous term that you think you know describes a growing business trend. I want the book to offer a practical tool kit to help retailers and e-tailers build clicks-&-mortar strategies.

Read this book as vision, fact and guide. It's a book for all of you who are interested in discovering the value of clicks-&-mortar enterprises: e-tailers, large and small retailers, marketers and advertisers, journalists, economists, e-commerce players, information technologists, Internet professionals, students of these disciplines and everyone interested in the future of consumerism.

For e-tailers, the book has an instructive purpose. I hope that by decoding this term I make the vision of a clicks-&-mortar future a reality for you. I want to show you how to analyze your brand and how to evaluate the strategic worth of a clicks-&-mortar arrangement to it; how to ascertain potential partners' compatibility with you; how to identify the right "mortar" to establish a deal with; and how to achieve execution.

Retailers, I hope to offer you the same experience, whether you're the CEO of a multinational chain or running a small to medium enterprise; whether you're in the process of forming a clicks-&-mortar alliance, think you need to do so or think you have no intention of embarking upon such a venture. In short, I want to help you find a path that arrives at the best clicks-&-mortar destination for your brand.

To marketers and all of you in the advertising industry, I hope that the book says this: clicks-&-mortars are providing a new branding environment. I want to familiarize you with this emerging business arena and help you discover how to build brands within the clicks-&-mortar framework.

For journalists, professionals and students in economics, e-commerce, information technology and the Internet, and all who want an understanding of where business and consumers are heading, I hope this book will increase your fluency in the language of clicks-&-mortar enterprise, will introduce you to clicks-&-mortar operational strategies; and will enable you to meet comfortably with clicks-&-mortars, as you will do, more and more, over the coming years.

What's this book about?

Clicks-&-mortar businesses are the inevitable result of the consumers' desire, on the one hand, for online convenience, range of selection, global access and rapidity of response and, on the other, of their inalienable and self-defining need for human interaction and sensory stimulation.

By now, bricks-&-mortar retailers need alliances with online competitors. The former can't compete with the latter on product price and breadth of selection, two crucial drivers in consumer choice. The online world also offers retailers a new brand polish that comes of association with innovation and communications efficiency. In a clicks-&-mortar relationship, retailers also gain wider customer bases and broader functionalities, like the capacity for cross- and upselling. Equally, e-tailers gain infrastructure, established distribution channels and consumer-handling experience from old-world partners. More crucially, clicks companies are confined to visual and aural communication; they can't compete with their bricks-&-mortar counterparts' command of the multisensory environment.

Sensory satisfaction and familiarity are fundamental consumer drivers.

Both are related and both contribute to the cultivation of the most precious of business assets: trust. It's the trust factor that young online e-tailers need to acquire from mature, real-world retailers. Trust is pivotal to business success and brand-building. In fact, trust = brand. Thus, branding is inextricably related to this book's clicks-&-mortar subject. You'll find branding discussed parallel with every aspect of clicks-&-mortar development.

The book's title, *Clicks, Bricks & Brands* should express the centrality of branding to clicks-&-mortar prosperity. My expertise is in brand-building and my marketing experience straddles both offline and online brands. I believe that clicks-&-mortars are the future of consumer life and that effective branding is what will help emerging businesses survive. My convictions are the book's *raison d'être*: it makes no sense for many e-tailers to remain exclusively online, as much as it's vital that retailers meet the Net threat by colluding with it. According to Forrester Research, 83% of American retailers find that by offering consumers multiple purchasing channels they increase overall sales: that retail customers who move to the Net then spend 22% more in retail stores on top of their online purchases.

DualBook.com: clicks-&-mortar in action

Clicks, Bricks & Brands lives as a DualBook™, between the covers of this volume and online at DualBook.com. It's a pioneering concept, the first DualBook™ in the world, and it allows you to combine your offline and online reading as a clicks-&-mortar experience. *Clicks, Bricks & Brands* has no final page: it lives online to accommodate its rapidly evolving subject. Every chapter in this volume is open-ended, an invitation to go online and experience the book's interactive dimension. Use the tangible book as

Visit the "Activate your Membership" area of DualBook.com to begin your free four month membership.

an entrée to the subject, then keep your involvement with it alive and relevant by visiting DualBook.com for all the updates every chapter promises. The Web address is printed at the bottom of each page. Of course, you can enjoy this book conventionally, without entering the book's interactive dimension. But because this DualBook™ is an important milestone in clicks-&-mortar development, your purchase of *Clicks, Bricks & Brands* entitles you to four free months of access to DualBook.com.

Clicks, Bricks & Brands is designed to perform the very function it aims to explain. It should stand as a brand itself, while being an artefact of online and offline synergy. You are the junction in this enterprise. You are the consumer that it's serving. This is the principle of *Clicks, Bricks & Brands*, and its message: marry your online and offline worlds and seamlessly deliver the service your customer expects from the marriage broker, the brand.

A note on *Clicks, Bricks & Brands*

Put the book into action

Most chapters in this book end, not only with a handy summary, but with a practical guide to enacting the principles explained in each chapter. These Action Points are intended to work cumulatively. If you work through each chapter and follow the Action Points as you arrive at them, the book should help you a) establish an understanding of your brand's clicks-&-mortar future and b) compose an initial clicks-&-mortar operating strategy.

By following the steps described in the Action Points you'll prepare a strategy that's appropriate for your brand as well as developing the channel strategy, goals identification, alternative revenue model creation, trust development and maintenance which all form the operating strategy. Encompassing the strategy is the duty of partner identification and, following this, the joint responsibility of developing synergy in all operating areas.

- The Action Points at the end of Chapters 2-5 guide you through the development of a clicks-&-mortar operational strategy to suit your brand.
- The Action Points at the end of Chapter 6 guide you through partner identification and the development of operating synergies.
- The Action Points at the end of Chapter 7 help you assess your brand's m-commerce options and potenial.
- The Action Points at the end of Chapter 8 assist you in refining your customer's online experience.
- Chapter 12's Action Points are designed to help you assess your brand's application to the Webster market and Chapter 13's help you explore the infomediary path as a revenue option for your brand.

Finally, the Action Points at the ends of Chapters 9 and 10 embrace the bigger picture, offering hints on online brand-building and brand global-isation initiatives.

Chapter 1

The Power Shift

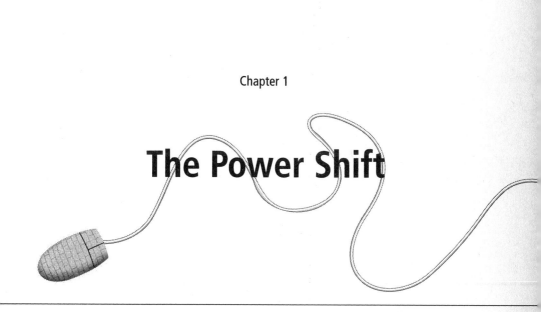

Once upon a time, the storekeeper had the power over the consumer's purchasing choices. Then, over the past century, this power was stripped from the merchant. It became prized territory and was fought over in the battle for market dominance. The trophy was wrested from the hands of the vanquished and held briefly by successive victors: the consumer, the manufacturer, the brand, the retailer. And now ...?

The consumer's assumption of power over purchasing choice parallels the rise of the self-serve supermarket. This shopping environment, in which shoppers walk freely up and down aisles, hunting and gathering according to their own and their clan's needs, preferences and desires, enabled consumers to recover the power over their own commodity choices, a power which, until then, had been held by the retailer. The generic products that filled store shelves were soon overcome by branded alternatives. Thus, brands began driving consumer choice. It was so until the Internet recovered the middleman's power. Now e-tailers and retailers are facing off. The power of directing consumer choice is swinging back to the bricks-&-mortar retailer whose command of consumer trust and dominion over the consumer's predilection for sensory experience is harnessing consumer preference. E-tailers will need to co-opt these assets if online entrepreneurship is to survive. The power shift is making the rise of clicks-&-mortars inevitable.

Model 1.1: *Control over consumer choices*

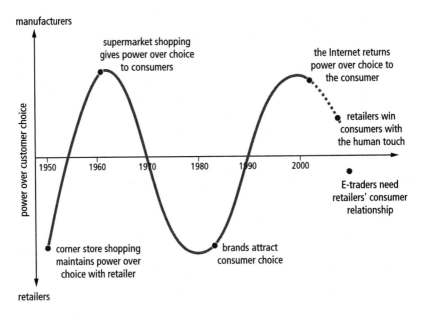

The Shopping Evolution

Over the past half-century consumer habits and procurements have been modelled by environmental engineers. Cultural and physical environments have manipulated and been manipulated by our evolving consumerism.

The Fifties and the Generic Shopping List

It's difficult for today's child to imagine that, when their grandparents were children, there were no supermarkets to dash into. Daily visits to the corner store were the order of the day. And this frequent household chore was a matter of personal contact between the customer and the store keeper. You stood in front of the counter while the grocer presided over his domain behind the till. He took your order and fetched every item for you. Your shopping list would have been a generic one: sugar, milk, flour, and so on. Over time, generic descriptions gave way to brand-oriented products. But the power of choice remained with the grocer. It was he who collected your comestibles from his shelves and, over time, he came to know your purchase patterns as well as you knew them yourself.

Model 1.2

The Sixties: the Birth of Choice

But, in the early sixties, the grocer's dominion began disappearing. The advent of the supermarket changed the world of shopping and the retailer's power over consumer choices shifted to the consumers themselves. The new stores really were "super", surpassing all others and making their intention transparent by adopting the Latin prefix *super*, meaning "above".

Now shopping was the domain of individual choice. It was no longer up to the grocer to decide what you did and didn't want. The interesting thing was that now, for the first time ever, the customer was exposed to the possibility of developing relationships with FMCG (fast-moving consumer goods) brands.

Also, "retail price maintenance" systems emerged. In the old days, the retailer decided product prices and routinely charged more or less than the manufacturer's recommended retail price to attract customers. This risked compromising the consumer's perception of a brand and, thus, risked diluting the brand's value. By adhering a fixed price to a branded package the retailer was pushed totally out of the game and manufacturers controlled prices. The practice guaranteed profit margins, forced retailers into obeisance and removed the prime motivator (apart from geographic location) in the consumer's choice of one retailer over another. Price and the selection in all stores were now the same. Consumer loyalty to particular retailers was transformed into brand loyalty. Now it was up to brands to make and keep promises — promises, not only of price, but of consistent quality and reliability. In the process, brands built platforms on which to establish consumer trust.

Model 1.3

So, by the sixties, a shift in the power over consumer purchasing choices had occurred, from the grocer to the brand. And this was reflected in a dramatic increase in new brand launches. In 1965 there were 400% more brands introduced than in 1960.

The Eighties: Branding Power

Over the past fifty years, the power of brands, the weight of reputation they carry, has grown. We now take the power of branding for granted. But it was Procter & Gamble that paved the way for branding and fashioned this consumer experience. Product identities are now part of our literacy and consumer items can exist as icons and metaphors for their own function.

CASE STUDY Procter & Gamble

We Make Every Day Better… In Every Way We Can: Procter & Gamble's Domination of the Household Product Market

Tide, Tampax and Oil of Olay. Jif, Pampers, Crest and Cascade. From toilet paper to peanut butter, from household cleaning aids to medical products, there are over 300 Procter & Gamble brands sold to nearly five billion consumers in 140 countries. Those statistics make P&G products an intimate part of everyone's world.

Two brothers-in-law, William Proctor and James Gamble, started their candle- and soap-making business in 1837. The business immediately bore the trademarks of innovation and enterprise when they branded their candle boxes with a moon-and-stars moniker to distinguish them from their competitors.

P&G was one of the first US companies to build research laboratories and invest in product development. So, when the onset of electricity rendered candles obsolete, nothing was wasted. Years of developing pulp technologies for soap and candles paved the way for P&G's expansion into paper products. But most importantly, it was P&G's in-depth understanding of consumer needs, the result of pioneering market research methods, which fuelled the company's successful research and development programs.

P&G first discovered the power of brand advertising in 1886 when it spent $11,000 promoting the purity and long-lasting properties of Ivory Soap. Within a decade P&G became advertising innovators, regularly placing product advertisements in national newspapers and magazines.

By the early 1930s, P&G had evolved a brand-management system to maintain its brands' position in the market. A specialised marketing team with its own separate marketing strategy was appointed to manage each brand. P&G soaps sponsored the first radio serials, and as these serials gained loyal followings, so their listeners extended their loyalty to the brand that sponsored them. The programs subsequently became known as "soap operas". This consumer loyalty was recognised and P&G continues this successful marketing strategy this day. P&G now produces as well as sponsors the popular television soap operas *Guiding Light* and *As the World Turns*.

P&G maintains that the interests of the company and the individual are inseparable. So, the company uses sophisticated research techniques to ensure it understands the consumer's needs. John Pepper, the ninth chairman of the board, describes P&G as "first and foremost a research and development company". But it's P&G's understanding of the complex relationship between brand identity and consumer spending that keeps it in the lead.

In the late eighties, the power over consumer choice shifted again. Over two decades, the retail world had taken steady doses of branding medicine and learnt how to create brands itself. The local supermarket became part of a chain, affiliated with hundreds and, in some cases, thousands of other supermarkets nationally and internationally. Brands like Marks & Spencer, Sainsbury's and Toys "R" Us have become brands themselves.

The Nineties: Retailer Power

Suddenly retailers realised that they themselves often accounted for a sizeable proportion of manufacturers' business. Conversely manufacturers discovered they could be threatened by this relationship. Gradually they learnt to give in to whatever demands the retailer made. In the eighties LEGO, for example, manufactured private label products which could only be purchased in certain branded toy stores like Toys "R" Us. Coca-Cola developed special six-pack promotions for private label use. Kodak produced promotional packages targeting individual chains. Such manoeuvres forced brands to create points of differentiation that were based on the client-store needs. This turned the tables on the consumer's prime loyalty, to the brand, and resurrected consumer loyalty towards the retailer.

Model 1.4

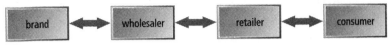

So strong had retail chains become that, in the nineties, they inspired debates among marketers trying to define the future role of brands. Were brands dead, buried by the retail giants? Or were they simply living quiet lives that needed reviving and redefining?

In the meantime, chains like Sainsbury's and Marks & Spencer established an even stronger market position by introducing their own private labels: sub-brands to be sold at a low price and marketed under the umbrella of the retailer's name. For those who understood this concept, who perceived the basics of brand building, this development opened up a goldmine.

In just five years retail brands gained in strength and market dominance, becoming so successful that even the strongest FMCG brands in the world had trouble surviving. One of the victims was Coca-Cola, arguably the world's biggest and most heavily hyped brand. Over a three-year period it lost 60% of its sales in Sainsbury's because of the competition posed by Sainsbury's own cola product. Häagen-Dazs and Ben & Jerry's soon also fell victim to such private-label dominance. Retailer brands are fully controlled by their owners and creators, the retailers, who can monitor consumer response to the products and adjust them constantly to ensure brand popularity and, ultimately, loyalty. Most retailers have realised that they need to offer own-label products, generic products and branded equivalents to be successful. It's the brands that attract customers; generic products retain customers and offer confirmation that a store is cheap or good value; and private label products act as negotiation tools to push the branded products' prices down.

Own-label branding put the retailer in charge of consumer product choice once again, recalling pre-supermarket shopping conditions when the grocer had the power over the consumer's purchasing decisions. Loyalty wasn't necessarily connected to FMCG brands but to the stores' own private labels. Ironically, experience has revealed that retailer earnings for private label brands are limited. *The McKinsey Quarterly* Current Research bulletin titled "How profitable are own brand products?" states that "…DOB [distributor own brand] products are often allocated an excessive amount of space in relation to brand leaders, which means they generate lower ratios of profit per cubic metre…than brand leader counterparts."

Retailer Branding Overtakes Product Branding

But the resurgence of retailer power over consumer choice didn't stop at private-label brand-building. During the nineties, stores like Toys "R" Us spread all over the world. The brand suddenly became the small player in the big competition for consumer attention. Consumer loyalty followed the options it was offered and shifted from individual brands to retail identities. These retailers now offered warrantees, price reductions, handy locations and, often, private-label brands. Customer attention was captured, rather than captivated, by the sheer numbers of brand stores that they could identify across the world, and by the benefits derived from the enormous negotiation power these numerous stores now wielded.

The result for the marketer was a decade in which acquiring advertising space in supermarkets and large stores was like winning a lottery. Chains, like Tesco in the UK, introduced POS (point of sale) guidelines which allowed only certain brands, using Tesco-approved colours and design, to occupy specific floor areas. That the power over consumer product choice had shifted away from brands and back to retailers was reflected in the costs of store floor and shelf space. Every metre of floor and shelf space was calculated and valued and the store's real estate defined optimal product positions which brands then competed and paid for.

Shopping DNA: Customer Behaviour Mapped

The nineties was the decade in which the DNA, figuratively speaking, governing consumer behaviour in shopping malls and stores was mapped. As a result, brands no longer had simply to offer discounts to be represented in stores. They had to pay an extra fee to guarantee preferred shelf position. If a brand wanted to benefit from a particular position on the shelf, it paid a premium for the privilege.

To keep a handle on this mini real estate, retailers and brand owners established complex planograms to assist in optimising the use of every centimetre of space in the store and to help the parties negotiate floor space value.

As more floor space became, ostensibly, more optimal, value difference slowly disappeared. With every position in the store being apparently of premium benefit and value to the brand that would occupy it, the store's negotiation power waned. What was the solution to this development? What could retailers do to harness custom now that the floor space differential had been exhausted?

Retailers conceived and introduced loyalty programs.

Every Little Helps: The Tesco Community of Grocery Shoppers

With over 600 stores selling 60,000 product lines, Tesco is one of the largest food retailers in England. The company injects much energy into convincing shoppers that it is unwaveringly committed to providing value for money and that it understands that "every little helps": that Tesco appreciates that every penny the customer saves helps the household budget. Tesco customers can expect cheaper prices, better service and, importantly, Tesco's embracing commitment to the local community.

Tesco's own-brand products form an integral part of the value-for-money strategy and they account for 40% of Tesco's UK sales. Maurice Pratt, managing director of Tesco Ireland says, "Own-brands are clearly winning a place on our customers' shopping lists; if they did not offer the value, price and quality sought — they would not."

In the 1990s Tesco began an active program of acquisition, buying supermarket chains in Central Europe, Ireland and Thailand. With each new expansion, Tesco reiterates its promise, offering the "valued customer" the greatest range of goods, value-for-money and corporate dedication to contributing to the well-being of the local community. This philosophy of community involvement underpins Tesco's strategy of acting locally in the interests of its global identity. Every Tesco store becomes a vibrant part of the community it moves into, employing people from the neighbourhood and establishing firm relationships with local suppliers.

With an emphasis on promoting the customer's relationship with the store, Tesco operates the "Clubcard" program, a reward-earning program available to all customers. For every pound a customer spends at any Tesco store or affiliate, they earn a reward point. These points can be redeemed against the weekly shopping bill or saved up and used on a variety of Clubcard deals ranging from discounted travel to a full tank of petrol. The ten-million-member-strong Clubcard program, obviously, encourages and rewards customer loyalty.

Tesco's own-brand product lines represent the point at which the chain's promises (of wide selection and value-for-money) and philosophies (which emphasise community involvement and responsibility) converge. Customers educated in these promises and philosophies are inclined to bestow their loyalty upon Tesco, the trusted brand, and its products. And this loyalty is measured in Clubcard program membership. Within the first three years of operating in Ireland, the program acquired 800,000 new Clubcard members, just part of Tesco's loyal following of shoppers who know that Every Little Helps.

Loyalty Programs and Data Exploitation

Loyalty programs harnessed the consumer's loyalty to the retailer, thereby protecting that hard-won choice driver from the retailer's biggest enemy, the brand.

From 1988 to 1998, 100,000 loyalty programs were established around the world. Airlines led the battle charge making it possible to buy all sorts of things for points earnt through loyalty. The bricks-&-mortar chains were quick to follow the trend. Today Sainsbury's serves more than fifteen million customers a week.

Australia's largest retail corporation, Coles Myer, claims twenty-five cents in every dollar spent by Australian consumers. More than ten different store concepts huddle under the Coles Myer umbrella and share in the FlyBuys™ loyalty concept. Every time you bank at the National, rent a car from Budget, or book a vacation through Traveland you earn points. Other FlyBuys participants include Elders Real Estate, Katies clothes and Sports Direct. Computer related items from Harris Technology, alcohol from Liquorland and Vintage Cellars, and car accessories from MyCar. The list goes on. There are up-market and budget department stores that participate, and every time you pay your Pulse gas and electricity bill you will earn a few more FlyBuys. The program has 2.1 million members — 15% of Australia's population.

By the end of the nineties retailers realised they had accumulated a goldmine of behavioural data. But only a minority of them were able to influence sales by extricating useful statistics from this overwhelming amount of data.

Data mining and analysis is a complex and costly process. For this reason, retailers have been reluctant to capitalise on the consumer information their loyalty programs have captured for them. One of the many ironies in retailing history is that this information, so material to retail recovering its power over consumer choice, was sold by retailers to research companies like AC Nielsen. Among the research companies' clients are the manufacturers who, armed with the retailer-derived information, are equipped to thwart the retailer's recovery of the power over consumer choice. But the retailers that did manage to harvest relevant information from their customer profiles discovered a key tool in recovering their role in directing consumer decisions. The data not only informed retailers of consumer behaviour in the store; it also allowed retailers to predict consumer behaviour. It's this crucial predictive ability that can help retailers differentiate their offline selection from their online competitors' offerings in cyberspace.

Enter the Internet

While retailer attention was focussed on keeping the enemy, the brand, at bay, by making floor plans, planning chain expansions and orchestrating loyalty programs, the Internet crept up on the adversaries' flanks. A power shift was again about to occur, this time moving the power over consumer choice away from both brands and retailers to e-tailers.

With the advent of the Internet, manufacturers saw the possibility of bypassing the stores, traditionally their link to the consumer, and communicating with customers directly. By using the consumer data acquired from research companies, the data that the retailers' own loyalty programs had accumulated, manufacturers could interact directly and relevantly with consumers via the Internet, promoting brands through direct-marketing campaigns. Thus, the manufacturer regained some control over the consumer's choice. The Net enabled brands to direct customers into co-operating stores and to control consumer flow in a low-profile fashion: broadcast promotion was superfluous now that direct communication with consumers was possible. Paper-based direct-marketing campaigns had been outrageously expensive, especially for cheaper FMCG brands like Pepsi and M&M's. The Internet made the direct-marketing exercise affordable by offering manufacturers the means of building an e-marketing dialogue between brands and consumers.

Model 1.5

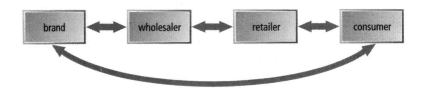

The Internet bridge thwarted the retailers' ability to intercept consumers as they had been able to do, for example, with POS materials. But also, because the dialogue happened on a one-to-one basis, the Internet prevented competitors from obtaining the full picture of what went on between competition brands and their consumers. Even more significantly, the manufacturer could now act as retailer: the consumer could visit the manufacturer's online stores rather than patronise the real life store. The

Internet turned the battle for power over consumer choice upside down one more time, creating a new and unexpected retailer enemy. The surprise of the attack was reflected in responses such as this: "If any supplier opens up a direct Internet sales link with the consumer we will stop selling their products." (Target Corporation, 1999)

Internet shopping and marketing offered what retail had failed to deliver: no queues, no geographic barriers, low prices and unlimited selection. A consumer dream world had appeared. A survey conducted by AC Nielsen in 2000 posits that 15% to 20% of consumers say they prefer to shop online than in real-world stores.

E-tailing Drags Territory from Bricks-&-Mortars

Apart from offering manufacturers the means of recovering direct communication with consumers, the Internet established a new business arena. Upcoming Internet brands reconfigured the landscape of consumerism and their sudden births and rapid growth captivated the market's attention. Amazon.com, for example, in just eighteen months caused the United States' largest bookstore, Barnes & Noble, to realise that their well-established company with its comfortable market lead suddenly had a rival which could not be ignored.

Even though they all saw the threat, few retailers challenged it or adopted the Internet as a tool. General opinion held that the Amazon.com thing was singular and not likely to be repeated in any other product category. But, of course, general opinion was mistaken.

By the end of the nineties the consumer's focus had turned away from retail stores, now labelled as "bricks-&-mortars", in favour of whatever the e-tailer could offer. Internet hype primed the consumer with high expectations of e-tailer service and, as Christmas 1999 approached, an educated consumer was demanding that e-tailers keep their promises.

E-tailer Testing Season

The online hype which had attended dotcom e-tailing was, by Christmas 1999, replaced by educated consumerism. In the United States, the Internet had penetrated life to such an extent that dotcom addresses were cited as the first point of contact in 80% of brand communications and the consumer had started to trust the process of using a credit card online. In short, consumers were ready to make the deliberate choice of buying from e-tailers rather than retailers.

But that Christmas season turned out to be many e-tailers' last. More than 20% of e-tailers failed their first test, a test to prove to consumers that using the Net's services instead of bricks-&-mortars' is worthwhile. Because, in spite of the Net's claim to advantages like "no waiting in lines", "the biggest selection in the world", "friendly service" and so on, its service proved to be less than satisfactory.

In many cases, the promises of no-wait service were confounded by downloading time (more than forty seconds, in some cases, just to get into the homepage), delivery problems on popular products, and half-hour waits on the phone to get assistance with user problems. In fact, a test by USA Snapshots in January 1999 showed that not one of the world's top-ten most visited e-tailer brands was able to deliver as promised. According to BizRate.com, only 74% of deliveries were made on time. Of a total of 34 million online orders, 8.8 million were late. Eighty per cent of customers using home connections waited an average of twenty-one seconds for sites to load, and sites were accessible only 90% of the time.

In general, the e-tailers squandered their opportunity to persuade consumers away from bricks-&-mortar services. Online shopping can't achieve preferred-choice status while basic services — like there being someone on hand to answer queries, reliable supply and delivery, product demonstrations, and so on — which bricks-&-mortars handle daily, aren't available. It doesn't take new and hard-won Net customers long to tire of deficient service. Just a couple of bad experiences will steer them back to the conclusion that traditional shopping is the easiest. As it was, Ernst & Young statistics for the 1999 Christmas season reveal that US online buyers spent only 26% of their holiday spending (averaging $1,080 per capita) online, while they devoted 67% of their total holiday expenditure to instore purchases. The remaining 7% they spent on catalogue products.

Good brand building is about anticipating and exceeding consumer expectations.

Frustrating consumer expectation not only leads to a backlash on e-tailing generally, but annihilates new brands as well. Without established brand strength and consumer recognition, and if the consumer rejects the online environment, infant e-tailing businesses don't have the chance to garner custom. Consumer trust depends upon their expectations being matched by reality.

Most e-tailers run on venture capitalist (VC) or initial public offering (IPO) money. They're born quickly and sent forth into the world before their backyards are established. It's possible that the many users who experienced the worst of e-tailing during the 1999 Christmas season won't give online brands another chance. As it was, BizRate.com statistics show a fall in initial online purchases from 1998 to 1999, while first-time purchases from offline merchants rose over the same period.

Model 1.6: *Initial purchase variations*

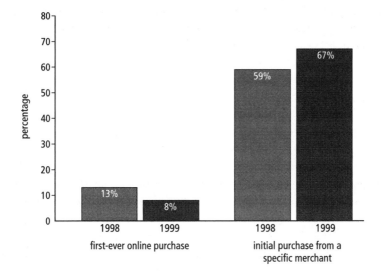

And this leads me to the truism that good brand-building isn't just good advertising. It's anticipating and handling consumer expectations and ensuring that what's being delivered is *better* than what the user expects.

Until now, e-tailing has been guilty of disappointing its customers by delivering service that was worse than expected. Christmas 1999 was heralded by e-tailing promises of queue-free shopping, of large product selections, cheap prices and rapid delivery. Many e-tailers weren't able to honour these promises and, by the end of the holiday season, the professional e-tailers could be distinguished from the e-amateurs.

The 2000 holiday season told a graphic tale. More than 90% of e-tailers closed down in the period up to January 2001.

Visit **DualBook.com/cbb/ch1/EtailingNow**
to learn more about how e-tailing is faring right now.

Bricks-&-Mortar Recovery

The Internet challenge to the bricks-&-mortars was an unanticipated source of competition, and one which drew some energy from the apparent perception that bricks-&-mortar retailing was antiquated when compared with e-tailing's potential for efficiency, choice and selection. But it quickly became apparent that bricks-&-mortar businesses held many of the keys to ongoing commercial success, including brand strength and distribution efficiencies.

Brand Strength

Even as I write, consumers don't yet trust the Internet. But they trust brands, especially offline brands. They know them, relate to them and identify with them. Brands have proven to be the survival kit for companies on the Internet. Yet just a few companies have managed to gain leverage from the value of their brands and taken those benefits to the Net. This is evident in the fact that established manufacturers, like Levi Strauss for example, with years of consumer loyalty and marketing experience behind them, spend about 18% less than online startups when building a website (*Red Herring* and Forrester Research, July 2000).

A key contributor to the steady dominance of offline brands is consumer trust in them.

When drugstore.com merged with offline pharmacy chain Rite Aid, businesses around the world began to realise the value of combining offline and online brands, of creating clicks-&-mortars. A study by Cheskin Research and Studio Archetype/Sapient titled "e-Commerce Trust Study" (January 1999) pointed out that more consumers were familiar with offline Rite Aid than online drugstore.com and that more consumers would trust the former than the latter. So drugstore.com had this advantage to gain by association with the real-world chain: consumer trust born of familiarity.

The fact is that only forty-two out of the world's top 500 best-known brands have been born online. The other 458 were created offline, during the decades of bricks-&-mortar marketing that predated the rise of the Internet.

Visit **DualBook.com/cbb/ch1/Top50Brands**
to see the top-50 brands update.

Distribution Efficiencies

Distribution systems will also strengthen the threat posed by offline brands to brands born online. Even though many companies have claimed that distribution is not an infrastructural priority for online brands, one of the largest investments Amazon.com made in 1999 was in establishing distribution centres to manage increasing consumer demand for its books.

Of course, many factors influence the e-tailer's distribution considerations: the product's retail price, the physical requirements of the product to be shipped and the delivery speed required for the product category. For e-tailers, the price point is a crucial determinant in distribution and business-viability decisions. *The McKinsey Quarterly*'s study, "How e-tailing can rise from the ashes" (June 2000), shows that the fulfilment costs associated with FMCG products are so high that price points below US$70 will fail to achieve break even. Digital products (like software, softbooks and digital music) will satisfy online distribution needs at almost any price point because they require no physical distribution. However, products that require wrapping and/or shipment naturally have high distribution costs and these pressures are exacerbated by the fact that consumers, realistically, need delivery of their purchases straight away. For almost everything apart from software and music — drugs, food, cars, clothes, the list goes on — same-day fulfilment can be vital. *Red Herring* and Forrester Research (July 2000) claim, not surprisingly, that 58% of US consumers demand same-day fulfilment on prescription drug orders while only 8% demand same-day fulfilment of toy orders. Yet these statistics indicate that even the most ephemeral of items demand same-day delivery. In these cases the best distribution centre is the retail outlet closest to the consumer, making personal collection or speedy individual delivery possible.

> *58% of US consumers demand same-day fulfilment on prescription drugs.*

So, the bricks-&-mortar store holds the advantage over its online rivals in the distribution stakes: the retailer's delivery costs, relative to product retail costs, are lower than those facing e-tailers.

Retailing Evolution: the Fittest Survive

Great companies are created through a Darwinian competitive process: the fittest survive. What we've seen on the Net to date is the first stage of this evolutionary process. The second stage will see the vengeful resurgence of offline retailers. They have lower costs, purchase in larger quantities, have long-standing relationships with suppliers and more highly-tuned supply and distribution chains than their online equivalents.

Future business will acknowledge the value of offline brands and accurately perceive the worth of cyber brands. Yes, Internet-born brands are flexible, independent of old traditions and capable of adjusting to fluctuating market conditions. On the other hand, a solid reputation, which is the advantage offline brands currently hold over their online competition, is impossible to establish quickly, no matter how fast Internet brand development becomes.

The e-tailer's rush for success probably explains bricks-&-mortar survived. E-tailer haste ignored essential consumer needs and, thereby, gave retailing the upper hand. But this reprieve will be short-lived. Sooner rather than later e-tailers will rectify their errors and establish the knowledge and service retailers have worked so hard to build over the decades. But, most importantly, they'll learn to focus on what they're good at and avoid interfering where they know they can't succeed.

But why was so much of what we learnt in the past, about the importance of power over consumer choice, forgotten? All the knowledge retailers accumulated through the eighties and nineties; knowledge that could be used by e-tailers in fashioning online success was neglected.

People Sense

Remember: consumer behaviour hasn't changed much even in the face of dramatic developments within the Internet industry. Human beings are still subject to their five senses and to motivations born of whim as well as wisdom. As far as possible, humans like to touch, smell and taste products, as well as see and hear them, before making purchasing decisions. It's no surprise that more than 80% of consumers still prefer to shop at their local merchant's establishment because they can actually *touch* the products it proffers and because they're familiar with the environment. (*Red Herring*/ Forrester Research, July 2000).

Ironically, it was the e-tailing threat that elucidated retail's chief virtue. Until the tremendous successes e-tailers achieved in 1999 and in the first quarter of 2000, retailing seemed oblivious to, or at least neglectful of, the advantage it held in sharing the tangible world with its customers. The chasm between the online environment and sensuality has highlighted bricks-&-mortar retailers' dominion over the charms of physicality.

E-tailers are one half of the meeting between two utterly different worlds. This encounter between online and offline environments indicates the future direction of commerce: the marriage of clicks with bricks. Data on consumer behaviour and preferences, monitored, evaluated and mapped during the last two decades of the twentieth century, are more relevant than ever. This information will direct the design of the "perfect" shopping experience in cyberspace and in the real world. The clicks-&-mortar partnership will acknowledge and accommodate all consumer needs.

The traditional retailer's ability to connect with all five of the consumer's senses had, until the advent of the e-tailer, been largely overlooked by the offline trader. Of course, we've been able to sample delicacies in food halls, try perfume before we buy it, sit in sofas and lie on beds before we decide upon the right models. What I'm referring to is the neglected potential of total sensory experience: retail environments designed to envelop consumers in whole concepts; concepts which infuse consumers with brand knowledge via appeals to every sense. Singapore Airlines, for example, has used this potential. The music the airline plays, the aroma held in the warm towels its gracious cabin crew distribute, the cabin's décor and ambience are all deliberately designed to convey the airline's image. Singapore Airlines is one of the few passenger airlines in the world to have every one of its on-board announcements scripted by an advertising agency, the purpose being to ensure this cabin detail also conveys the same image story to the passenger.

Until e-tail competitors challenged offline retailers, the latter had no need to consider the potential of sensory communication with consumers. Remember the endless aisles and shelving systems of hypermarkets in the eighties? Some of the shelves put products at such a height that the consumer's eye was barely considered let alone any of the other senses. The Internet's failings have highlighted the retailer's neglected advantages so activities which were cut in the interests of cost savings are now seeing a comeback: food and product demonstrations, visits to stores by experts, instore entertainments are all finding their way back into the retail program. Retailers will never be able to compete with e-tailers on product selection, price, lack of queues or instant access to information. These benefits belong firmly to the online world. But the power of sensory experience belongs to the bricks-&-mortar world: the shopping experience, the ability to touch, feel, smell and taste products, the potential to be entertained.

Consumer Loyalty

As I hope I've demonstrated, it's important to be mindful of the past half century's shifts in the power over consumer choice. The examples we've witnessed over this time might become the best guidelines for our decisions over the next couple of years. When evaluating all the shifts, one thing stands out: the constant hunt for the loyalty of consumers to brands — retail, FMCG and dotcom brands.

Brand loyalty is like a friendship which, if nurtured, grows and strengthens. Brands like Disney and LEGO still survive despite the mass distribution of their products in almost every possible format via every possible delivery channel. The brands are still there, and so is the consumer loyalty towards them. The crucial focus is on maintaining the relationship between brand and consumer no matter where the loyalty is born and matured: offline or in cyberspace.

Summary

- In the late nineties retailers recognised the goldmine of behavioural data they had accumulated. But only a few were able to extricate useful statistics from it and thus influence sales. This behavioural information has been retail's key tool in recovering its market position. The data not only informed retailers of consumer behaviour in the store, it also allowed retailers to predict consumer behaviour. It's this crucial predictive ability that can help retailers differentiate their offline selection from the offerings in cyberspace.

- Good brand building isn't just good advertising: it's anticipating and handling consumer expectations and ensuring that what the brand delivers is better than what the user expects.

- A key contributor to the steady dominance of offline brands is the trust factor. Consumers don't yet trust the Internet, but they trust brands, especially offline brands which they know, can relate to and with which they identify.

- Great companies are created through a Darwinian competitive process: the fittest survive. What we have seen on the Net so far is the first stage of this evolutionary process. The second stage will see the resurgence of offline retailers. They have lower costs, purchase in larger quantities, have longer standing relationships with suppliers, and have developed highly-tuned supply chains.

- E-tailing can only appeal to the consumer's senses of sight and hearing. The power of sensory experience belongs to the bricks-&-mortar world: the shopping experience, the ability to touch, feel, smell and taste products, the potential to be entertained is the domain of the offline retailer.

- The shifts in power over consumer choice that have taken place over the last fifty years could become our best guidelines for future retailing decisions. When evaluating the power shifts, one thing stands out: the constant importance to brands and retailers of earning consumer loyalty.

Action Points:

SWOT analysis of your own and your competitors' businesses

Summarise your business's strengths, weaknesses, opportunities and threats. Determine what threats your offline or online store is facing from your online/offline competitor and what features would be most likely to lure your customers to your competitor.

Create a list of the strengths your existing offline or online store enjoys and identify which of these explain why the consumer visits your offline or online store rather than your online/offline competitor.

Look closely at all your online/offline competitors and list all the techniques they use to attract and maintain their customers. Use this knowledge to determine if your existing strategy should be adjusted and improved.

Look at your closest online/offline competitors. List down not only all the values and strengths they represent but also all the weaknesses.

Based on these data create a full chart of all strength, weaknesses, opportunities and threats your offline or online store has to face. Prioritise each of the points according to what your customer would see as being the most important.

Based on this evaluation determine what threats your offline or online store is facing from the online/offline world. Determine which online/offline player/s, not only represent the greatest threat but also which seem to use techniques most likely to attract your customers and maintain their custom.

Now decide whether you're going to beat them or join them. Don't conclude this yet. Read Chapter 2 and then make up your mind.

Chapter 2

Second Round:
Retailers versus e-tailers

By 1999 retailers had started addressing the threat posed by their e-tail competitors, and e-tailers had begun recognising the values inherent in old-world experience. The result? Some offline operators abandoned their stores and headed straight onto the Net; others established partnerships with online foes to create clicks-&-mortar entities; and a handful of e-tailers, finding online financial returns dismal, entered clicks-&-mortar relationships with skilled traditional retailers. Have these strategies been reflex reactions or considered responses? Before executing any online or offline transition, you must analyse retailing's and e-tailing's comparative advantages.

Why the second round? Because the bout for market dominance between retailers and e-tailers continues.

Retailers won the first round after the World Wide Web appeared in 1994 because the idea of surfing the Web was too new and too unfamiliar for the consumer. But now we're into the second round. The spectators have learnt that surfing the Web is an everyday consumer activity and the contenders in the marketing ring have learnt a lot about technique and strategy from each other.

The Bout's Trophies: Multichannel Versatility and Consumer Loyalty

One resultant perception is that retailers are unable and/or unwilling to recognise and adapt to the Internet's potential. Yet the fight has taught many retailers that they may not have option of neglecting multichannel strategies.

And now that e-tailing is over its first-round injuries, it can see that the best strategy for winning the match is gaining consumer trust. Trust begets loyalty, and consumer loyalty contributes to a healthy bottom line. E-tailers have learnt that offline retailers hold the crucial advantage of consumer trust, cultivated over years, and they can see that this asset has been missing from their own training regimen.

> *Retailers don't have the option of neglecting multichannel strategies. E-tailers don't have the option of neglecting the advantage that retailers hold over them: consumer trust.*

Retailers have learnt that, theoretically, owning a database containing millions of loyal Internet users predisposes an online company to a successful outcome almost before any product has been launched. Retailers have also learnt that there are, theoretically, infrastructure savings for Internet companies when compared with the expenses they face themselves. Both contenders should also have learnt that such theories should be treated with caution.

As I discussed in the first chapter (under Bricks-&-Mortar Recovery: Distribution Value) e-tailer profitability depends in large part on logistics: the suitability of products for online sale and distribution. For pure-plays (Internet retailers that operate exclusively online) the costs of packaging and shipping products to customers can annihilate profit, making many FMCGs unviable as e-tailing goods. According to *The McKinsey Quarterly* "How e-tailing can rise from the ashes", even Amazon.com loses about US$7 per non-book order, the loss being due to shipping and fulfilment costs. Model 2.3, later in this chapter, shows how e-tailers lose money on transactions.

In its early days, Amazon.com, inspired the presumption that pure-plays were bound to annihilate old world competitors with rapid brand-building and accurate, efficient delivery of competitively-priced products to consumers. We now discover that the presumption was erroneous. Since 1999 we've learnt that success isn't a matter of being 100% online or offline: it's about the right mix between clicks and mortar allies. So most business-to-consumer sites are going to have to work some offline presence into their business plans. Equally, retailing has to face the fact that without an online presence it could succumb to the power of choice and price that the Net players wield. In the words of Joanna Barsh, Blair Crawford and Chris Gross (*The McKinsey Quarterly*, 2000 No. 3), "Pure-play Internet retailers haven't made a profit and probably never will. The winners will be experienced retailers that can execute a multichannel strategy."

Clicks-&-Mortar: Charles Schwab's Seamless Blend of the Real and Virtual Worlds

Charles Schwab's was among a number of nimble Internet companies that sprung from nowhere in the mid-1990s. But Charles Schwab's business statistics astound the best of those new entities. In a four-year period, Charles Schwab quadrupled its revenue from US$1.4 billion in 1995 to almost US$4 billion in 1999. Over the same period, its mutual funds family went from US$20 billion to over US$100 billion. There is no doubting that Schwab's Internet strategy has been an enormous part of the company's success as the world's largest online brokerage house.

Charles Schwab is not a new company. On the contrary, it started life in San Francisco as a traditional, full-service financial broker. It underwent its first transformation in the mid-1970s when it became a discount brokerage firm. Charles Schwab embraced technology way back then, when it decided to stop outsourcing its IT work and bring it all in-house. At times the company's investment in technology was so great that it seemed almost to have bet its business on it. But this history of integrating hi-tech into the company's corporate culture paved the way for incorporating the Internet into the business strategy. As co-CEO, David Pottruck, said, "We didn't just slap 'dotcom' onto our name. We embedded the Internet into all of our operations — and most importantly, into the lives and thinking of our employees."

By 1995 Schwab had formulated a web-based brokerage service and by 1996 it began trading as a separate division under the name eSchwab.com. For a greatly discounted fee of US$29, eSchwab.com investors paid for a no-frills, no-contact service. Another option was offered to online investors who also wanted face-to-face contact. They had access to a regular Charles Schwab account along with online access, although this cost them more. Both sections of eSchwab.com prospered exceedingly well although neither group of customers was entirely satisfied. The no-frills group felt they needed more contact while the contact group felt they should be getting a greater discount.

Working on the assumption that a simpler offer at a greater discount, along with access to personal service, would greatly increase its number of transactions, Charles Schwab made a bold business move. In 1998 it eliminated the divisions and merged the two groups. So, for the same US$29 (a reduction of more than US$50 off their standard fee), Schwab offered all their regular services along with online access.

Inherent in this lesson was the realisation that the traditional office — the bricks-&-mortar store — had a vital role to play in this new business model.

Charles Schwab was already a well-known brand in the investor world. This immediately carved a clear pathway to their cyberspace door but, more powerfully, the service and steadfastness of the brand in the real world had to be maintained in the virtual world. And the secret of this was to be found in mastering the integration of technology with the strength of the people. Only people in the real world can unscramble confusion, respond efficiently to e-mail queries, put out fires and reassure concerned customers. The people compose the mortar that holds the bricks of a business together.

Ten per cent of Charles Schwab's initial transactions were once conducted online. In 2000, that figure was closer to 80%. Charles Schwab had an active hand in effecting this increase. The company held over 10,000 seminars in 2000 to familiarise its customers with the Charles Schwab website. Despite this, it's important to note that 70% of new assets still come to the business through the doors of its branches.

Clearly the integration between the clicks and the mortar sides of the business is working for Charles Schwab. The schwab.com website receives an astonishing 76 million hits daily. There were 225 branch offices in 1995. In 2000 there were over 350, with plans to expand the 4000-people call centre. These bricks-&-mortar factors are necessary to servicing the 153,000 online trades Charles Schwab handles, worth US$2.6 billion a day.

Rather than pursuing a traditional bricks-&-mortar business model or forcing an Internet-only strategy upon its clients and employees, Charles Schwab has taken advantage of integrating clicks technology with the very best of bricks service. This seamless synthesis has created a new model for doing business on the Internet, and resulted in a most favourable outcome for customer and company alike.

Operational Cost Comparisons

The Internet has already caused upheaval for retailers, and the future promises more surprises from unforeseen competition. What car dealer a few years ago would have suspected a software company like Microsoft would be one of their biggest competitors? Could banks have guessed just a couple of years back that online stockbroker Etrade would siphon off their retail customers so easily, or that Microsoft Money would be one of their key competitors?

Model 2.1: *Potential growth for Internet shopping*

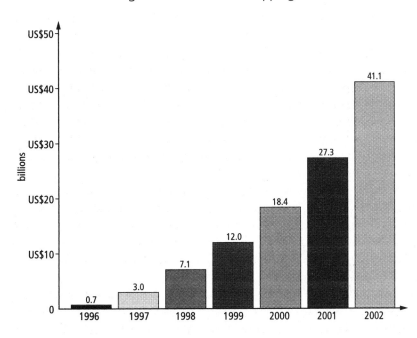

Yet an AC Neilsen study conducted in 2000 showed that only 20% of shopping will take place on the Internet over the next half-decade. This estimate was down from the 30% predicted the year before. Whatever spectators have been learning from the retail/e-tail battle has refined consumer cynicism and defined consumer demand, the result of this education being cautious acceptance of online shopping. And this leaves bricks-&-mortar retailers as potential second-round victors. Goodwill and the capacity to offer consumers personal contact and sensory experience are still firmly planted in the retailers' garden. What retailers need to do if they're going to survive in the ring is understand how to make these

A crucially advantageous role for retailers lies in supplying consumers with the sensory experience which can only be met within the physical world.

plants, which they've historically grown successfully, continue to bloom. What e-tailers need to do is learn how to co-opt the benefits of the longstanding relationship between retailers and consumers.

In short, retailers and e-tailers need to understand what they do best. Virtual and real-world retailers enjoy mutually exclusive assets. The trick of establishing a clicks-&-mortar partnership is to capitalize on these and minimise each side's disadvantages.

Marketing Expenditure

Catalogue retailers, with minimal infrastructure and personnel costs, differ from dotcom businesses only in that they communicate with customers by mail or e-mail rather than via a website. With years of traditional retailing experience behind them, catalogue retailers have been able to grow successfully online. They manage to attract customers more cheaply, spend

Amazon's business model is based on retaining each customer for a significant number of years to justify the investment—up to an astonishing twelve years by some analysts' forecasts.

less of their revenue on marketing and convert buyers into repeat customers more successfully than pure-plays, according to a study of 400 online retailers by Shop.org and Boston Consulting Group. Yet the following model shows that in 1999 e-tailers, store- and catalogue-based clicks-&-mortars all spend proportionally more of their marketing budgets on acquiring customers than on retaining them. The model also illustrates that multichannel retailers with shopfronts are twice as successful in creating brand awareness as pure-plays, even spending half the amount on customer acquisition as do online-only traders.

Statistics from Shop.org and the Boston Consulting Group show that the average pure-play spent US$82 to acquire a customer in 1999, a 95% increase over the $42 spent on average in 1998. Much of that increase can be attributed to Net companies' struggle to build brands during 1999, which caused Net firms to increase offline advertising spending by a massive 518%. By contrast, offline-based companies spent an average of US$12 to acquire each new customer in 1999, down from the $22 of the previous year. As Model 2.3 illustrates, online firms spent an unsustainable 119% of their revenue on marketing in 1999. And even with the advantage of their established brands, offline companies spent a high 36% of their revenue.

Model 2.2: *Percentage of marketing budget spent on consumer acquisition and retention*

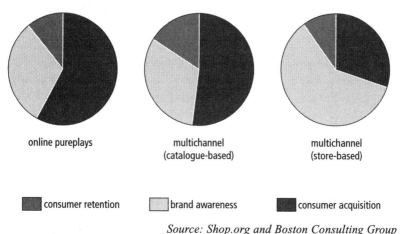

| online pureplays | multichannel (catalogue-based) | multichannel (store-based) |

consumer retention   brand awareness   consumer acquisition

Source: Shop.org and Boston Consulting Group

Model 2.3: *Marketing expenditure as percentage of revenue*

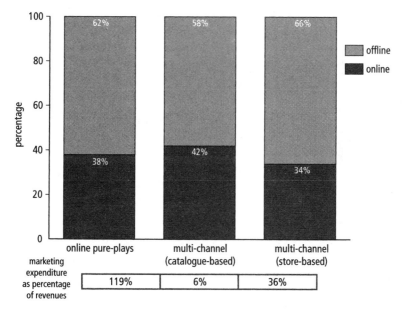

Source: Shop.org and Boston Consulting Group

As the above model demonstrates catalogue retailers know how to acquire and maintain a profitable client base, spending only 6% of their revenue on marketing. Net firms count on advertising to drive customers to their sites and find that just 3.5% of unique visitors make a purchase. (Internet statistics don't count the same user as several users if that same person returns to a site several times. One user is one user and described as unique.) That's

> *For destination websites to make economic sense they must attract repeat visits from customers, with each visit adding even greater loyalty.*

better than the 1.8% of unique visitors buying from clicks-&-mortar companies, but much less than the 42% still buying from catalogue firms. But bricks-&-mortar companies are proving their might through repeat buyer visits and repeat purchases. Repeat customers make up 34% of their consumer base and account for 45% of their revenue. Net players' repeat buyers constitute an average 27% of their customer population and account for 30% of their revenue.

How effective has costly online marketing been? A Forrester Research study, one of many conducted throughout 2000, showed that consumers, time after time, could remember only a few of the dotcom brand names mentioned on television or in print. The few brands they could remember were mostly those that had enjoyed first mover advantage (FMA): brands that became successful (and well-known) because they were first of their type and were, therefore, able to grab consumer attention. Yahoo!, Excite.com and Amazon.com are examples. The following model demonstrates FMA is a key factor in reducing leading brands' advertising expenditure. Being first clearly counts.

Model 2.4: *The FMA awareness advantage*

Dot-com Brand (Company)	1999 Advertising Spending ($MM)	Q1 2000 Top of Mind Brand Awareness	"Branding Bang for the Ad Buck"
Ebay	$5.5	22%	4.000
Excite	$3.2	8%	2.500
CDNow	$10.5	22%	2.100
Yahoo!	$29.2	38%	1.301
Amazon	$35.2	45%	1.278
Buy.com	$17.0	6%	0.353
IWON.com	$18.4	6%	0.326
AOL	$83.2	22%	0.264
Priceline	$49.6	5%	0.101
Monster	$29.0	2%	0.069
Etrade	$124.2	5%	0.040
Ameritrade	$103.7	1%	0.010

Sources: Competitive Media Reports, Greenfield Online for HMS Partners' Brand DNA and studiomotiv, June 2000

Visit **DualBook.com/cbb/ch2/ValueMarketing**
and get the latest information on how to get value for
your marketing dollar.

Order Fulfilment

One advantage pure-plays retain from having built e-commerce systems
from the ground up is in order fulfilment. The average e-tailer spends
US$12.50 fulfilling an order where bricks-&-mortar stores part with
US$18.10 to complete the same task. How do bricks-&-mortars justify the
extra US$5.60 they shell out to fulfil orders? Can they define where the
extra value lies for the consumer? Is it in quick access to products? Do
products arrive fresher? Are they preceded by product demonstrations?
When a retailer is competing with an e-tailer, such justifications will need
to be apparent in order to retain customers. It's vital that retailers focus on
service elements which truly differentiate their stores from e-tailer sites.

The figures I've quoted in the preceding paragraph are only part of a
bigger statistical picture which compares the e-tailer's revenue flow with the
retailer's. The fact is, retailing remains more profitable than e-tailing because
bricks-&-mortars still deal in large volumes of product and, therefore,
benefit from volume discounts. And they still have lower marketing and
customer retention costs than their online counterparts because offline
brands have achieved customer acquisition already. As I mentioned in the
first chapter, within most product categories FMCG products that are priced
under US$70 can't be profitable in an e-tail environment. As the model
below shows, most e-tailers lose money on every transaction, fulfilment
costs (picking, packing, shipping and delivering) rendering a variety of
products unviable as online consumer items that require immediate door-to-
door delivery.

Model 2.5: *E-tailer transaction costs and losses*

	Estimated costs per order fourth quarter, 1999 (US$)				
	Drugstore.com				
	Prescriptions	**Merchandise**	**Fogdog Sports**	**Webvan**	**eToys**
Total revenue	64.07	23.50	61.82	81.30	62.00
Product cost	60.29	20.75	47.01	66.20	40.04
Shipping	0.80	4.88	9.01	18.00	12.00
Fulfilment	14.29	14.29	11.00	10.00	14.00
Total loss per order (US$)	−11.31	−16.42	−5.20	−12.90	−4.04

Source: The McKinsey Quarterly, *"How e-tailing can rise from the ashes", July 2000*

However bricks-&-mortar retailers still have to compete with products sold online over the US$70 price point. So offline retailers need to maintain vigilant control of their costs and ensure constant optimisation of their vital points of differentation. I'll discuss these at length later in the chapter and later in the book (Chapter 4, on trust, and Chapter 8 on the shopping experience and environment) but, briefly, they centre on personal service, the capacity to appeal to all five senses, and the enjoyment of long-established consumer trust.

Infrastructure Costs

Fulfilment costs are, as I mentioned, just part of the complex cost-structuring to which all retail businesses are subject. High infrastructure costs can represent both a pivotal problem for traditional retailers and a key advantage for their e-tailer adversaries. The Web's cost efficiencies, compared with the high infrastructural investment demanded of bricks-&-mortar business, have seen, for example, Amazon.com spend only US$56 million on fixed assets while Barnes & Noble has spent US$472 million on its one thousand (or more) stores. A direct comparison would lead you to conclude that Amazon.com's strategy is more profitable than Barnes & Noble's. But before concluding this, you'd have to remember to ascertain the advantages of a number of intangibles like: the value of street-level visibility against a less visible cyber existence; the value of impulse buying in a real store against the structured online environment which precludes impulse provocation, and so on. And this isn't the whole story.

Setting up any online or offline infrastructure isn't cheap. Amazon.com, in addition to its US$56 million in fixed-asset investment has spent about US$200 million on more than three million square feet of warehouse space (in Coffeyville, Kansas, McDonough, Georgia and Campbellsville and Louisville, Kentucky) and US$300 million on shipping operations. Amazon.com's warehouses can accommodate US$15 billion in sales according to Jeff Bezos, the CEO and founder of Amazon.com who calls Amazon.com's infrastructural program "the biggest peacetime build-up of warehouses and distribution facilities in history".

My discussion of the marketing, order fulfilment and infrastructure costs concentrates on investment areas that have starkly different effects on online and offline retailing. It's somewhat misleading to attempt to compare the retailer's and e-tailer's comparative advantages in these operational areas because every case depends on its own complex circumstances. Ultimately, you can't avoid the difficult task of de-tailing your plans; of defining your business objectives and determining the point of differentiation that makes your on- or offline business a leader in its category and which justifies your cost structure.

The Human Factor

Consumers report a range of reasons to explain their ongoing preference for bricks-&-mortar retailing. According to a Forrester Research study (*Red Herring*, July 2000), the fact that consumers can actually touch products in the store is the reason most of the survey group preferred to shop there. Also, the local merchant's ability to fulfil their shopping needs immediately is high among their priorities. The fact that it's easy to return products to the bricks-&-mortar store accounts for 55% of consumers' preference for the local shop over the Net. And 30% of respondents say that a real live salesperson is the attraction of the bricks-&-mortar store over an e-tailer equivalent. The model below highlights a number of other people-contact reasons for preferring the real-life store over Net shopping. But consumer attitudes change daily. I reckon that by 2005, 25% of all FMCG sales will be online. In the meantime, our senses and our preference for human contact remain the chief reason behind the offline retailer's dominance over e-tailing.

Model 2.6: *Why consumers prefer shopping at the local store*

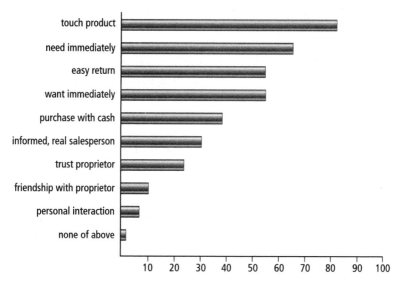

*Source: Forrester Research (*Red Herring, *July 2000)*

Back in the eighties, general opinion held that small retail outlets would die in northern Europe, their customers being lassoed by the emerging hypermarkets.

But, the consensus was wrong. The view was predicated on the assumption that shoppers would be passing by the hypermarket on the way to and from work and, because the hypermarket's prices were cheaper and the selection larger than that of the small retailer, the passer-by would be unable to resist the temptation of popping in for a carton of milk. What the assumption didn't take into account was that consumer shopping behaviour isn't necessarily driven by price or efficiency. Small specialty shops still managed to survive. What was it that they could offer that the hypermarket could not? You guessed it: a shopping experience.

The parallel between Internet and hypermarket shopping is obvious. In a rational and efficiency-driven world you might predict the imminent death of the bricks-&-mortar retailer. But humans are not necessarily guided by rationality or objectivity. They are won over by appeals to their taste and sensibilities.

Let's glance at some interesting similarities between the promises the hypermarkets made in the eighties and the advantages e-tailers are articulating now. In 1999, 98% of e-tailers promised cheaper prices. A similar percentage of hypermarkets made the same claim in 1985. Faster service and no queuing was foreseen by 96% of e-tailers while, in 1985, 92% of hypermarkets promised fast service according to an AC Nielsen study. In 1999, 92% of e-tailers were making the same promise of large selection that the hypermarkets were making in 1985.

Hypermarkets never died, but they never entirely usurped small retail business' trade either. In the late eighties, the retail winners were concept shops: chains that built their identities on soft values and replicated their shopfronts worldwide.

Retail and Soft Values

"Soft values" refer to unquantifiable qualities like comfort, peace, ecstasy: pleasurable human experiences. Concept stores, like The Body Shop, Starbucks Coffee and Mambo Juice did the same thing in the nineties. Their success was based largely on soft values — like ecological responsibility, cultural sensitivity and global awareness, the clear vision of its founder in The Body Shop's case; a taste of Italy just around the corner, peace, quiet and relaxation at Starbucks; and Mambo Juice's healthy living image — and very little on price, selection or efficiencies.

Just think about it. Why are we so willing to stand in queues for hours at theme parks to enjoy a ten-minute ride? Why do we go to tradeshows or to concerts? Why have cinemas remained steadfastly on the scene despite the logical prediction that the video recorder and cable television would kill the business? It's for the human experience, the feeling of belonging, of enjoying the world with other people. There wouldn't be much fun in visiting a fun park all by yourself, would there?

So, a crucially advantageous role for retailers lies in supplying soft values like entertainment, enjoyment, cosiness, harmony, relaxation, and so on. Sensory, experiential values which can only be met with in the physical world. The following model highlights the consumer's preference for real contact with products and people and exhibits this as an explanation for the consumer's reported and demonstrated reluctance to shop online. The major reason shown in this model concerns the vital issue of trust. See Chapter 4 for more on this key consumer driver.

Model 2.7: *Reasons people won't shop online*

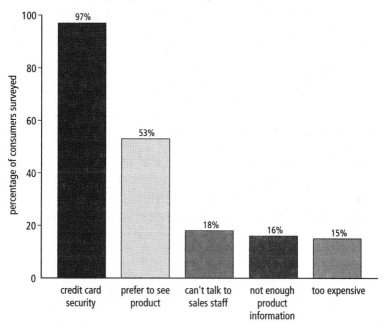

Source: Ernst & Young Survey; Jupiter Communications, June 2000.

Retail outlets are, therefore, likely to become showrooms or places of entertainment, just until technology learns how to gratify our senses anyhow. One day we'll be able to visit theme parks, like Disney World, in cyberspace. We'll fulfil our hankering for the Disney experience by visiting online superstores that will offer us sensory fulfilment that isn't yet available online. And believe me, there have been multiple attempts at creating the virtual shopping experience. Perhaps the best known is the Apple Store which was an online replica of the real-life original. A visit to the virtual store was meant to offer a parallel experience to that offered by the real-life store. Every shelf was positioned as it was in the real store and every product was right where the shopper expected to find it. The 1995 concept wasn't a success, at least from a revenue point of view. From a PR point of view it was potentially highly successful. But, in practical terms, the consumer didn't see any value in the virtual store's complicated navigation. "Why pretend to walk down the street? Why not just click on products and buy the stuff?" was the most common response to this and similar experiments.

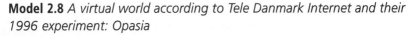

Model 2.8 *A virtual world according to Tele Danmark Internet and their 1996 experiment: Opasia*

Internet failures such as these, as well as the World Wide Web's rising success have prompted the retail world to analyse its unique features. At last, offline retailing has discovered that the principle of physical contact — between consumers and products, consumers and brands, consumers and consumers — is central to retail's real-world advantage. In 1998, Estée

Lauder's recognition that the offline advantage lay in focusing on human interaction was reflected in the company's decision to replace traditional glass counters with open displays. This simple piece of environmental engineering encouraged customers to handle the cosmetics, test out products and browse freely without having to seek help. The strategy increased Estée Lauder's sales by almost a quarter.

E-tailing and "Now"

The nature of retailing has also changed as a result of the Internet's "now" quality. During the past five years, consumers have become habituated to the rapid response Internet communication allows. Consequently, consumers don't expect to have to wait for service, for answers to queries, or for products to become available. If you want to order flowers for a friend, you needn't wait until you go up the street. You can go online immediately, order the flowers and cross the job off your things-to-do list. If someone recommends a book to you, you can jump online, read a couple of reviews and order the book. In the old days, you'd have forgotten about the book by the time you next visited the book store. So the "now" factor is an important one in garnering sales for e-tailers.

But immediate purchases and delivery doesn't suit all product categories. You probably wouldn't go online and purchase a house in haste. You could conduct the research but you'd probably prefer to actually see the place and its vendor before making such a substantial investment. But you've probably already started buying small articles online, like books. If your purchase fails, so what? You don't lose so much.

The practice of purchasing small items is exposing consumers to online shopping culture and preparing them to accept it as an ever-growing part of their lives. As habits take hold, larger investments will become commonplace. Product by product, service by service, e-tailer and consumer experience will evaluate the articles which are and are not suitable for the Net, and will determine the transaction and fulfilment processes necessary in each case. Eventually we'll even buy cars online without test-driving them first. The following model posits Forrester Research's predictions for percentages of total US sales, by category, that will happen online by 2004. Note that most of these categories' products can be assessed by the consumer's use of just two of the five senses: sight and sound.

Model 2.9: *Percentage of goods (by category) purchased online (Canada)*

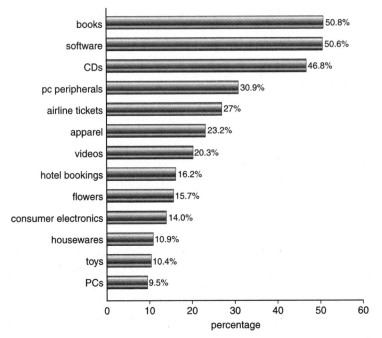

Source: Jupiter Communications June 2000

Model 2.10: *Percentage of sales (by category) predicted to happen online by 2004 (USA)*

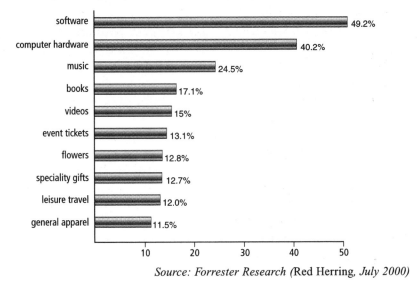

Source: Forrester Research (Red Herring, July 2000)

Despite the predicted drop in e-tail sales which I mentioned earlier in the text (an AC Neilsen study conducted in 2000 showed that only 20% of all shopping will take place on the Internet over the next five years, down from the 30% predicted the year before), such figures are just predictions. The fact is, the Net has entered consumer life and rapidly found a relevant role there. Humans are adept at habituating themselves to changing circumstances, and the presence of online retailing will inevitably alter consumer habits and influence overall retail strategies. Change simply takes time.

CENTRAL CLICKS, SATELLITE BRICKS
Ethan Allen Services Online Clients from Traditional Stores

Case study by Don Peppers and Martha Rogers, Ph.D

The single most difficult task preventing an existing company from setting up a successful e-business is resolving the conflicts that exist between the cyber world and the real world. The cyber world of direct-to-consumer deliveries threatens most companies' real-world channel structures, and the self-help customer service offered online is often inadequate unless it can be linked with real-world service calls or repair scheduling. Resolving these conflicts, by using real-world strengths to leverage an online presence, has proved overwhelmingly difficult for many firms. Barnesandnoble.com, for example, has never been able to leverage its hundreds of bricks-&-mortar bookstores to pull an end-run around Amazon. And Compaq had to stop shipments of its Presario PC through its Web outlets so it could rethink its e-strategy.

But lately there have been some interesting success stories in this space. Circuit City allows online customers to order products on the website and pick them up at the nearest retail store. Ethan Allen is also trying to turn itself into a true clicks-&-mortar enterprise.

Ethan Allen may have found a way both to turn the tables on channel conflict and to leverage its substantial retail presence. As it prepared to start selling via the Web last autumn, the furniture retailer tried to design an initiative that wouldn't upset the independent licensees who manage and own nearly three-quarters of its 310 traditional stores. So far, the licensees are embracing the plan.

Here's why: In 1999, original plans called for Ethan Allen to sell only smaller, easily shipped items over the Internet. But in May 2000, Ethan Allen chairman and CEO, Farooq Kathwari, halted the move because he felt the stores already have a distribution network that is well-equipped to handle larger deliveries — beds, sofas, tables, etc. — and the resulting service calls. Why not use this

CASE STUDY: Ethan Allen

www.1to1.com

network to offer a full, serviceable product line on the Web while relieving the managers' and owners' concerns?

So the plan now offers a way for the bricks-&-mortar licensees to share in profits generated by online transactions. The website's product line will include almost all of the company's wood merchandise and a limited selection of sofas and chairs. These items will be shipped and serviced through Ethan Allen's retail distribution structure while smaller items, which typically don't require servicing, will still be shipped through UPS. Stores providing delivery and service for an online sale will get 25% of the sales price; 10% if the online item is shipped directly from the factory to the consumer within a store owner's territory.

Ethan Allen's new strategy destroys any bricks-&-mortar resistance, and solicits their help in providing service and delivery. "It's more than what they expected," says Kathwari.

Witness the success and leadership of Dell Computer. The company started in 1984 with the mission of selling personal computers directly to the customer. Dell is today the second largest manufacturer of computer hardware in the world and holds the largest share of the personal computer market in the US. Fifty per cent of its direct sales and customer support activities happen online and, at the time of writing, Dell sells US$10 million worth of computers on the Net every day.

But far too often, new products are launched prematurely, in untested markets. If a market isn't prepared for a product, it's likely that product will flounder. Premature e-tailing developments risk the same failure.

Gradually the Internet will capture a share in every product category. But e-tailing alone will never capture the full market. Until products are tested for suitability to the Net and appropriateness to the market, the e-tailer's job is to conduct detailed consumer research combined with detailed revenue forecasting to determine how well any e-tailing concept will survive. Market research isn't new in the bricks-&-mortar world. But for some reason, it's a necessary developmental step that's often forgotten by e-tailers.

Visit **DualBook.com/cbb/ch2/OnlineBrandTest**
to learn the latest trends in market testing of online brands.

Before focussing on future e-tailing, let's consider two fundamental issues that simultaneously define offline advantage and online deficiency and which promote the case for clicks-&-mortar development: trustworthiness and goodwill.

Trust and Goodwill

It takes time to establish goodwill and the trust that promotes it. They're not commodities that can be bought or synthesised. Goodwill is earned over time. Being new in town, the stakes are high for online retailers who don't deliver. Consumers with no loyalty to the online provider have little tolerance for deficient service delivery. This fact should lead retailers and e-tailers to the conclusion that it's better to have no online presence at all than to be online purposelessly. A retailer's non-serious presence on the Internet is likely to result in inadequate customer service. This frustrates consumer expectations and, as a consequence, dilutes the value of the offline brand and the bricks-&-mortar stores that supply it. Unfortunately, most retailers still think that some online presence is better than none. Consider the following sobering facts.

Goodwill and the trust that promotes it are not commodities that can be bought or synthesised in any way. Goodwill is earned over time and is an asset that retailers can offer e-tail partners a share in.

Online Failures

A Boston Consulting Group study, "Insight into Online Consumer Behavior", was conducted among 12,000 consumers in the United States and Canada in 1999. The study showed that 57% of Internet users have shopped online, and 51% actually purchased goods or services online. The typical online purchaser completed ten transactions and spent $460 online over the previous twelve months. Yet 28% of all attempted online purchases failed, and four out of five consumers who made purchases online experienced at least one failed purchase attempt over the same period. These failures resulted from technical problems consumers encountered with the sites, difficulties in finding products, and logistical and delivery problems after the sale. Twenty-eight percent of consumers who suffered a failed purchase attempt stopped shopping online; 23% stopped purchasing at the site in question.

But the study also showed that consumers who enjoy a satisfying first-purchase experience online are likely to spend more time and money on the Net. The satisfied first-time purchaser typically engaged in twelve online transactions and spent $500 during the previous twelve months. The dissatisfied first-time purchaser spent only $140 on four online transactions. The scariest data indicated that 6% of users who had bad online shopping experiences also stopped patronising the retailer's physical store.

Eighty-seven per cent of Consumers Prefer Bricks-&-Mortar Shopping

While the Boston Consulting Group's study results indicated that a bad online experience will deter a large proportion of Net customers from returning for more, the same is not the case for bricks-&-mortar businesses, which can sometimes get away with bad service without losing a customer. (This is partly due to the geographical location of bricks-&-mortar businesses. Even if service is lousy, a customer may be persuaded by a store's convenient location to return and suffer the bad service again.) In the bricks-&-mortar parallel only 8% of consumers who suffered bad service stopped shopping offline.

Studies by Forrester Research and McKinsey, in June, July and August of 2000, show that consumer tolerance with offline supplier failure lies in branding. Strong branding is a reflection of consumer loyalty, and vice versa. Loyalty manifests bonds of trust between the brand and the consumer.

So, when an online purchase attempt fails, it's not necessarily the brand that suffers. Eighty-seven per cent of users claim that they simply prefer to continue their patronage of the brand with a bricks-&-mortar supplier. Why? Because they perceive the offline retailer to be more trustworthy than the online e-tailer who has just disappointed their expectations. The next model indicates the importance of trustworthiness in inspiring online consumer patronage. When choosing an Internet store, consumers aim to minimise the Net's perceived drawbacks like loss of privacy, delivery inefficiencies and shipping costs.

Model 2.11: *Factors determining patronage of specific e-tailers (2000)*

Percentage of online shoppers who indicated this was one of the three most important factors motivating their choice of online merchant	
Trust the site will keep my personal information private	57%
Lowest product prices	53%
Free shipping and handling	35%
Detailed product information	33%
Site operated by a store/catalogue retailer I trust	21%
Delivery within a specified time frame	20%
Easy to shop site	20%
Access to customer services	17%
Large selection of merchandise	16%

Source: E-Retail Intelligence System, PricewaterhouseCoopers LLP

A harmonious relationship between off- and online branding — the clicks-&-mortar synergy which I'll discuss in detail in Chapter 6 — is necessary for sustaining consumer trust in brands. As a Forrester Research study (conducted in Australia in 1999) shows, a positive synergy between off- and online brands can be highly influential upon a customer's relationship with a brand. A good online experience will, in 9% of cases, lead to offline-generated sales in same-brand stores. Consumers having positive offline experiences are, in 32% of cases, open to trying the store online if they have access to the Internet.

In a clicks-&-mortar relationship, the retailer's special plants, goodwill and trust, can be cultivated and harvested to the advantage of both their offline owners and online borrowers. Goodwill and trust are the keys to maintaining positive synergy between retail and e-tail activities that come together as clicks-&-mortar ventures.

Retailer Options

According to an AC Nielsen study conducted in 2000, 39% of consumers in the United States are buying less offline than they did only five years ago. Analyst Michael De Kare-Silver claimed in his book, *E-Shock 2000*, that a decrease of 15% in turnover will push retailers' earnings into the red. If 39% of consumers are shopping less in the store and more online, a substantial percentage of income is being diverted from the traditional store. So retailers will have to be prepared for a loss of the market share they command today. Preparation means either altering their existing business models so retailers can afford narrower margins; or investing in such strong marketing that consumers will be persuaded to pay more for retailers' products and services. Or, of course building an e-commerce component into their business strategy.

Yet, against this forecast, is one by Forrester Research that predicts Internet sales will reach just 7% of total US retail sales within the next four years. While e-tailers have captured the adventurous consumer's imagination, and online retailing has shown remarkable growth, most retail sales remain the province of bricks-&-mortar stores.

According to the US Department of Commerce, "non-store" sales (like catalogue sales, TV direct marketing and Internet sales) grew from US$1.3 trillion in 1990 to US$1.8 trillion in 1998, representing a rise from just under 1% to a mere 1.4% of total retail sales.

Here's the message: retailers can't afford to neglect executing multichannel strategies. And e-tailers will have to harness the potent reputations and physical presences possessed by traditional retailers.

Before leaving this chapter and discussing the processes involved in retailers planning a move online (Chapter 3), e-tailers moving offline and both parties seeking each others' advantages in clicks-&-mortar relationships (Chapter 5), I want to introduce you to a couple of independent retail transitions that illustrate the comparative advantages of the off- and online environments that this chapter has outlined.

Online Auction Sites

As Chapter 1 discussed, the advent of Internet shopping has returned some power of choice to the consumer. In just three years, consumers were released from the grip of retail branding and allowed to assume a new place in the consumption paradigm. The result? The retailer no longer decides the right price — the consumer does. In the eighties and early nineties the price of products was entirely controlled by the manufacturer. However this changed in the mid-nineties when Priceline.com and other online auction sites appeared on the Net. These sites allowed consumers to set prices by pledging what they were willing to pay for a product. At Priceline.com you type in what you're prepared to pay for a flight from San Francisco to London, for example, and the site will respond to your offer if an airline is prepared to sell you the ticket at the price you bid. This practice turns the consumer/product relationship upside-down. It forces the brand to ask the consumer about value rather than dictating price to the customer.

There are more than 15,000 online auction sites in the United States alone. More than 8% of consumers in the United States visit and use online auction sites every month. My own forecast is that the online auction concept will eventually become part of everyday transactions, even in supermarkets, so that prices on shelves will be unfixed and open to offers. The communication tool will be the mobile phone which will connect the bidding consumer to the auctioning supermarket.

Don't necessarily bring the customer to the site; instead bring the message directly to the customer at the point of need.

Now retailers are on a steep learning curve that many of them may not surmount. Try learning to play an instrument or learn a new language when you're forty! The older you are, the harder you find it to change, to learn and to act upon new knowledge. This is the challenge facing retailers.

The auction approach doesn't yet dominate the consumer/brand relationship: retailers still rule the pricing roost. But most retailers are being forced to analyse their identities. They've spent their existences ostensibly putting the consumer first. In fact, retailing has been governed by merchant prerogatives rather than consumer primacy. The customer's influence has been, ultimately, eclipsed by the retailer's needs, profit margin directives, distribution deals and seasonal demands and availabilities, all of which determine fixed prices. Price has had nothing to do with the consumer and everything to do with the retailer.

The tough fact is that dealing with the new flexibilities demanded by the online environment will be beyond many retailers. Those who don't meet the new challenges are likely to die. But this doesn't mean brands will expire with them. Most brands will survive and the strong ones will thrive in an environment in which the consumer has ultimate control over price: lesser-known brands will become auction fodder while leading brands will retain the advantage of higher prices.

Line Extension
Being one of those generic products with no point of differentiation between brands, petrol stations don't usually attract a clientele because of brand loyalty. Motorists usually fill up at service stations that are geographically convenient for them.

But petrol competition has become tougher since oil companies have found traditional retailers moving in on their territory and offering customers the chance to fill up while they stop for groceries. So, petrol outlets like Shell's have had to hang on to their consumer group by matching the competition with equal services. The introduction of grocery stores to gas stations was an immediate attraction for a consumer group with no real product loyalty. In fact, consumers were exhibiting a growing loyalty to the incidental grocery stores. So petrol companies like Shell were forced to turn many of their outlets into "Shell Select" stores.

Until the mid-eighties, Shell was well known for its petrol and oil products, but not much more. You wouldn't have thought about the Shell brand in connection with a convenience store.

Yet this smart offline transition wasn't a big move. The store was there; the staff were there; the shelf space was available; and the customers were already lined up in front of the cash register. In reality, the Shell Select store concept was just an extension of existing business activity. This practice is called "line extension". For Shell, it created a bridge between the old petroleum-focused brand and the new convenience-oriented brand. Shell's successful achievement of this brand transition, manifested in the Shell Select stores, is a key reason behind Shell's maintenance of a strong market position.

Some other brands have managed successful line extensions. Virgin, for example, is an umbrella brand for everything from wedding shops to publishing offices to cola, airlines, online and mobile service and train systems. The brand has managed to establish a platform which remains intact, independent of the products under it that may come and go.

Offline to Online Transition

How would you handle the challenge of starting up a new business activity under an existing brand name? Until now most companies have treated the situation as an extension of their extant business, just as Shell did when it launched its Shell Select stores. The fact is, however, that going online from an entirely offline environment should be treated as a totally new challenge, like starting up a new company. Let's look at a couple of instances in which two leading companies handled the same online-offline dilemma in opposite ways.

In 1999 Nike did what many observers expected the company to do in 1998. Nike Retail Services Inc. introduced Nike iD, an interactive site that allows visitors, professional athletes and everyday consumers alike, to design and order customised shoes. Almost simultaneously Levi's deleted its customised service from the Levi's site because the service wasn't achieving the results Levi's had expected.

Nike introduced Nike iD late, right in the middle of the customisation trend. Levi's, on the other hand, was one of the trend's pioneers. Were they too far ahead of the trend to reap the desired results from it? Or was customisation on the Internet not suited to jeans retailing?

Visit **DualBook.com/cbb/ch2/CustomProduct**
and discover how customisation is leading products into
one to one branding.

The presence of true customisation on the Net removes a major enticement for consumers to visit stores. Why should customers visit the Levi's store to buy customised jeans? They can't take their new jeans with them anyway. And they can't actually see and try the jeans. They may even have to pay up-front for them, just as they do if they're buying from the website. The added value of visiting the store is, therefore, nil. Thus it would seem that cutting the customisation service from the Internet might support Levi's stores.

In 1999, Nike was faced with the same issues. What would motivate the consumer to visit Nike iD for customised shoes? There's no apparent motivation at all: the well-branded Nike Town stores offer impressive expertise. Given this fact, Levi's' logic would result in a decision not to go online with a customisation service. Yet Nike chose to introduce Net-based customisation. Was Nike behind the times? Was it charging recklessly ahead on the path that Levis wisely abandoned? Or was Nike going to reap the benefits of a perfectly timed e-tail service introduction?

And what of Levi decision? Did they jump the customisation ship too soon? Levi's might have been wise to remove their customisation service from the Internet, though it seems a strange decision to have taken when the customisation boat had set sail and, finally, become serious business on the Net. What we don't know is how many millions of dollars the customisation exercise cost Levi's to maintain on a yearly basis, and what added brand and loyalty value was earned in return for the investment. Conversely, the Nike introduction seemed late. But Nike might well have timed the initiative just right. All the e-tailing hype had subsided by then and transformed itself into serious e-commerce, with revenue returns instead of immeasurable public relations results to count on.

Levi was one of the first e-tailers to take the customisation chance. The jeans giant led the pack and, in so doing, captured early knowledge about online customisation. The learning experience has, for many site owners, been the prime reason for going online.

The Third Round Referee

Time and again attitudinal surveys reveal the shopper's preference for the human contact that retailing offers and which e-tailing denies. The surprises and twists of personal encounters, the delight in unplanned product discoveries, the entertainment of the shopping experience are all major factors that explain the retailer's current survival. Consumer retention in the real-life store preserves the potential of impulse buying, customer return and ongoing viability.

Yet the Net offers advantages which directly contradict these: structure which precludes impulse purchases; data which negates the need to try before you buy; immediate access, twenty-four hours a day, to the stores consumers need, free of the delays personal contact can create, unburdened by the hassles of parking, and undistracted by peripheral demonstrations, entertainments and other instore diversions.

Will the third round go to the educated consumer, who has entered the ring to dictate product price, quality and delivery channel preferences? Spectators may yet take over from brands to referee the fight for retailing survival while retailing's challenge to e-tailing is in a "catch-24/7" dilemma. Read on.

Summary

- Retailers don't have the option of neglecting multichannel strategies. E-tailers don't have the option of neglecting the offline advantage: consumer trust. The solution is for experienced retailers to develop multichannel strategies: to develop clicks-&-mortar relationships.
- Virtual and real-world retailers enjoy mutually exclusive assets. The trick of establishing a clicks-&-mortar partnership is to capitalise on these and minimise each side's unique disadvantages.
- Setting up any online or offline infrastructure isn't cheap and ultimately, you can't avoid the task of detailing your plans. Define your business objectives and determine the point of differentiation that makes your on- or offline business a leader in its category.
- Humans aren't necessarily guided by rationality or objectivity, so online retailing can't rely on its ostensible efficiencies to attract and retain consumers. Consumers are won by appeals to their taste and sensibilities.
- A crucially advantageous role for retailers lies in supplying soft values that recognise the consumer's human condition: sensory, experiential values which can only be met with in the physical world. The principle of real contact is central to retail's real-world advantage.
- The Internet's "now" quality and the consumer's resultant expectations of immediate satisfaction have introduced efficiency challenges to retailers. Yet the advantages the Net offers directly contradict those offered by retailing. Online purchasing structures preclude impulse purchases. They provide immediate access, twenty-four hours a day, to the stores consumers need, free of the delays personal contact can create, unburdened by the hassles of parking, and undistracted by peripheral demonstrations, entertainments and other instore diversions.
- A bad online experience will deter a large proportion of Net customers from returning to online shopping and 6% of users who have bad online shopping experiences also stop patronising the retailer's physical store.
- Goodwill and the trust that promotes it are not commodities that can be bought or synthesised. They must be earned over time.

Action Points:

Develop a clicks-&-mortar strategy (Stage 1)

Analyse the rational and emotional reasons that persuade your customers to favour your brand. Consider what mix of clicks and bricks would coalesce with your customers' choice drivers. Analyse your motivations for developing a clicks-&-mortar strategy and identify a business concept that responds to these motivations. Your subsequent operational strategy will include a channel strategy which will define what resources you need to dedicate to your online and offline channels.

Plan the clicks and bricks mix
Think five years ahead and consider the rational (price, selection, efficiency, convenience) and emotional (social, enjoyable, warm, exciting, fun) drivers governing consumers' choice of your brand.

- List and prioritise the ten top reasons your offline customer would have to visit your bricks-&-mortar store. Arrange these reasons in two columns: rational reasons and emotional reasons.
- Now imagine an online version of your store and conduct the same exercise.
- If you've listed more rational reasons than emotional ones, your future could well be online or as part of a clicks-&-mortar partnership. Make your best estimate of the right mix of clicks-&-mortar for your business and set this out as a draft plan.

Survey opinion on the clicks and bricks mix
Ask your customers, suppliers, your industry's experts, your distributors as well as your board their opinions of your rough clicks-&-mortar plan.

- Having your suppliers on side is essential to a workable clicks-&-mortar strategy. Ask them whether they'd be willing to maintain their support of your business if it were to go 100% online. Are they prepared to receive and execute orders online? Are they prepared to respond within strict timeframes? Are they prepared to support guarantees like a no-questions-asked return policy? Are they prepared to fulfil orders by delivering directly to the consumer?
- If your company is public, or dependent on industry opinion, you must involve expert industry observers and players in your survey. Analysts, journalists, researchers and unions will all have a position on your proposal which is relevant to its outcome. Ask how they think your clicks-&-mortar strategy would be received in the market place. What problems do they think your clicks-&-mortar strategy might encounter (union, staff, regulatory restrictions, taxation ramifications)? What opportunities should the concept be prepared to take on? What badwill is the concept likely to engender? What is competitor response likely to be and will this affect the brand's accumulated goodwill?

- Your distribution network is your brand's lifeline. Ask your distributors what problems your clicks-&-mortar draft strategy suggests and what benefits they see in the proposal from a distribution point of view.
- Consolidate your survey results and prioritise the positives and negatives it reveals.

Develop a clicks-&-mortar operational strategy that includes a draft channel strategy

Develop your clicks-&-mortar draft plan into an initial operational strategy. Take your direction from the positives and negatives your survey revealed, your business goals and the business motivations that lie behind your clicks-&-mortar proposal. (Increase brand PR? Grow revenue? Stymie competitor? Build consumer trust?)

Analysis and definition of motivations and goals will: a) suggest a skeleton for an initial channel strategy; b) provide a means of measuring progress towards operational synergy; and c) a means of communicating company direction to staff.

- Ascertain the percentage split between the proposed clicks channel and its mortar ally for marketing expenditure, resource allocation, revenue generation, distribution costs, communications responsibilities, infrastructural responsibilities, etc.
- Consider how operational areas will be integrated across channels and put *channel* governors in place to ensure the fulfilment of each channel's role and goals.
- Ensure that your whole organisation understands the operational strategyis geared toward the mix, and that you have in.

Don't race any further ahead with your clicks-&-mortar strategy. Chapter 3 will tell you why!

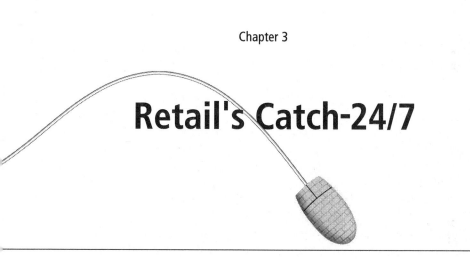

Chapter 3

Retail's Catch-24/7

The online onslaught is obliging the retail industry to redefine itself:
service, delivery, customer and supplier relations, infrastructure and
distribution systems and all the attitudes and assumptions that mould
retail culture are under review. But the tactical response is fraught with
catch-22 conundrums, typified by the "catch-24/7". Online shopping is
available twenty-four hours a day, seven days a week and this forces retail
equivalents to be similarly accessible to the consumer. The catch is that
retailers won't survive if they don't keep up with the demands of catch-
24/7 but, at the same time, they'll be ruined trying to achieve them. And
then, the more stores that open twenty-four hours a day, the more people
will need to shop twenty-four hours a day: catch-24/7!

Ask the captain of a huge oil carrier to turn his ship around 180° — fast! No matter how much he'd fancy offloading you and returning you to port, his ship would be incapable of skidding to a halt and spinning around. Most bricks-&-mortars, large and small, are facing a similarly difficult feat: turning businesses around that are laden with years of pre-Net experience.

Even businesses like those in the advertising industry, which should be capable of the early adoption of new thinking, haven't yet made the mental or technical transition to online operation. Almost no advertising agencies have managed to adapt their offline activities to the new media and a bricks-&-mortar advertising agency has yet to appear among the top five most innovative agencies. All dotcom-born, these are Agency.com, Organic.com, Razorfish.com, MarchFirst.com and RedSky.com.

Many consulting agencies like Boston Consulting, McKinsey, Andersen Consulting, Ernst & Young and PricewaterhouseCoopers are struggling to turn their ships around too. In the unwieldy process they're losing staff to dotcom companies all over the world.

So if specialists, who for decades, have offered analysis and advice to companies on their strategic problems and business directions, have such difficulty in managing the online challenge, what hope have retailers?

The Seven Catch-22 Problems

There are seven main reasons behind retailers resisting the online transition. These are catch-22s because they define the very nature of retail culture. How can retail operate beyond its culturally-moulded behaviours? Yet all seven factors are substantially to blame for the bricks-&-mortar delay in moving online. Most retailers have some online presence, but very few have taken the venture seriously enough to see it as their primary revenue channel in the near future. This resistance not only reflects lack of management motivation and consequential staff inertia, but also an introverted focus which is almost entirely dedicated to the reluctant retailer's existing offline presence. Retail resistances lie in:

1. the fear of destroying distribution networks;
2. failure to analyse online potential and to identify ways of adding value by going online;
3. unwillingness to cut into the profit margin;
4. lack of patience;
5. fear of cannibalising existing business;
6. unwillingness to fund an online presence with offline financial resources; and
7. fear of losing control.

Rethink Distribution Networks

Retailers depend heavily on the efficiencies of their distribution networks. It's their organisation's most important infrastructural component because it determines how well they meet their customers' demands and, consequently, has a direct impact on turnover.

For retailers considering the move online, anxiety over disrupting and alienating distribution networks can halt the transition process. I'll draw an illustration from Coca-Cola's history.

The brand weathered significant problems with its established retail outlets when it started installing vending machines. Even though follow-up tests showed that the vending machine presence actually benefited all parties, that the strategy was a classic win/win arrangement, retail outlets were offended by Coca-Cola's seemingly cavalier attitude towards the retail support they provided the brand.

In 1998, Coca-Cola faced enormous problems when the CEO, M. Douglas Ivester, decided to reduce the company's distribution network. Ivester downgraded the role of the plants and neglected to involve local players in decision-making. This, along with a range of other factors (including a crisis in which 300 Belgian children were poisoned by the drink, the vending machine issue and weak management), affected sales which plummeted dramatically in the late nineties. After only a year the backlash was reflected in Coca-Cola Inc.'s falling share price, which reached its lowest point in fifteen years in July 1999. Ivester left Coca Cola in January 2000.

Nike ran into problems when it first opened its own Nike Town stores. Nike, as Coca-Cola had done before introducing the vending machines, carried out detailed consumer surveys that clearly demonstrated the role the Nike Town concept could play in strengthening the brand in the interests of all parties. The Nike Town stores would reinforce the brand name and showcase the product. This would generate increased demand and sales in established channels. Subsequent market success demonstrated the point that a win/win situation is achievable but often not initially perceived as such by all parties.

So, experience shows that the slightest signal from a retail chain's headquarters that it may be going to cut down the retail outlet's role in favour of Internet activity has, for almost all organisations that have gone through the process, resulted in major conflicts. The chief response from retail staff has been a general feeling of disempowerment. And, from the distribution side, the response has been based on the fear of being out of business within years. As a result, in most situations, retail businesses have taken conservative action. For example, Barnes & Noble, the USA's largest book retailer, took two years to go online and meet the Amazon.com competition on the Net. The chain's online transition in the nineties wasn't achieved without difficulty. The company had to resolve a range of conflicts with its existing distribution network and had to weather tax jurisdiction complications which prevented full integration of the website with local store operations in some states. (This was a significant issue because it put Barnes & Noble at a disadvantage not suffered by its competition, Amazon.com. The online pioneer, operating entirely online, didn't encounter the same tax problems that dislocated Barnes & Noble's website and store operations.)

It's no wonder the retail industry is protective of its distribution networks. Distribution is what has made most retailers what they are today. Shifting too hastily away from these lifelines and towards the dotcom platform might engender so much staff insecurity that the move could be counterproductive. Gradual evolution over a few years is more likely to work compatibly with existing workplace cultures. Research from Forrester Research (February 2000) indicates that only 25% of existing retailers will become e-tailers within the next seven years. A recent study by USA Today (November 2000) shows that more than 80% of all e-tailers have closed down since 1994. This predicted hesitancy to enter the dotcom environment must persuade tactical thinkers in retail businesses to consider the move to cyberspace even more carefully.

On the other hand, several players have already achieved major successes by either cutting away their retail distribution network or starting new concepts, independent of traditional distribution.

Companies have adopted divergent strategies to tackle the online opportunity. Dell Computer was never concerned about its move into cyberspace as the company was born on the Internet. Egghead, with 350 stores across the USA, just did it: they literally closed most of their stores overnight and moved online. Drugstore.com teamed bricks-&-mortar with clicks. And Levi Strauss, as you will have read in the previous chapter, gave up the online option.

Placing all its Eggs in One Dotcom Basket

In the early 1980s we began buying computers for personal use at home. Egghead opened its first store in 1985 with a mission of translating the jargon-heavy techno-talk that confused software customers into easy-to-understand language that would allow them to make suitable purchase decisions. Egghead stores marketed their philosophy through a nutty persona, Professor Egghead, who offered too-good-to-be-true deals to a clientele that was growing by the day.

Egghead software boutiques satisfied this burgeoning market and by 1989, with 112 stores, the company listed on the stock exchange. This rapid growth, however, caused problems. Stock movement was not managed well, Egghead having inadequate precautions against theft in place; and the turnover of qualified sales staff who could help customers understand the increasingly complex world of software was high.

According to George Orban, who would steer Egghead's drive to Egghead.com, "The company grew too fast, with little discipline and no vision or business strategy." One of the missed opportunities occasioned by this fast growth was Egghead's failure to diversify into hardware. Superstores specialising in everything to do with the home computer began appearing everywhere. Since these stores made their margins on hardware, they could afford to discount the software. Sales of personal computers had overtaken those of televisions, and were being sold with software packages as part of the deal.

By 1993 Egghead was steadily losing market share. At the end of the1995 fiscal year, sales had dropped some 20% below those of 1994. The company appeared to be in turmoil. There was cost cutting across the board, and there were three CEOs in as many years. It was time to rethink the Egghead strategy.

First the company reduced prices to match discounted goods in the superstores. Then it redesigned its stores and offered a selected range of hardware. But the new-look stores, with their wood-veneer shelves, failed to stem the downward trend. By March 1996, Egghead was showing losses of over $11 million.

In January 1997 George Orban became the CEO. He assembled a team to guide the company through these difficult days, when all they knew was that Egghead needed serious change to survive. So they set out to stop the company's haemorrhage. They closed stores and embarked on a rethink about consumer software needs. By now there were fewer uninitiated users than knowledgable ones: the market was on familiar terms with hardware and software.

Orban had contacts with a small computer hardware and software surplus liquidation company called Surplus Direct, and in Surplus Direct Egghead saw a match. Egghead had the brand; Surplus Direct had the hardware knowledge. Before Christmas 1996 the two opened Egghead Computer Surplus, a huge space that looked like an overstocked warehouse. It was a great success, and despite the fact that Egghead continued with other store closures, the company seemed to have a viable means of competing on superstore level.

Not wanting to miss another opportunity in the newly evolving computer-based landscape, Egghead launched its first website in 1997. Extensive print and banner advertising supported its introduction and Egghead offered a Dodge Viper as an incentive to one lucky winner. Over the next three months the online site attracted an encouraging 700,000 visitors.

Egghead still had 80 retail outlets and one huge superstore and there were more superstores on the drawing board. But the smaller Egghead retailers were being closed. Leasing and stocking the new superstores was a capital-intensive exercise. And finding the right locations for them was made more complicated by reluctant landlords who were conscious of Egghead's simultaneous closures. The Internet seemed a more and more attractive option.

Combining with Surplus Direct, Egghead now had an auction site which earned $2.7 million in its first three months of operation. So in December 1997, the management team made a crucial, life-altering decision for Egghead. It decided to abandon every last brick and redirect all Egghead's resources into clicks.

Within six weeks Egghead had closed its remaining stores, including a distribution centre and its corporate headquarters. The 2,000-strong staff were reduced to 300; the organisation offered 40,000 varieties of hardware products, 10,000 software products and a plethora of accessories. Egghead had become Egghead.com.

Egghead.com invested in operating structures with sophisticated systems to manage online ordering, customer handling and marketing messages. It entered major advertising agreements with crucial Internet sites and signed deals with Yahoo!, GeoCities and CNET. Egghead.com embarked on campaigns in conventional media to inform online consumers that it offered "Three intelligent ways to shop for the best values on the web: Superstores ("with over 30,000 products online"); Auction ("action-packed online bidding"); and SurplusDirect ("the online liquidation dealer").

By the end of 1998, research company Media Metrix reported that, in terms of growth, Egghead.com ranked as the fourth most popular Internet shopping site. Once Egghead had decided to dismantle its bricks-&-mortar business in favour of an online enterprise, the company's fortunes were significantly improved.

The story doesn't end there. In late 1999, CEO George Orban suggested that establishing new Egghead stores might not be out of the question. He's on record as saying that he believes "the biggest threat to online companies is from more traditional companies". It seems that Egghead.com may yet revisit the bricks-&-mortar option.

Analyse Online Potential

From the extreme of reluctance to go online, many retailers have succumbed to near-panic in a desperate attempt to win back, or retain, market share.

The temptation of going online can be like the impulse to join a gold rush: desperate souls, smitten with gold fever, rush to the gold fields without ever considering whether their chances of finding gold make the effort worthwhile. It's clear that there isn't necessarily good value for *all* retailers in going online.

Yes, if their product is compatible with the Internet platform, retailers will gain massive benefits by going online. But in some cases almost no value can be gained by going online. Some types of clothing, low-price FMCGs and beauty products spring to mind as product categories which don't see many benefits from e-commerce.

Going online must achieve added value from both the customer's and the company's perspectives. Does the customer feel any advantage in purchasing online? Is access to products easier? Is the selection larger, the price lower or the service better than buying in a retail environment? Does the company gain value buy being online? Does it enjoy greater customer loyalty, lower transaction costs or faster response capabilities?

The decision to go online comes down to the question of what value the manoeuvre will add to the brand. Answering this question requires careful and realistic analysis of a company's existing core business and future objectives.

Ask the Customer A key consideration is that, no matter what channels your business adopts, your's consumer's expectations must be satisfied. Problems occur when there's a gap between consumer perceptions and the reality you offer. So, identify these expectations by asking, not just your existing customers, but your potential customers, your competitors' customers and the younger generation of customers as well.

Regardless of the channels your offline business adopts, you must anticipate, must be prepared to accommodate and must satisfy your consumer's expectations.

"Asking" needs to result in useful answers which will suggest a direction for your clicks-&-mortar concept. Unfortunately, a classic truth rules: consumers don't know what they want. You have to tell them. But what a consumer survey can usefully achieve is problem identification. The airbag, for example, was a great and simple idea that has saved thousands of lives. Consumers didn't suggest this as a solution, but they did identify the problem that it addressed. ABS brakes, the microwave oven, the video recorder and non-stick Teflon surfaces were all developed as a result of consumers identifying problems and needs.

So ask the consumer about what they find negative in the shopping process. Price and affordability? Having sufficient time to shop? The downsides they perceive in Internet versus real-world shopping? Look for patterns in the feedback and find ways of categorising the identified problems: lack of time, lack of advice, lack of money, lack of trust, lack of inspiration might be problem clusters you can see. Once you've identified the problems and understood their causes, you can turn them into opportunities.

I'll give you an example. Your respondents may have passed on comments such as "I hate shopping because it's boring." Such responses may suggest a category of problems broadly caused by lack of inspiration. This problem proposes solutions: you may think about an instore entertainment program; or you might consider revamping your image to ensure that full information is available to customers legibly, comprehensively and entertainingly. The aim of your consumer survey is to gain a clear understanding of the best direction for your business. Make up a table like the example below. Use it to tabulate the problems detected by consumers and the solutions you come up with to turn those negatives into opportunities.

Model 3.1: *Problem and opportunity survey*

	Sample survey table	
Problems and negatives identified by consumers	**Problem clusters**	**Solutions and opportunities**
no time to shop	lack of time	offer extended hours phone/Net order options
shopping is boring	lack of fun/inspiration	introduce in-store demo program; competitions
too difficult to get shopping home	delivery problems	offer delivery deals i.e. free with $X worth of shopping
too expensive	lack of money	offer payment options; in-store reward program

Cut into Profit Margins

Charles Schwab is the largest investment company in the USA. The company invests private people's money in all sorts of investment products. When Charles Schwab combined two organisations — the offline Charles Schwab and the online eschwab.com (now known as schwab.com) — the company faced a major decision. Online, it was offering its customers substantial discounts. These weren't offered for the same products offline. So the company had two choices. Either it could increase the fees online or decrease the fees offline.

Charles Schwab decided to cut the price by 25% offline, in all its retail stores, with the risk of a potential revenue loss of US$125 million in year one. The result, however, was that Charles Schwab increased its total earnings in the first year of operating with the off- and online strategies.

You could conclude that the concerns the organisation had over potential revenue loss were unfounded. But the Charles Schwab case is a dream scenario. The organisation's existing market position (number one in the USA), and its ability to react quickly to market opportunities and threats (like eTrade.com, an aggressive online investment site operating in direct competition with Charles Schwab) were factors which contributed to the success of the Charles Schwab strategy. And the product category with which the company deals is media-transparent: it can move seamlessly to the Internet without any disruption to operations because the product is virtual. Investing online is just as easy, easier, than investing by phone or in person at a branch office.

Learn Patience

Many dotcom business plans prepared in 2000 don't expect their finances to be in the black until 2003-2004. That sort of time demands patience. On the other hand most, if not all, retailers need to have a black bottom line on a daily basis. It's required by their investors and boards and the same is increasingly the case for dotcom companies. Investing in the Internet demands a change in this attitude: startups need time to succeed.

Patience is counter to retail culture but it's a virtue which retailers need to cultivate if they're to competently manage the one to one (see Chapter 15), clicks-&-mortar future. Minute-by-minute monitoring of sales figures and the need for daily changes and corrections — like putting products on sale, changing the shelf position of products, activating a newspaper campaign or stopping one if it isn't working, figuring out what your competitor must be doing to have decreased your customer flow — has trained industry players to react quickly. This has had the simultaneous effect of nearly eliminating patient habits from the retail culture. So, retailers are rarely mentally equipped to fashion realistic time frames for online development strategies. It's a major challenge for them to have to wait for the online channel to return a profit.

This lack of patience infects senior management, board and shareholder vision and the resulting short-sightedness is probably the reason behind most retailers' opinion that it's not worth going online.

Analyse Cannibalisation Threats

Many retailers have convinced themselves that an online version of their business will interfere with and dilute their existing revenue model.

It's likely that the introduction of an online revenue stream will have an effect on existing bricks-&-mortar business, but this need not be deleterious. In introducing online products to their businesses, for example, banks are eliminating the relevance of fees on many transactions which can be conducted on the Net. Often, a range of online services can add extra and desirable dimensions and revenue channels to existing services and products. But the car industry provides us with an example of cannibalisation in action.

Securing a loan through a car dealer can be a pain. You've finally found the car you want and now you have to go through the tedious loan approval process which delays your acquisition of the new vehicle. A range of online car sites has now developed concepts which help the consumer with finance and loan documentation. So, when buying a vehicle from a bricks-&-mortar yard, the online finance company can approve your loan within five hours and send your cheque to the retailer by courier within twelve hours. At the same time as offering this service, online car sales sites are diluting the role of the car yards. With the loan being handled more quickly and painlessly by an online car loan company, any consumer loyalty there may have been towards the car yard moves from the dealer to the online finance company. Online car purchases are the next step and the car yard will potentially disappear from the vehicle buyer's sight.

To handle the fear and threat of cannibalisation, you need to conduct a cost-of-opportunity analysis. The purpose of this is to quantify the cannibalisation that could occur and what the cost of avoiding such cannibalisation would be. Determine the threats (like discounted product prices, sold via the online channel), put a dollar value on each of them and prioritise them in order of expense. Then identify the opportunities the potential cannibalisation will annihilate and value these losses. What opportunities are you losing by not executing a clicks-&-mortar strategy? What services is your online or offline competitor likely to capture from you? How do these potential lost opportunities and threats affect your revenue plan for the next five years?

Here's a warning. The fear of cannibilisation is strongest when you don't know what to fear and in 80% of cases, you'll be trying to rationalise your own and your colleagues' gut feel. By identifying every part of your business that you feel is vulnerable to erosion if you introduce an online business channel, and by valuing each of these elements and the costs of the opportunities lost or gained, you'll decrease the cannibalisation fears that are delaying your transition to a multichannel strategy.

Fund the Online Presence

Most retailers will recognise this conundrum: how to finance an infant online presence by using the company's offline resources — financial and human. Withdrawing the necessary funds from the bricks-&-mortar end of the business will inevitably damage the company's bottom line and dilute its value, while offering no guarantee that the offline company can provide enough funds for the online setup to gain substantial market presence. On top of this it's clear that most online experiments find it impossible to break even after the first year. In the offline world, this would be required to justify an offline investment.

There's no doubt that the best way to establish a serious online presence is by separating the setup costs totally from the existing bricks-&-mortar operational costs. Establishing the online entity as a separate company will make it easier for investors to understand the losses. It will also open up an opportunity for outside investors — welcome support during serious online growth.

So how do you liberate funds to foster a startup? First, separate the startup's financial and expansion plans from those of the current business. This way you limit damage to the existing business if the online venture fails. Then identify small and large goals and time frames within which to achieve them. These are then milestones against which you can measure progress and justify the online venture's development. Revenue, infrastructure savings and share values should set the parameters for one set of goals. But don't neglect customer satisfaction and retention and goodwill measures, all of which are connected with service and information quality and the synergy, the smooth operation, between the offline and online entities. (Read more about synergy in Chapter 6.) Nailing down goals from the beginning is an imperative part of paving the way for accountability and of liberating the board's collective mind and disposing it to look favourably upon an emerging startup.

Fear of Losing Control

Fear of losing control is a powerful inhibitor to retailers going online. To dilute a revenue channel which they know, own and run with high success in favour of something unknown is a disconcerting prospect. An understandable concern, though often unfounded, as illustrated by the Charles Schwab experience. The irony is that, by resisting the establishment of online business ventures, retailers may be counting themselves out of opportunities and, thereby, losing control to even more complex concerns like being stuck in a business model that may be redundant within five years.

Ultimately, resistance to any change is rooted in culture. Retail players will need to adopt a mindset that can encompass strategic alternatives like online auctions (as eBay.com did, capturing millions of dollars from the local classified pages), One to one production (which General Motors plans to launch within a few years) or fully digital and automated online trading (which Etrade.com is pursuing). These concepts all demand startup investment way ahead of any revenue returns. Retail's internal culture will need training in patience, in constructive self-criticism and in the active adoption of improved trends if the industry wants to avoid seeing its enterprises unravelling and dissolving in the face of online competition.

Catch-24/7

7-Eleven started the trend back in the seventies. As its name indicates, the convenience store was open from 7.00am to 11.00pm. The term 24/7 has become shorthand for twenty-four-hour-a-day, seven-day-a-week service. This 24/7 trend ushered in twenty-four-hour consumers for whom opening and closing times no longer exist. They expect stores to be open whenever they require their services.

In 1999, *USA Today* ran an article titled "I Want It Now". It described a society in which consumers are becoming increasingly impatient and intolerant; one in which they know what is possible and are unwilling to accept anything less than the best. The article was one of the first to articulate the fact that lack of time has contributed to the creation of impatient consumer behaviour; of a consumer generation that has experienced, through e-mail, a decrease in response time from a couple of days to less than twenty-four hours; and of a consumer environment that demands instant gratification.

A study conducted in 2000 by David Lewis Consultancy showed that 77% of US consumers and 73% of UK consumers would find it useful being able to shop outside normal opening hours. The future consumer will do a lot less pre-shopping planning than we might have expected ten years ago. Forget about long shopping lists and detailed budgets. Forget about planned shopping trips and weekly food schedules. Most of these habits were formed when shopping hours were limited and you had to make sure you didn't forget the milk after 6.00pm on Saturday to avoid a milkless Sunday.

More and more grocery stores in metropolitan areas are now open twenty-four hours. This educates the consumer out of planning habits and into the habit of impulse and as-needed shopping. For small independent retail stores, the pressure to stay open is as great as the impracticability of doing so. For these retailers, opening stores for extended hours can be more costly than having the shop closed. The birth of the Internet has exacerbated this "open-all-hours" pressure.

Unfortunately, catch 24/7 is a fact of our time, and it's probably here to stay. But this doesn't mean that every store that's not open twenty-four hours a day, seven days a week will expire. What it does mean, though, is that retailers will need to clearly understand which consumer problems (as elucidated by the problem-detection survey I discussed earlier) they're offering to ameliorate and they'll need to promote these as points of differentiation. Survival and viability will be a matter of retailers identifying and focussing on their strengths. Many of these will lie in the retailer's ability to effect personal contact and sensory experience. More about these important retail assets in Chapter 8.

Cruising Thailand's Virtual Aisles

7-Eleven is the largest network of convenience stores on earth. At any time, day or night, you can buy your fresh eggs, garbage bags or slurpees from any one of the 18,000 affiliated or franchised stores throughout the world.

7-Eleven opened its first store in Thailand in 1989. The chain took its name from the sixteen-hour-a-day service it offered. Now, the Thai stores are pioneering a new kind of shopping by removing the physical restrictions of walls and expanding into the limitless shopping aisles of cyberspace. 7-Eleven Thailand plans to adopt an e-commerce service by building a business-to-consumer network throughout its 1,400 branches.

Over the next few years 7-Eleven Thailand plans to install computer kiosks in every store. Here customers will browse 7-Eleven's virtual aisles for consumer items not regularly carried on the shelves, will make their selections, place their orders, and come back a few days later to pick up and pay for the goods.

This e-commerce initiative will offer a convenient solution to shoppers who don't own computers, who don't have Internet access or don't have credit card facilities. It will also benefit those customers who are reluctant to give out their financial details online.

The 7-Eleven cybermall will initially offer local products, but there are plans to establish links with producers further afield, constantly broadening consumers'

CASE STUDY: 7-Eleven

choices. Additionally, 7-Eleven has plans to be an online shopping network for emerging t-commerce (television) and m-commerce (mobile) players.

Piyawatt Titasattavorakul, the managing director of Thailand's 7-Eleven network says, "We want to develop the outlet to be a centre of the community where people can come to buy food, drinks and other consumer products, and use related e-commerce services in one place."

If this 7-Eleven business-to-consumer initiative finds its market, it will considerably boost Thailand's e-commerce economy.

Brand Migration: Be Prepared

Let me say upfront: an online channel isn't appropriate for every retailer and a clicks-&-mortar partnership isn't the solution for every e-tailer. These alternatives depend on many variables including the suitability of the product to the Net (its retail price against total fulfilments costs, as discussed in Chapter 2), current competition within the product category on the Net, and customer preferences and problems. But no matter how little you believe your business needs a clicks-&-mortar strategy, it's important that you examine the option and determine when or if such a transition should take place. Circumstances change constantly, and you must be prepared for the strategy if its adoption became imperative. The purpose of the following exercise is to instruct retailers on being ready for a clicks-&-mortar launch and on not missing the boat if it sails. Be prepared to migrate your brand to an alternative revenue platform.

Where does Your Business Fit in an Online Future?

To click or not to click The questions you need to ask yourself as a retailer are:

- How would your online presence affect and be received by your existing distribution network?
- How would your failure to go online affect your business in five years' time?

Compare the forecasts you make in answer to these questions and assess which scenario (adopting an online presence or remaining exclusively offline) offers your business the better outcome.

Assess the clicks and mortar mix Now assume that 25% of your potential revenue will, within seven years, come from online activity. How would this assumption affect your online plans over the next seven years?

- Would it persuade you to identify and capture new offline business?
- Would it direct your offline business into new revenue-earning areas?
- Would it force you onto the Net as a pure-play?
- Would you go online by becoming part of a clicks-&-mortar partnership?

Analyse and define online success What is your definition of online success? When framing your answer take into account the fact that it's unlikely any online presence will make money in its first three years. Estimate the infrastructural cost savings an online business, running parallel with your offline business, would achieve. Typically, online channels save money on staff costs, volume purchases and the smaller commercial premises needed to house reduced staff numbers and stock quantities. The desirability of an online presence comes down to an assessment of the costs of opportunity gains and losses and to determining the added value to be gained by an online presence.

Define online goals Use your definition of online success to identify goals and to locate them within a time frame. Your online development strategy should use the goals that fashion it as milestones against which to measure success.

Redefine Revenue Models

Retailers and brands are being forced to rethink and reposition their existing marketing platforms. It takes the discipline of thinking laterally to redefine business: put question marks against all your established operations, assumptions and habits. The ultimate aim of redefining and/or repositioning your business in the market is to ensure it becomes more convenient, easier, cheaper, faster … in short, better. When opting to add an online stream, by establishing a clicks-&-mortar partnership, or when taking any new business direction, the added value for the consumer must be clearly present and perceptible.

In June 2000, The Body Shop announced Body Shop Digital, an online concept complementing the existing bricks-&-mortar chain. At the same time as introducing Body Shop Digital, the organisation revisited its existing model to ensure it was achieving and harmonious match with the online channel. This is a clicks-&-mortar necessity and one which should confirm that the brand and the business models through which it lives is in synchronicity with consumer demands.

Every retailer has been through some repositioning process. Notable examples are Shell Limited's creation of the Shell Select stores, Egghead's closure of all its stores in favour of a purely online reincarnation as Egghead.com, Nordstrom's transfer of almost all its goods and services online, and Gateway's decision (in 1996) to diversify from its exclusively online business model by opening more than 200 retail stores in the United States. Gateway's move was based on the assumption that Gateway customers wanted personal contact when purchasing computers.

The wisdom each of these organisations displayed was in identifying market preferences in their product categories and being prepared to flexibly adopt considered alternative business models when the market dictated the need. Shell established a second revenue platform to differentiate the brand and recover it from generic anonymity and consumer indifference. Egghead fulfilled an apparent need for a 24/7 software and computer service. Nordstrom added credibility and innovative values to one of the United States' oldest and most respected retail stores. And Gateway promoted the importance of human contact to its corporate identity.

Let's consider ten services which are likely to be redefined (or already are in the process of being redefined) by clicks-&-mortar or pure dotcom solutions. None of these solutions existed two years ago. And in most cases, each of the categories these services and products belong to were struggling to find added value models for going online.

24-hour loans Who says that a fixed price for a certain loan is mandatory? Several online loan providers are currently working on the development of online, twenty-four-hour auction sites at which consumers say how much they are willing to pay for loans and under what conditions. The site then auctions this to the best loan offer within twenty-four hours.

Automatic home delivery If you've been serving a customer for some time and have noticed what the consumer's buying pattern is, you're able to predict what groceries your customer will need from week to week. Home delivery is now available for all sorts of products. It's a fast-changing service that's being transformed by the virtual shopping list. Now online whitegoods are being installed in the garages of consumers' homes enabling the online home delivery company to assess needs and deliver groceries and household items. In many cases, the online appliance is aware of grocery needs which the owner hasn't noticed.

Virtual software You needn't buy software offline. Buy it and have it downloaded online. Software is more expensive when purchased offline and offline purchases don't include the service packages which are offered with the online product. Most software companies offer a discount of 25% if their products are purchased online.

Flexible warranties Companies like WarrantySuperstore.com sell warranties for the products of your choice — online. These warranties carry the conditions we've been used to and offer some more flexible options. You can also insure small things, like your $100 vase, as well as large items worth hundreds of thousands of dollars. The processes are all simple in either case: no questions, no waiting time and low fees.

Personalised music It's a difficult task these days selecting music from among the thousands of CDs that are on the vibrant music market. Several online companies offer predictive modelling to help consumers choose their music. Predictive modelling extracts customer profile information and marries it with purchasing histories to isolate items that are likely to appeal to each customer's exhibited tastes. Some retailers, like Tower Records and Imix.com help you create your own CD compilation and then have the facilities to design and print your own personalised CD or DVD covers.

Micro-gaming These are services in which you play online games free of charge. At various points in your gaming career you reach new levels where you, as the key player, will be asked to prepare yourself for the game's continuance by purchasing ammunition or other tools. The more you purchase the stronger you are in the game. Millions of people play online games, and the business viability lies in low-cost (two cents per game too, for example) but very frequent product sales.

Personalised cars You no longer need to compromise your needs by taking any old car on the lot. Now you can design your own vehicle. Volvo offers twelve million ways to combine your car online, a service that's impossible to handle in the bricks-&-mortar stores.

Shopping reminder Upselling and cross-selling in stores has always been a challenge, requiring vast knowledge from staff and demanding a lot of their time. In the consumer world of the future, cross- and upselling will be ably handled by wireless technologies. Imagine you've just dropped a pack of pasta in your supermarket shopping basket. You might then receive a message on your phone informing you of some special offer — buy another pasta product and get pasta sauce for half price, for example. Wireless commerce, or m-commerce, is set to become a discipline for promoting, communicating, transacting and branding products via a mobile device. Read more about m-commerce, WAP (wireless application protocol, a software development platform) and i-mode technologies in Chapter 7.

Virtual photos Several online photo albums, like Onlinephotolab.com not only offer to develop your pictures offline and send digitally formatted versions of them to you, they also store the pictures in online photo albums that allow access at different levels to family, friends and colleagues.

Visit **DualBook.com/cbb/ch3/RetailTrends**
for the latest on retail trends.

Consumer Expectation and Service Response

All businesses, whether there's a niche online for them or not, must recognise changing consumer demands and expectations and understand how evolving service expectations should be met. Let's consider a couple of hypothetical examples and examine how consumer expectations and retail service delivery might evolve.

First, expect to have thrown out all your currently-held service understandings by 2005. For example, what retail consumers expect to receive free of charge these days may attract a fee online. If you purchase a can of soup and need instructions on how to prepare it, your mobile phone will give you direct access to the supermarket's online chef who'll provide the requisite "serving suggestion" advice for a per-use or subscription fee. Such service introductions will be necessary components in future revenue models.

On the other hand, things for which consumers expect to pay a fee today may be supplied free in the clicks-&-mortar future. Parking space will have to be free as this will be one method of encouraging consumers to visit real-world product showrooms. Delivery will be free because retailers will be competing with online services. The price for shopping late will be the same as shopping during business hours because the 24/7 arrangement will become a must-have and not just an extra retail service.

Consumer expectations, online and offline, change constantly. And they're are as various as the people that hold them. So retailers need constantly to analyse their product/service category's relationship with consumers and ensure that their own business isn't becoming disconnected from general expectations.

For example, in 1999, Kodak introduced an online photo development lab which offered consumers digital versions of their photos as well as conventional paper versions of the same shots. But digital photography had already captured a major share of Kodak's traditional film and photo development business, weakening Kodak's relationship with the consumer. The industry leader had left its response to the online threat too late. It hadn't kept pace with its product category's relationship with the consumer, a fact which robbed Kodak's brand image of its potency.

So, if Kodak was learning from this experience, it would be looking, not to maintain its existing product, but to establish a new revenue platform towards which a brand migration could be staged. This lesson, of anticipating and being prepared to accommodate consumer expectation, is valid for every conceivable product.

But what, for example, are banks doing to prepare for brand migration to a new revenue platform? Now there are dotcoms to handle all banking roles: lending, transacting, saving and investments can all be handled online by non-bank operators. Etrade.com, Quicken.com, Schwab.com, Ebank.com and so on have decimated the money management monopoly which banks once held. I'd be interested to know if any banks have established migration plans for their brands.

In Chapter 5 I'll discuss how formulating and executing migration plans.

Visit **DualBook.com/cbb/ch3/FreeServices**
for updates on the trend of offering services free of charge.

Summary

- There are seven main reasons behind retailer resistance to making an online transition. They're catch-22s because they define the very nature of retail culture:
  - the fear of destroying distribution networks;
  - failure to analyse online potential;
  - unwillingness to cut into the profit margin;
  - lack of patience;
  - fear of cannibalising existing business;
  - unwillingness to fund an online presence with offline financial resources; and
  - fear of losing control.

- A key consideration is that, no matter what channels your business adopts, your consumer's expectations must be satisfied. Ask consumers what they find negative in the shopping process. Once you've identified the problems and understood their causes, you can turn them into opportunities.

- Retailers need to anticipate and be prepared to accommodate changing consumer expectations. Constantly analyse your product/service category's relationship with consumers and ensure that your own business isn't becoming disconnected from customer expectation.

- An online channel isn't appropriate for every retailer and a clicks-&-mortar partnership isn't the solution for every e-tailer. Going online must achieve added value from both the customer's and the offline company's perspectives.

- Prepare alternative revenue platforms and be ready to migrate your brand to them in response to consumer demand, competition, technological development and emergent opportunities.

Action Points:

Analyse your business's compatibility with online opportunities and prepare a brand migration plan

Prepare alternative revenue platforms and be ready to migrate your brand to them.

Apply your consideration of these questions to the draft clicks-&-mortar operational strategy you developed in chapter 2's action points. Your answers will indicate how compatible your business is with online operations and suggest a brand migration plan.

Assess the costs of online opportunity gains and losses

- How would your online operations affect and be received by your existing distribution network?
- How would your failure to go online affect your business in five years' time?

Compare your forecasts and assess the opportunity gains and losses of each scenario. Which offers your business the better outcome?

Propose alternative revenue models towards which you can migrate your brand

Assume, hypothetically, that 25% of your potential revenue will, within seven years, come from online activity.

- How does this assumption affect your online investment plans for the next seven years?
- Would you execute a line extension and move your brand into another revenue category?
- Would you aim to harness new market sectors?
- Would you adopt a clicks-&-mortar strategy to broaden your brand's customer base and access flexible operating options?

Set brand migration goals to measure new revenue model success

What's your definition of success for your brand? Or, think of the question this way: what four points would qualify a strategy as a success in the eyes of your board? When framing your answer take into account the fact that it's unlikely any online presence will make money in the first three years. Quantify the infrastructural cost savings you think an online version of your existing business would achieve. Attach a time frame to the success drivers so that these become goals against which the success of the business in transition can be measured.

Review

Now you should have turned your draft clicks-&-mortar operational strategy into one which includes specific and quantifiable goals and options for alternative revenue models, including online components. Read Chapter 4 and consider the vital importance of consumer trust to your brand's future success.

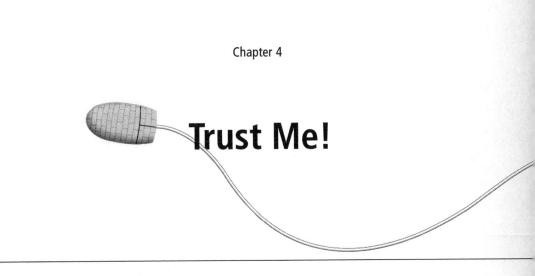

Chapter 4

Trust Me!

"Trust me!" An imperative statement full of implications: that you can trust the speaker; that you should trust the speaker; that there are a million reasons why you can't and shouldn't trust the speaker. On the Internet, as in all consumer interactions, trust is crucial, essential to inspiring consumer ease about fundamental issues such as security and privacy. Without trust, e- and m-commerce cannot realise their optimum viability.

Imagine some guy approached you on the street, opened his coat and, displaying his pendant range of Rolexes, said, "PSST! Wanna buy a watch?" Would you buy one? Probably not. And why? Because you don't know the guy and, what's more, you won't know who or where he is once the transaction's complete.

Not many of us would risk buying a watch on the strength of our own judgment and in the absence of any infrastructure to give even the illusion of reliability, traceability and credibility. But if two thousand people invested in the watch guy's wares, their concerted and demonstrated opinion would coax an individual into feeling justified in making a similar investment. What would make the difference? Word of mouth. The recommendation of others would direct your choice.

The more we become used to certain procedures, the more universally they are known and spoken of, the more we rely on them. Over time, reliance becomes the basis for the creation of trust. Trust is not a procurable commodity. Earnt over time, it grows from superficial familiarity into deep confidence. In commercial terms, brands are the vehicles for garnering and retaining consumer trust. As a product becomes familiar to consumers they begin to develop trust in the brand the product represents. Not surprisingly, therefore, trust is responsible for branding success. Don't underestimate it. Trust = brand.

Consumer trust is responsible for branding success: trust = brand.

In this chapter I'll take you through the elements that can inspire consumer trust in your online and/or offline business. I've dedicated a whole chapter to this topic because trust is the key to successful online, offline and clicks-&-mortar commerce.

Trust = Brand

In the earliest days of the World Wide Web, word of mouth was an enterprise's strongest and cheapest promoter. People trusted each other more than advertisements. As more sites are being born on the Internet (as I write the Internet consists of more than three billion pages and is growing at a rate of more than 250,000 new pages a day) the more promises advertisers have to make of their products to compete with the explosion of alternatives available to the consumer. And the more alternatives consumers face, the more information they need in order to make educated decisions amongst an increasingly confusing plethora of choices.

Unable to make contact with the majority of our senses, online brands are obliged to lasso consumer attention by appealing to our sight and hearing.

This limitation, coupled with the youth and exponential growth rate of Internet enterprises, makes the establishment of trust a real challenge for online brands.

Mismanagement Creates Mistrust

Consumer trust in online brands is decreasing every day. Users demonstrate, not only *lack* of trust in websites and online brands, but *mistrust* of them. According to an AC Nielsen study conducted in 2000, more than 75% of users are sceptical about the information they're exposed to on the Net and almost as many fear an invasion of their privacy online and doubt the security of online purchasing systems. This lack of trust is a symptom of weak brand management and mismanagement of consumers.

I once conducted an experiment in an attempt to ascertain the validity of consumer suspicions about online privacy. I created an email address for the sole purpose of using it as my junk mail address. The exercise didn't involve me in becoming a heavy Web surfer. I occasionally signed up as a member of a site if I liked the look of it, but I never ticked the boxes that allow the site manager to bombard my inbox with "additional material which may interest [me]".

After three months, the results of my experiment shocked me: 623 emails managed to find their way to my address, yet I had offered my new address only fourteen times! No wonder consumers are suspicious about being asked to volunteer personal information. The following model exhibits Internet fears held by a survey group of teen Web users. These fears have to do with the teens' regard for their personal privacy and for the importance of trust. The reported fear of privacy being invaded or compromised inhibits these users' trust of online dealings, a fact reflected in general user attitudes.

Model 4.1: *Fears that inhibit teenage consumer trust in the Net*

	Total	Males	Females	Ages 13–14	Ages 15–19	Website owners	Non-Website owners
Sample Sizes	2759	539	2220	1118	1641	1181	1537
	%	%	%	%	%	%	%
Loss of privacy	22	24	22	19	25	20	24
Internet crime	8	12	8	7	9	9	8
Dangerous info	6	6	6	6	6	6	6
Censorship	5	13	3	3	7	7	4
Viruses	5	8	5	6	5	5	5
Hackers	2	3	2	3	2	4	1
Stalkers	2	2	3	3	2	2	3
Getting scammed	–	1	–	1	–	1	–

Source: Cheskin Research and Able Minds, Inc
*(*Teens and the Future of the Web, *August 1999)*

The Trust Business

Between 1998 and 2000, websites offering consumers assistance in evaluating various sites' trust factors appeared. Sites like Truste, VeriSign and BBB Online help consumers manage their choices and their personal data. The latter issue is grounded in the fact that consumers' personal and behavioural data is becoming a valuable commodity to e-commerce operators. As well as the privacy and security concerns the promulgation of one's personal data raises, the information is of value, and consumers are learning not to give it away. After all, this data isn't confined to birth dates, addresses and average incomes. It encompasses shopping behaviour and interests and highlights likely future consumption patterns.

What's really interesting about the emergence of these sites is that they're educating consumers in the value of their own personal data. They're teaching consumers to be sceptical and careful when choosing transaction partners, whether online or in the real world. Consumers need to know who they can trust.

Online and offline businesses, too, are reassessing this most important and valuable of assets, consumer trust. It's an asset that has come to be treated blithely by the bricks-&-mortar retailers that possess it. Yet consumer trust should be nurtured, cultivated and coaxed into clicks-&-mortar deals with extreme care.

Far too many web sites tarnish their brand's image by bombarding consumers with information they neither want nor need. This is a crazy tactic when companies could be systematically using the intelligence gained from their site to tailor messages and restrict communications to items of relevance.

Consumers may know and respect an online brand, but their trust in that brand is what keeps them coming back to the site — and the brand. Maintaining your consumers' trust in your brand requires respect for consumer privacy and guaranteeing that the consumers' inboxes won't be packed with superfluous emails once they hand over private information.

Trust: the Reward of Goodwill

Disney is one of the few clicks-&-mortar brands that controls its brand image online. The difference between Disney.com and other dotcom brands is that Disney.com benefits from its longstanding consumer familiarity and thereby inspires the trust that a small club of online brands, like Yahoo!, AOL and CNN.com, have established and maintained. I reckon most consumers trust the Disney brand enough to click "yes" when asked by Disney.com to hand over their credit card numbers. Can the same be said for dotcom gambling brands such as goldenpalace.com? At this stage, most consumers hesitate to hand over personal information to most dotcom brands.

Model 4.2: *Disney.com benefits from consumer familiarity*

You can't buy goodwill and trust. As I've emphasised earlier in this book, these assets are earned over time. Considering no online brand has existed for more than a few years, consumer trust has been earned by a mere handful of Net-born brands. However, to maintain and extend consumer trust, established brands like Disney have realised they must apply the same principles that inform and guide their offline brand management to their online efforts. Primary among these principles is respect for the customer. Disney identifies the qualities that earn respect and trust (family values, safe community, etc.), builds its image upon them, and ensures these values are transferred online.

Clicks, Bricks and Trust

Trust is an indispensable goal in online and offline operating strategies. But consumer trust in dotcoms is falling at just about the same rate as Internet business is expanding. A study conducted by Cheskin in July 2000 shows that only 10% of consumers perceived little or no risk when purchasing on the web; 23% of users felt threatened by hackers; and 16% were concerned about unauthorised acquisition and abuse of their personal information. And a study conducted by CNN/Time in March 1999 shows that only 13% of kids between thirteen and seventeen trust the Internet.

It's clear that establishing consumer trust in the etailer is a fundamental objective if consumers are to be convinced to buy online. So the issue is how do e-tailers inspire trust in their online clientele?

Compare these facts. In June 2000, Greenfield Online, in the United States, reported that 50% of respondents to its study rated the offline store as very/somewhat important. Only 15% felt the bricks-&-mortar presence wasn't important at all. Perhaps surprisingly, it was the youngest members of the survey group, the under-25s (who you might expect to be more habituated to e-commerce than older interviewees, that placed the most importance on the store's offline availability with 61% of this group rating it very/somewhat important.

Combining offline with online enterprise is, therefore, clearly beneficial for online brands that are still trying to cultivate their consumers' trust in them. One of the most effective ways for online brands to establish trust is via a clicks-&-mortar relationship.

Bricks Give Clicks Trust

Alliances between established offline operators and online e-tailers can bestow credibility upon the online business. This assists the online partner in developing a relationship of trust with its customers. Trust and confidence are necessary motivators for people to become consumers of any particular product. Hence, more and more online brands are establishing unions with bricks-&-mortar businesses to gain leverage from the offline brands' solid market position. Well-established real world operators, who've been in town for years, not only have a physical presence for their customers but an intellectual, even emotional, one too. The store is represented by the real people that constitute its staff; it's patronised by real people in the form of friends and family who've shopped there as long as you can remember. This familiarity is described as "transparency", a quality which helps build trust. Companies with a non-transparent image are unfamiliar, unseen and, therefore, untrusted. Consumers trust what they know, can see and understand fully.

Online brands have a long way to go in the trust stakes when compared with their offline equivalents. But, during 1999, Internet brands did gain some level of consumer trust in their own right. Research conducted by Intertrust (in August 2000) of 102 high-profile sites reveals that the most trusted brands are also the best known brands. In order of the consumer trust they enjoy, the top ten were:

1. yahoo.com
2. netscape.com
3. blockbuster.com
4. usatoday.com
5. microscoft.com
6. walmart.com
7. go.com
8. excite.com
9. dell.com
10. lycos.com

The least trusted e-commerce sites were:

1. monsterboard.com
2. cyberkids.com
3. jennicam.com
4. spinner.com
5. well.com
6. carpoint.com

Visit **DualBook.com/cbb/ch4/BrandTrust** and discover which brands consumers trust and which brands they don't.

Clicks Give Bricks Market Access

Because offline companies enjoy the consumer trust that their online competitors have yet to harness, you might wonder what reciprocal benefits the retailer can gain from a clicks-&-mortar partnership.

The reciprocated benefit is that dotcom companies are able to offer the bricks-&-mortar partners instant credibility as innovative Internet players. Consumers might trust a certain brand, but this won't guarantee that the image-conscious consumer will find the brand attractive. So, as I discussed in Chapter 3, offline retailers are wise to respond to consumer expectation and offer multichannel access to their products. By going online, traditional retailers gain access to a new market segment. The clicks-&-mortar setup, as the experience of Gap Kids' (children's clothing retailer) and Victoria's Secret (women's lingerie outlet) reveals, gives skilled retailers a means of extending their revenue platforms and strengthening their already well-established market positions.

Visit **DualBook.com/cbb/ch4/ConsumerTrust** for the latest on consumer trust issues.

Old Bricks And New Clicks: Toys "R" Us and Amazon.com Join Forces in a Toy Venture

Since opening its first baby furniture shop, which also sold toys, in 1948, Toys "R" Us has grown into a toy giant. The toy shops gave way to toy supermarkets, and over the past fifty years or so, Toys "R" Us evolved into an $11 billion-dollar operation with over 1,450 stores around the world. The bricks-&-mortar retailer is now one of the most trusted toy brands and enjoys a reputation for variety, service, quality and value for money.

No offline giant could afford to ignore the sheer number of e-sales that rocked the retail world during the Christmas season in 1998, particularly a retail chain specialising in toys. A study by Jupiter Communications conducted around that time determined that online toy sales were noticeably eating into the sales figures of the offline stores. Determined to be part of online toy shopping in time for Christmas 1999, Toys "R" Us actively set out to establish a commercial web presence.

With no expertise in the field, and lacking a starting point, the Toys "R" Us route to the online highway was fraught with wrong turns and dead ends. Toys "R" Us initially entered into halting negotiations with rivals Toysmart.com and Brainplay.com. Toys "R" Us then joined forces with a Silicon Valley venture capitalist, Benchmark Capital. The deal looked good. Toys "R" Us issued statements decalsing its hope to "be the clear leader in the online retail market for toys and children's products by fourth quarter 1999". For a variety of reasons, this deal also came undone.

Despite the money that the company poured into their website, Christmas 1999 was not a good online experience for shoppers or the company. There were technical failures and order glitches. Toysrus.com failed to meet many a Christmas shipment deadlines and was forced to offer compensatory gift vouchers along with protracted apologies.

On the other side of Cyber Street, things didn't look that good in the virtual toy department of Amazon.com, the earth's biggest online store. Amazon.com ran out of Pokemon paraphernalia while, at the same time, being forced to offload a significant quantity of excess stock.

In August 2000, Amazon.com and Toys "R" Us announced that they had joined forces in a ten-year strategic partnership deal. The arrangement would allow both companies to exercise their strengths, co-branding Amazon.com with Toysrus.com in time to capitalise on the next holiday season. Amazon.com undertook to do what it does best, taking care of technical capabilities, warehousing, customer service, billing and delivery. Toys "R" Us bought and held the partnership's merchandise.

Toys "R" Us chief executive, John Eyler, said, "The strength of the Toys "R" Us brand and our merchandising expertise combined with Amazon.com's unbeatable Internet savvy will create an online presence second-to-none."

Building Trust

Partnerships with offline entities donate credibility to dotcom companies as well as bestowing an inheritance of consumer trust upon them. I'll discuss the trust issues associated with clicks-&-mortar partnerships later. Right now, let's look at looser partnerships and various means of building trust — through association, by buying it, building it through advertising and building it independently — which apply to offline and online enterprises.

Building Trust Through Association

One way to instantly achieve market place trust is to work with a partner with an established, well-respected, well-known brand. Even though trust can't be bought, it can be borrowed, reflected upon one partner by an alliance with another.

Visa is a globally-recognised identity. The company offers association with thousands of online and offline companies all over the world through a number of services, like payment avenues. The seventh most-recognised brand in the world, according to the American Advertising Association, Visa's association with smaller companies is of significant benefit to those little operators. If the consumer isn't familiar with a certain website or retailer, the Visa brand's presence can allay the consumer's suspicions and replace them with a sense of confidence in the business.

However, a 1999 study conducted by AC Nielsen offers a contrary reading of this observation. When the American Express symbol was shown to a survey group almost all of the 264 respondents recognised the symbol, but only one fifth of the group affirmed that its presence would increase their trust in a business associated with the symbol. Consumers aren't naïve. They're educated, often cynical and not likely to be persuaded by propaganda unless it suits them. Consumers have keen perceptions and recognise where their confidence lies. The association of brands like Amex and Visa with brands that are new to consumers doesn't necessarily communicate a guarantee of a store's quality. It simply telegraphs the understanding that payments can be made safely to that store.

Partnerships are solidly-forged relationships between business allies with compatible aims. They exchange and share brands and develop products, advertising campaigns and marketing promotions jointly. In 1998 Visa teamed up with Yahoo! and created a special Yahoo! Visa payment card. It's difficult to imagine a stronger form of partnership: Visa's part in the partnership gives approval to the Yahoo! brand. The benefits of this association for Visa are that it gets direct access to a new market segment, one that attaches value to innovation and e-commerce's convenience and style.

As online brands gain consumer trust they, too, become attractive partners for other dotcoms. One example is Drugstore.com. In 2000, Amazon.com. acquired yet another stake in Drugstore.com indicating Amazon.com's faith in predictions that the online pharmaceutical industry will become major e-commerce business. Instead of Amazon.com building another product offering, it chose to plug into existing expertise and the reputation that accompanies it. Of course the benefits were mutual. Unquestionably, the Amazon.com brand enjoys high-level credibility and trust which its association with Drugstore.com reflects upon that partner.

Buying Trust

Since 1996 a range of organisations has emerged especially to donate the appearance of trustworthiness to dotcom companies. Dotcoms solicit the association of services like Truste, VeriSign, BBBOnLine and Publiceye whose associations with sites are indicated by their logos. The logos, therefore, stand as seals of approval. Some of these third parties offer the consumer payment security. Others control privacy issues like how consumer information is used. Others monitor the dialogue the website enters into with the consumer.

Surveys carried about by AC Nielsen in 2000 showed that these "security brands" did manage to inspire consumer trust in the host organisation. If these watchdogs donate credibility to dotcom operations, as they seem to do, they're adding value to their host companies. A 1999 Cheskin Research/Able Minds Inc. survey revealed that teenage online consumers invest some trust in websites that carry "trusted symbols".

Of course, this type of bought trust is impermanent. The credibility lies in the watchdog's brand. Every time its logo is exposed via a host site, the watchdog brand itself becomes stronger (assuming that the watchdog's promises are being kept on the site) without necessarily helping the host brand gain its own strength or trust relationship with consumers. The very minute the watchdog's logo, which becomes for the consumer a "trust symbol", is removed from the site consumers will conclude some fault in the host site. The dotcom's bought trust will have evaporated.

Model 4.3: *Trusted symbols*

Survey respondents were asked to select the two symbols that would increase their trust if seen on a website

	Total	Males	Females	Ages 13–14	Ages 15–19	Website owners	Non-website owners
Sample Sizes	2759	539	2220	1118	1641	1181	1537
	%	%	%	%	%	%	%
Trusted Symbols							
Trust-E	60	56	61	63	59	62	59
Visa	45	42	45	42	46	42	47
Mastercard	37	35	37	36	37	34	39
VeriSign	26	34	25	28	25	30	24
BBBOnLine	24	26	23	22	25	25	22

Source: Cheskin Research/Able Minds Inc. in
"Teens and the Future of the Web" (August 1999)

Model 4.4: *Symbols, familiarity and trust — traditional versus web*

Survey respondents were asked two questions:
1. **Of the symbols shown below, please check all those you are familiar with or have seen before.**
2. **Please select the two symbols that would increase your trust the most if you saw either of them on a website.**

	Familiar	Increase trust	Increase trust by those familiar
Sample Sizes	315	315	varied
	%	%	%
Traditional Brands			
Visa (spinning)	83	24	27
American Express	84	18	19
BBBOnline	18	16	36
Mastercard	79	13	14
Visa (word)	70	111	13
Microsoft	58	9	13
Discover	72	7	8
Mastercard ShopSmart	34	6	10
IBM	19	4	11

continued over

	Familiar	Increase trust	Increase trust by those familiar
Sample Sizes	315	315	varied
	%	%	%
Web-Originated Brands			
VeriSign	36	25	53
Netscape Key	40	12	24
TRUSTe1	23	12	31
Excite Certified Merchant	33	10	21
Safe Secure Shopping Guarantee	20	9	22
TRUSTe2 (blue circle)	10	9	30
PublicEye	6	9	10
Lycos (Top 5% seal)	30	5	12
Cybercash	27	5	15
Handshake	23	4	14
RSAC	19	4	17
Excite Guarantee	11	4	14
BizRate	8	3	4
Shop.org	4	3	0
Ascend	12	2	3
Virtual Emporium	3	2	22
iCAT	13	1	2
e-merchant	0	0	0

Source: Cheskin Research and Studio Archetype/Sapient in
"eCommerce Trust Study" (January 1999)

Building Trust Through Advertising

Remember my Rolex man at the beginning of this chapter? You couldn't trust him because you didn't know him. He would have no reputation or credibility for you. Advertising's aim is to break down unfamiliarity, to install knowledge and, thereby, to create trust. So advertising communicates trust-creating values like stability, dependability, safety, competence, leadership, tradition and wisdom.

The reason for consumers placing more trust in television and radio advertising than they do in web advertising is that offline media itself is more familiar than online media. It's been around for decades. The familiarity and trust corollary means that consumers know and feel comfortable with print and broadcast media and its messages. They know where they're coming from; they can trust the culture. It's obvious that trust is related to time. The longer a medium has been known and integrated with daily life the more conversant the consumer is with it. Banner ads on the Net are at the opposite end of the spectrum. They're perceived by users as being untrustworthy and insubstantial, because they're new and because, being Net-based, they're capable of monitoring user behaviour.

Tests conducted by search directory company, BTLookSmart.com show that users trust banner ads less than plain links, even though the links direct the user to a commercial message. Why? Because links are triggered by key words, introducing themselves to users who may find some relevance in the product attached to the link. Banner ads, on the other hand, appear uninvited on the screen and offer general messages that are often irrelevant to the user.

Building Trust Independently

But for a few exceptions (like Amazon.com, Yahoo! and AOL, six years old and, therefore, the older, trusted generation of the Net world), Net companies aim to engender consumer trust within as short a time as possible. There are some, though, that are prepared to build trust "organically", to cultivate customer relationships over a long period. Organic trust allows for the most solid of customer relationships to develop because it grows gradually, and gathers strength slowly. Think of organic trust as a tree. A cross-section of its trunk will reveal slow growth over years in the concentric rings that form it (See model 4.5 overleaf). Every ring represents a time period and every ring adds strength, solidity and vigour to the tree's growth. The tree's growth slows over time, until it stops completely, paralleling the gradual growth of consumer trust, which eventually levels out. Then consumer trust in the brand is fully operational, having been built on the brand's reputation, reliability, value.

Trust Development

Let's analyse how trust grows. It begins with superficial first impressions, grows into passing familiarity and matures to become unquestioning confidence in a subject.

Model 4.5: *The trust tree*

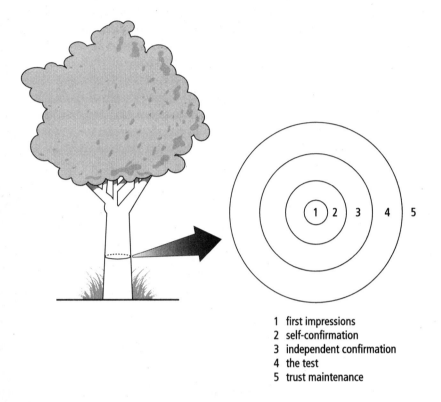

1 first impressions
2 self-confirmation
3 independent confirmation
4 the test
5 trust maintenance

Phase One: the first impression Model 4.5 illustrates the birth of trust in first impressions, the sapling of the trust tree. A brand that's new to consumers is greeted by them with varying levels of acceptance, scepticism and dismissal. Their reception of a new brand is determined by the product's applicability to them and/or by their experience of similar products. Consumers' awareness of a brand will grow over time, depending upon its relevance to them and the frequency with which they are exposed to it.

Phase Two: the self confirmation Self-confirmation is achieved with the brand's early maturation. If that brand, once new to the market place, demonstrates consistency in its quality, reliability and presentation, it builds itself a platform for trust growth. To instil this impression in the consumers' collective mind, to confirm your brand as being consistent, you need to invest in the brand's frequent and relevant exposure. This phase can be the most expensive and time-consuming of the trust development process. The more anonymous a brand is, the slower its trust building will be. The more distinctive the brand, the quicker its trust building will be, as long as its values are firmly, consistently and harmoniously communicated.

Model 4.6: *Self confirmation = frequent exposure*

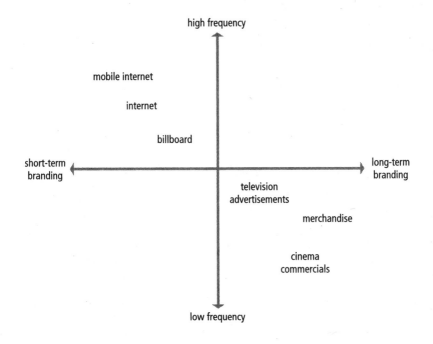

Phase Three: the independent confirmation Independent confirmation is the reward of a brand's growing reputation, one for which independent observers can be called upon to make positive testimonials. After a while, it's important to have an independent party confirm the image your brand has been promulgating for itself. Your brand needs the persuasive power of recommendation when developing consumer trust in itself. This independent confirmation can occur through customer testimonials, partner endorsements, any positive brand exposure that greets the consumer from an apparently objective perspective — as long as the confirmation is from a respected source.

Phase Four: the test Even though some advertising experts claim that perception can become reality, the reality is that poor product quality or substandard performance will negate brand-building and decimate trust-building. A brand's message must reflect its products' realistic promises and the promises must be in harmony with brand's identity. Many products might not be the best of their type in the world, but if the consumers' brand perception embraces this understanding, trustworthy communication has been achieved.

Phase Five: maintenance From this point on, consistency motivates consumer trust. Brands that surprise their consumers by adding value to products — more functionality, improved quality, better service, new innovations (like interactive distribution channels) — add strength to consistency-derived trust. Conversely, diluting product quality is brand homicide. Even lifetime-long friendships can fall asunder, so brands that let their consumers down more than once can annihilate the hard-won goodwill they've established.

Building Trust Through Clicks-&-Mortar Relationships

Building trust through a clicks-&-mortar alliance combines the strategies involved with association, advertising, bought and independent trust-building which I discussed earlier. Consumer trust in clicks-&-mortars is achieved by joint advertising, joint product development, joint promotions, joint distribution and joint identity. This is the dotcom's quickest access to the credibility its offline partner has established over time.

The clicks-&-mortar relationship donates well-established offline values, like competence, wisdom, dependability and stability, to the online partner. It's this donation that partly explains how online partners come to enjoy consumer trust or, at least, to enjoy the credibility reflected from their offline ally.

WebMD.com is an admirable example of an online brand which, in just six months, grew from an unknown Net player to being a well-known and trusted brand. The rapid acquisition of market recognition was because WebMD.com teamed up with a range of respected brands such as Dupont, CNN, Microsoft and Excite.com, all representing different sectors (software, media, the medical and communications industries) and all trusted by consumers. The aggressive technique implied this message: not only one, but several successful and respected brands can't be wrong.

Online partners also get to share in the trust consumers place in offline partners because of the real-world party's physical interface with the consumer. A physical presence is more important than any of the other trust-builders I've discussed (association, buying trust, building trust through advertising and building trust independently). The physical presence is an obvious offline trait. Drugstore.com has successfully proven this point.

When the online company teamed up with RiteAid in 1999, Drugstore.com managed to get its name in more than 3,800 stores across the United States. Some of the stores they found exposure in had existed for more than 35 years. By moving into the real world store, one-year-old Drugstore.com inherited the trust consumers had invested in stores they'd known for years. And for a category like pharmaceutical products, consumer trust is a particularly sensitive and vital ingredient. You could safely assume that pharmacists possess some intimate knowledge of their customers' habits, needs and lifestyles.

Trust-building and -maintenance

The aim of designing a trust-building program is to define brand values that inspire trust, to establish trust-building promotional activities and to ensure that the clicks-&-mortar setup gains leverage from the positive reputations already established by both the offline and online businesses.

Time and consistency build consumer trust.

The most important thing to start with is to define what trust values you would like to see related to your company. Even though trust is the "final" goal, a lot of other values will accompany the outcome. The way to define these values is to ask consumers what trusting your brand means to them. Your respondents might suggest that a competent privacy policy would encourage them to trust your brand. They might place an emphasis on delivery guarantees, product expiry-date vigilance or product innovation. The values your survey identifies will form the foundation of the many activities you will have to pursue in building brand trust.

Model 4.7: *Trust-building plan*

What does trusting Brand X mean?	
Customer responses	**Value this represents**
Competent privacy policy	Respect for consumer privacy
Reliable delivery	Delivery guarantees
Honest value	Best prices available

It's one thing is to establish trust. It's another to keep it. Remember: establishing trust is only part of the story. Your company needs to dedicate energy to maintaining consumer trust on a daily basis. Your staff must ensure that consumer expectations are met or exceeded at all times. To achieve this, you need to operate a trust-maintenance program.

Using model 4.7 add an extra column to accommodate your answers to the question: What activities are in place to achieve constant exposure of this value? If the surveyed trust-building value reported by the consumer group was "never offer products for sale that are beyond their expiry dates" the action to insert in the final column would be a strategy to ensure out-of-date products are never on the floor. Your trust-maintenance program might also include a service guarantee protecting your customers from any lapse in the policy.

Model 4.8: *Trust-maintenance plan*

What does trusting Brand X mean?

Customer responses	Value this represents	Activities to achieve exposure of this value
Competent privacy policy	Respect for consumer privacy	Adopt trust symbols; solicit testimonials
Reliable delivery	Delivery guarantees	Publicise on-time delivery over peak periods
Honest value	Best prices available	Offer survey results of global pricing

In 1999, Cheskin Research and Studio Archetype/Sapient conducted a study on consumer trust in e-commerce. The study highlighted criteria necessary for maintaining consumer trust and its results are summarised in model 4.9.

Model 4.9: *Building blocks of e-commerce trustworthiness*

Seals of Approval	Information about other companies that specialise in assuring the safety of websites
Network Level 1	Icons symbolising security of the computer network as a whole, such as TRUSTe or Verisign
Network Level 2	Text accompanying the items
Technology Level 1	Icons symbolising commerce-enabling functions, such as MS Commerce Server, ICAT, IBM e-business mark, and Browser compatibility marks
Technology Level 2	Text accompanying the icons
Merchant Level 1	Icons symbolising merchant service security like Mastercard, VISA, Amex
Merchant Level 2	Text accompanying the icons

continued over

Brand	Importance of the company's reputation in choosing to do business with them
Overall brand equity	Consumer awareness of what this company does for consumers outside of the Web
Web brand equity	How well the company's website fits with consumers' sense of what the company is about generally
Benefit clarity	On one's first visit to the site, how easy it is to discern what the site is promising to deliver
Portal/aggregator affiliations	Mention an affiliation to portals and aggregators such as Yahoo, eXcite, ivillage, Lycos etc.
Co-op third party brands	Promotion of "third-party" quality brands
Relationship marketing	Sending updates and other notices to consumers
Community building	Facilitating interactions between individual shoppers
Depth of product offering on the site	How many varieties of product type the site contains
Breadth of product offering on the site	How many types of products the site contains

Navigation	The ease of finding what the visitor seeks
Navigation clarity	Terminologies for navigation and content are apparent for the user to differentiate
Navigation access	The navigation system placement is consistent, persistent and easy to find
Navigation Reinforcement	There are prompts, guides, tutorials, instructions to aid and inform the user to perform transaction and or search tasks on the site

Fulfilment	The process one works through from the time the purchase process is initiated until the product is received
Protection of personal information	The information one provides is guaranteed to be used for no purpose other that what one gave it for, without their approval
Tracking	The site provides feedback or a confirmation number once the order is placed
Recourse	The transaction process allows for recourse if one has a problem at any time during the process
Return policy	How clearly the return policy is explained
Simplicity of process	How simple it is to buy something

continued over

Presentation	Ways in which the look of the site, in and of itself, communicates meaningful information to you
Clarity of purpose	The visuals/layout effectively convey the idea and purpose of the site — consumers would know they can purchase products when they get to the site
Craftsmanship	The degree to which, when one first views the homepage, one believes that the website developers were skilled in their efforts
Resembles other trusted sites	How much the site resembles others that consumers have come to trust

Technology	The ways in which the site technically functions
Functionality	Overall, how well the site seems to work
Speed	How quickly each page, text and images appears

Source: Cheskin Research and Studio Archetype/Sapient in
"eCommerce Trust Study" (January 1999)

Brand The better-known your brand, the more easily it attracts trust, as model 4.10 shows. But brand exposure must be managed carefully to define identity and communicate values consistently while avoiding disadvantageous associations. A solid reputation is built upon the promises a product makes being fulfilled. Positive consumer experience feeds the reputation that is so important in growing trustworthiness.

Navigation Consumers should be able to find what they're looking for with ease, both in the offline and online environments. Online, effective navigation is internationally comprehended and understood across all demographic groups and is simple and quick to download. Effective site navigation is a precondition to effecting trust. It demonstrates your brand's understanding and fulfilment of its customers' needs. Make your site an easy place for consumers to visit and find what they're after by offering superior navigation.

Fulfilment of product promises is vital to the establishment and later maintenance of consumer trust in your brand. Make sure your site clearly indicates how orders will be processed and provides information on how to source assistance if there are problems. Regardless of where a brand originated, brand reputation and the consumer's personal experience of it are vital contributors to consumer trust in the brand.

Model 4.10: *Relationship between familiarity with a brand and trust in it*

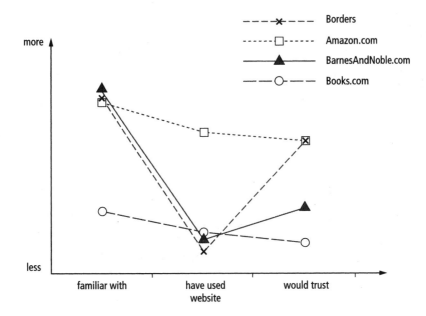

*Source: Cheskin Research and Studio Archetype/Sapient in
"eCommerce Trust Study (January 1999)*

Security guarantees Web-based seals of approval are displayed on sites by independent third parties that have subjected the approved website to due-diligence tests covering product delivery, warranties, website navigation and clarity, credibility with partners and industry peers. VeriSign and Truste are examples of companies offering this service which donates trust-by-association to the host website. These companies' seals of approval reassure visitors that the site's security has been established, tested and is being monitored. The companies that provide these seals of approval are referred to as "security brands" and their presence, even more than that of credit card symbols, communicates trustworthiness.

Information must be consumer-oriented. Fundamental to gaining consumer trust, it must clearly state company policies and offer consumers well-aimed, intelligently composed and relevant data. Parallel with this is the importance of presentation. Your design, as well as your language, must connote quality and professionalism. Consumer-oriented security and privacy measures and encryption information must be present and clearly articulated in any plan to maintain consumer trust. Ask only for necessary and relevant information, provide shipping and return guarantees, and offer consumers easy communication channels, online and offline.

Technology Up-to-date, intelligent and practical technology also communicates professionalism, a vital quality in building trust. So keep your site and your offline store equipped with the latest procedures as well as logical and accessible navigation. If your site is based on plug-in technology, like Shockwave or Flash, an effective download zone has to be established and tested for all environments. Using new technology is good and proper, as long as it is user-friendly.

The brand custodian A really good way to maintain consumer trust is to employ an independent brand custodian whose role is to keep an eye on your company's relationship with its customers. The custodian oversees all communications and ensures consistency, clarity, relevance and intelligence are used in every dealing with customers. This person, independently of the marketing or product development departments, reviews all material to be sent out online and offline, deletes junk messages and adjusts worthwhile ones. In short, the brand custodian ensures that the brand isn't destroying its credibility and consumer trust in it by throwing unwelcome and irrelevant material at the consumer.

Synergy and consistency

Consistency reflects values like stability, dedication and promise-keeping. So consistency between clicks-&-mortar partners' internal and external communications, the perceptions they inspire and the operations they achieve is key to developing consumer trust and a workplace culture that promotes it. Well thought out company policies that are service-focused and communicated consistently across all channels cohere staff, consolidate workplace morale and boost your brand's reputation.

Offline and online synergy Integration between off- and online operations is a fundamental necessity. Using one voice offline and another online is like creating a Dr Jekyll and Mr Hyde schism for your brand identity. Your clicks-&-mortar voices must be consistent with each other. Remember, your customers will include people who've had a strong relationship with your offline partner and have decided to bravely go online. The Internet experience is as uncomfortable for many consumers as driving on the opposite side of the road to that they're used to. So it's in your brand's interests that you help customers feel at ease with online practices. The online consumer's perception should be, "This is like visiting the store, only faster." But if the online experience is too different and the consumer has to consider what to do and how to do it every step of the way, your online channel is unlikely to acquire bricks-&-mortar customers. Worse, offline customers will feel let down, even betrayed by their brand.

Design consistency Changing your graphics frequently is a dangerous exercise. Your visual symbols and signals make your brand familiar to consumers. In a commercial world of rapid change, quick business births and, often, speedy deaths, consumers are looking for icons they recognise. A brand's logo, colours, typeface and other graphics convey a shorthand summary of its identity, purpose and values. In practical terms, this means that the same logo should survive with few changes over many years. The same principle applies to all design elements: colour schemes, uniforms, shop outfitting and site design should all be consistent with each other and be guided by your brand's values. Don't ignore details. Even name badges and price tags should form part of your clicks-&-mortar's design story. Your website and real-world store and all your communications should share the same identity so that messages to your customers are unequivocally from your brand. The more consistent the bricks-&-mortar store is with its online partner the more trustworthy the business will look from a consumer's point of view.

Message consistency It's vital that your brand's use of language and the messages it conveys are consistent across media. Unfortunately, too many clicks-&-mortars emit conflicting advertising messages and use disparate language registers, tones of voice and styles. Additionally, advertising and promotional messages must be consistent with operational outcomes. If your brand is well-known for high quality and service and not necessarily for low prices you'd be damaging your brand to covey promises of cut prices and minimal service. The example sounds extreme but I myself have seen a number of sites and stores, like Levi's and Gucci, fall prey to this mistake, one which leaves consumers thinking, "What does that business stand for?"

Clarity in all communications is fundamental and a quality which is assisted by consistency. Clarity doesn't necessarily mean simplicity but it does mean comprehensibility. This "easy-to-understand" principle results in an "easy-to-trust" response. Try it yourself. If you're being introduced to a new acquaintance and you have reason to question their motivation for wanting to meet you, it's likely you'll reserve your trust of the newcomer. Out of discomfited suspicion you may even try to terminate your conversation with him. So it is with new brands whose message, purpose and/or values are not conveyed with clarity to consumers. For consumers to devote time to investigating a brand, they need to understand the brand's function, how it might apply to them and where to procure it.

The Internet still poses fundamental uncertainties for consumers. These insecurities prevent consumers from engaging in e-commerce and they retard the development of trust. Your clearly and consistently communicated company policy should address consumer concerns before they surface. Forestalling concerns will be perceived as empathetic, a human quality that helps instil consumer trust and loyalty.

Navigational consistency Clearly define action steps for your customers and staff. Everyone knows what to do when entering a supermarket. The navigational language is, by now, pretty universal. The fruit and vegetables are near the entrance and the pet food and house cleaning equipment are in the farthest aisles. The same is the case for consumers entering Starbucks Coffee or McDonald's stores. Consider what steps you want customers to follow during their instore or online visits. If consumers feel uncomfortable or inadequate because your navigation and planning is too difficult to understand, they won't offer you their patronage for long. The only thing you will achieve is reduced visitation and consequential decrease in trust.

Summary

- Trust is responsible for branding success: trust = brand. It's the key to successful online, offline and clicks-&-mortar commerce.
- Time and consistency build trust. Brand trust is established when products consistently meet or exceed consumer expectations. Surprises can only afford to be positive and reflective of the brand's core values.
- Lack of consumer trust in a brand is a symptom of brand mismanagement.
- The most effective way to establish trust is to adopt an offline presence independently, or by forming a clicks-&-mortar relationship with a well-established bricks-&-mortar partner.
- Not only is it apparent that users don't trust the information they're exposed to on the Net, they fear abuse of their privacy online and doubt the security of online purchasing systems.
- Maintaining consumer trust in a brand requires respecting consumers' privacy and guaranteeing that their inboxes won't be packed with superfluous emails once they hand over private information.
- The familiarity and trust corollary means that consumers know and feel more comfortable with print and broadcast media and its messages

than with the same messages delivered by online media like the Internet and mobile Internet.

- Consistency reflects values like stability, dedication and promise-keeping. So consistency between clicks-&-mortar partners' communications, the perceptions they inspire and the operations they achieve is crucial to developing consumer trust and a workplace culture that promotes it.
- Employ an independent brand custodian whose role is to monitor your company's relationship with its customers by overseeing all communications and ensuring consistency, clarity, relevance and intelligence are apparent in every dealing.

Action Points:

Trust management

Employ an independent brand custodian whose role is to monitor your company's relationship with its customers by overseeing all communications and ensuring consistency, clarity, relevance and intelligence are apparent in every dealing.

Trust evaluation

Do consumers trust your brand? Ask your customers to rank your brand on a scale of 1 to 10, with 10 indicating complete trust in the brand. A trust-evaluation score lower than 7 (when averaged) indicates you really need to concentrate on trust-building. A score of more than 7 means your brand is being well received but trust-maintenance is a constant duty.

Trust identifying

Ask your customers:

- what trustworthy values they associate with your brand;
- to define what your brand delivers to support these associations;
- to nominate what characteristics they would like to see your brand exhibit in order to inspire their trust in it.

Analyse the results and assess which of your brand's characteristics are most positively influencing the development of consumer trust in it. Use the final part of the survey to assess what trust-building factors your brand strategy is missing.

Trust building

List your brand's existing perceived trust-inspiring features and those you'd like it to communicate. In a parallel column identify appropriate products/services/activities which will, over time, achieve the realisation of each feature.

Trust maintenance

Trust maintenance is dependent on your brand keeping its promises tirelessly. Add a third column to the list at step 3 and describe ongoing activities that will ensure your brand focus remains on each trust-building feature.

Trust and the channel strategy

Assess the trust-builders and the trust-maintenance activities you've identified in step 3 in terms of the channel strategy you developed (as part of the clicks-&-mortar operational strategy, last used at step 4, Chapter 3 action points). Next to each medium in your channel strategy (bricks-&-mortar store, mobile Internet, the Internet, WebTV) describe activities that will develop the trust-builders you've identified.

Constantly monitor trust development

Remember that your trust-maintenance activities will need constant revision in light of changing business priorities and consumer perceptions and expectations.

Chapter 5

Making Clicks-&-Mortars Click

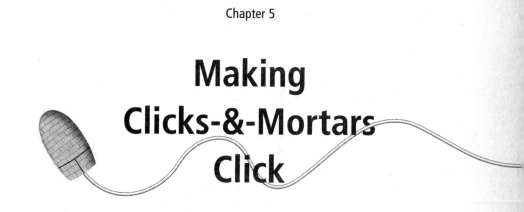

Offline retailing is facing online inevitabilities, but they're inevitabilities with options. Pure online, pure offline and online-offline combinations summarise the marketing future. The solution your brand arrives at should be driven by your consumer's preferences and expectations, your product's properties and tolerances and your brand's trust- and reputation-development needs.

Let's review our progress. So far I've discussed retailing history in an effort to explain how retailing has arrived at the online impasse (Chapter 1). I've attempted to analyse retail's and e-tail's comparative advantages and weaknesses and looked at offline's online adaptation options in light of these (Chapter 2). Chapter 3 faced the reality of retailing's catch-24/7 bind. And in chapter 4 I discussed the fundamental ingredient in any business's growth — the acquisition of consumer trust. Together we've arrived at an understanding of the online inevitability in retail's future. Hopefully, I've prompted you to engage in some self-, service- and consumer-analysis. Now, I want to introduce you to the options the Internet offers existing and potential enterprises.

Let's begin with a concrete understanding of the terms that are central to your future strategic considerations: bricks-&-mortar and clicks-&-mortar. And let's assess where these entities are in consumerism's evolutionary process.

Offline firms that operate from a store environment, communicate their services via traditional means (like letters, phone calls and personal visits) and which promote themselves via old-world broadcast media (like print, television, radio, billboards and so on) are known as "bricks-&-mortars". The expression communicates the fact that these businesses exist in the physical world rather than in the virtual world of "clicks" operations.

The term "clicks-&-mortar" was coined by Charles Schwab's public relations department. (Charles Schwab is one of the world's leading online investment companies, the largest discount brokerage company in the United States and one of that country's foremost mutual funds managers.) The expression was used to explain and justify the company's business strategy. Their tactic combined bricks-&-mortar stores with an online presence — a revolutionary concept which has since been emulated across industry sectors by integrating Internet and physical distribution systems. So, clicks-&-mortar refers to a combination of off- and online business activity.

Fact: E-tailing Alone is no Gold Mine

To be frank, as I've declared earlier in the book, e-tailing will never become a gold mine. In fact every research study conducted on e-tailing profitability indicates that online retailing will face some very tough times before achieving the merest shade of black in its bottom line. The majority of e-tailers lose money on every transaction. While Amazon.com makes about US$5 on every book order, fulfilment, shipping and product costs account for a loss of about US$7 on every one of the high-profile e-tailer's non-book orders. Glance back at model 2.5 in Chapter 2 and you'll see Fogdog Sports, a sporting goods outlet, loses US$5 an order while Drugstore.com loses about US$11 to US$16 an order.

There are a number of reasons for e-tailing's struggle to get into the black. Here are four of them.

Fulfilment costs and lack of scale The erroneous claim that online fulfilment are lower than those borne by bricks-&-mortars trapped many retailers into believing they'd have to offer huge discounts to compete with their online equivalents. When Amazon.com opened its shop in 1995 it offered discounts of 30% on bestsellers. Barnes & Noble turned up the heat online in May 1997 by offering 40% off its retail stores' titles. WalMart, one of the largest US booksellers, has a Web outpost slashing 45% off listed prices. And buy.com promises 50% discounts. Such savage discounting, fulfilment costs (which can be as high as US$16 an order for most dotcom e-tailers) and lack of scale all conspire to keep most dotcoms in the red. Online storefronts wear surprisingly high distribution costs — about 15% of sales for Web sellers like Borders or $US20.90 for every US$100 worth of sales according to Thomas Weitzel Partners (August 1999).

Many product categories, such as toys, are disadvantaged right from the start by their shipping needs. They're difficult and, therefore, costly to pack and ship, and they often consitute only small orders. Jeff Bezos', CEO and founder of Amazon.com, choice of books as the platform for his online store was not a matter of chance. His decision was the result of analysis based on criteria of his design. Two criteria were the product's fulfilment and shipping needs. For books, the process is uncomplicated and relatively cheap: they're easy to pack, unlikely to suffer damage in transit and can be shipped at minimal cost. Ebay.com, the auctioneer, is one of the few pure-plays to turn a profit, in part because it refuses to deal with fulfilment at all. Customers are responsible for shipping products themselves. Macromedia.com

> *The majority of e-tailers lose money on every transaction.*

survives because its product only exists in a soft version and so can never be tied up in high fulfilment and shipment costs.

Read more about fulfilment issues and the role they play in contributing to online/offline synergy in the next chapter.

Inexperienced inventory management Poor inventory management also causes major losses for many dotcoms. Most e-tailers are managed by personnel with no retail background. This fact, plus the inexperienced merchandising teams, brutal price copetition and inefficient product return systems that pure-plays work with result in poor gross margins for online-only players. Nordstrom, Gap, Old Navy and Target, however, have been successful online because they *are* retailers. Established retailers in categories like apparel and drugs enjoy the advantage of 2,000 to 3,000 basis points in gross margins. An irony is that direct sales to customers, which is online retailing's chief *raison d'être* (as far as brands and manufacturers are concerned), cause e-tailers with ill-developed fulfilment processes problems, the result being that up to 10% of products are returned by customers.

Online marketing costs Pure-plays have to build brands and consumer loyalty from scratch. Established brands, like Levi Strauss, gain leverage from their established brand loyalty and accumulated marketing knowledge. Experienced offline brands spend about 18% less than startups on establishing retail websites (*Red Herring*). Amazon.com and a handful of others achieved the feat because they were on the FMA team. Creating a brand in 1995 and 1996 was easier than it is now because there were few true e-commerce offerings.

Offline brands spend 18% less than startups.

But those days are over. E-tailer marketing costs are high. Online "rent", my term for the price of time and space on media channels for on- and offline brand marketing, inflated hugely over the last decade of the twentieth century. Barnes & Noble, as an example, paid AOL US$40 million to lock up space as AOL's exclusive bookseller for four years. Where a superstore, according to Thomas Weitzel Partners (August 1999), spends an average of US$2.50 promoting a product, e-tailers spend US$17.29 per product.

Online consumer-acquisition costs Right now, most consumers still need to be persuaded to go online. They need to be convinced that there's extra benefit for them in "risking" using their credit card online, waiting a couple of days for delivery and paying for the whole process when surfing the Net. At the same time, almost all e-tailers lose money on every customer. Their customers generate too few orders and too little profit per order to cover the costs of winning them, which can be as high as 65% per order. Bricks-&-mortars don't have the high acquisition and fulfilment costs that are threatening the viability of so many e-tailers. Traditional brands' consumer loyalty and the fact that offline customers deliver their own shopping are key retailer advantages.

According to a study by *The McKinsey Quarterly* in July 2000, for e-tailers to achieve comfortable contributions on each transaction, they'd need efficient order fulfilment processes, average orders of at least US$100 and gross margins of at least 25%.

The Online Dangers for Retailers

A well-established bricks-&-mortar player joining a clicks-&-mortar partnership can enable the online channel to break even. This is because of the offline ally's lower fulfilment, marketing and consumer acquisition expenses. Clicks-&-mortars dealing in brand-sensitive categories like apparel can spend as little as one third or even one fourth of the sums their pure-play rivals, with no established brand presence, spend on marketing.

Model 5.1: *High pure-play marketing costs*

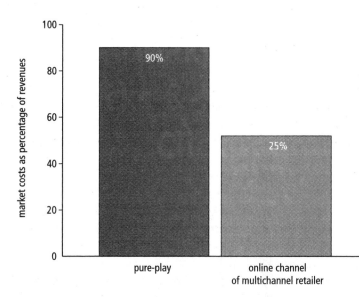

Source: BCG and Shop.org

As I write, US taxation regulations make electronic commerce taxable only if the outfit has a physical presence. The legislation varies from state to state, as do taxes when they are imposed. In September 2000, the California legislature considered a bill for the imposition of taxes on electronic businesses operating in the state, but at the time of writing the bill's fate has not been decided. Barnes & Noble's hands are tied because its stores and its website are run as separate companies. Barnes & Noble holds only a 40% stake in the site as being more involved with it could mean that the site would have to charge its shoppers sales tax. This gives pure dotcom e-tailers like Amazon.com a distinct advantage. With just a handful of physical locations it generally doesn't have to impose sales tax on its shoppers.

Another danger for retailers going online lies in the potential for mismanaging the cultural and personnel impacts of the clicks-&-mortar transition. Full communication is crucial to achieving the synergies that make for viable clicks-&-mortar deals. (See Chapter 6 for more on synergy.) Insufficient strategy explanations to staff and inadequately involving each staff member in the brand's migration will result in an atmosphere of competition between the clicks and the mortar partners, rather than co-operation.

Clicks-&-Mortar Economics: the Healthy Alternative

Maintaining an industrial-strength website and its associated backend systems costs between US$15 million and US$25 million annually, and this won't decrease over time, according to *The McKinsey Quarterly* (August 2000). If anything, expenses associated with hardware and software, which constitute about 30% of website costs, increase with site traffic. Other types of fixed costs, such as warehousing, typically grow as a percentage of revenues. These costs are generally huge initially then continue to depress earnings through depreciation and ongoing expenses like rents. Even if e-tailers made a profit on every order, sales would still have to be high to break even. Just to break even, e-tailers must achieve revenue of about US$1 billion a year, especially for low-priced products such as books (*The McKinsey Quarterly*, August 2000).

Clicks-&-mortar economics are more positive. The retailer's high gross margins make the per-order economics more profitable than they are for pure-plays. And the fixed costs are lower because the brand's reputation reduces marketing expenses. But the real value lies in the benefits of inter-channel synergy (See Chapter 6). More and more consumers are surfing the Net before purchasing products offline. According to an AC Nielsen study (October 2000) up to 34% of consumers check the Net before purchasing a product that costs more

34% of consumers check the Net before purchasing.

than US$100. Early experience suggests that bricks-&-mortar stores with an online channel enjoy increased consumer spending. So even if a clicks-&-mortar's online channel turns out to be a breakeven proposition, it may still be a worthwhile way of reinforcing and extending the franchise.

In short, the Web offers retailers both vexing problems and great opportunities. The e-tailing kings and queens will be experienced retailers, already skilled in direct marketing. There are strong similarities between catalogue retail business and e-tailing. The losers will be pure-plays that fail to build efficient fulfilment, shipping and marketing processes. In clicks-&-mortar partnerships, inexperienced online players can avoid this lethal mismangement by allowing experienced mortar partners to assume control of these areas.

Clicks, Bricks, Brands and Compatibility

Establishing a clicks-&-mortar partnership is costly and time-consuming so it's imperative to ensure that both potential partners are compatible, not only with each other, but with the online and offline environments their jointly-held brands will share.

Obviously, retailers need to undertake a range of considerations before teaming up with a clicks partner and online e-tailers must engage in the same thorough analyses before allying themselves with a mortar partner. Right now, let's look broadly at the clicks-&-mortar structure. It will necessarily be based on a dynamic model because business formats, values and priorities constantly change.

E-tailing winners will be experienced retailers that are skilled direct marketers.

Any business transition must achieve added value from the customer's perspective. Will your offline customer feel any advantage in purchasing online? Will e-tailer consumers perceive added value in being able to conduct business offline? Does an online arm increase your customer's product selection? Does it make your offline business more price competitive? Would your customers think the online service was more convenient than that offered in the retail environment? Increased customer loyalty, lower costs, faster response capabilities, larger selection and improved reputation are among the value gains you should expect from entering a clicks-&-mortar alliance.

Product Compatibility

Model 5.2 (overleaf) shows products and services and their comparative popularity as online consumer items. Physical realities mean that the online conduit just isn't practicable for some products and services. Service stations, for example, might not gain much by entering a clicks-&-mortar relationship, except perhaps when handling consumer loyalty programs which can be conducted online. Fulfilment costs for fragile, large and other difficult-to-pack-and-ship items make many product categories unviable online options.

Model 5.2: *Comparative shares of online sales by product category*

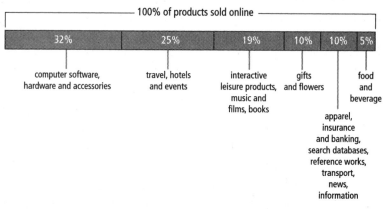

Source: "Brand-Building on the Internet" *(Andersen, Lindstrom 1997)*

Let's examine some product categories *vis-à-vis* their compatibility with the online environment.

Apparel

Among the most attractive online categories because of its large-order and gross-margin potential, clothing and apparel can achieve breakeven point at as low as US$100 million for the strongest traders (*The McKinsey Quarterly*, August 2000). These high per-order economics translate into excellent per-customer returns for established apparel merchants. Skilled traditional retailers who enjoy minimal consumer acquisition costs by leveraging on their established labels are the leaders in this category.

Drugs

This category has proven to be a challenging one in which to succeed. Scale counts only for pharmaceuticals while large volumes in front-end merchandise are often worthless. The real benefit comes from the solid contributions (about US$15 to US$25 per order) of high-frequency prescription sales. However, to reach this profitable level of prescription sales, pharmaceutical e-tailers in the United States must obtain the right to fill prescriptions covered by insurances, and this is where complications occur. The e-tailer, as in Drugstore.com's experience, needs a pharmaceutical-chain ally in order to co-opt the involvement of health insurance agents, a prerequisite in the United States and in most Asian and European countries to supplying prescription items. Failing this the online focus has to be on non-prescription products, like health and beauty items, which are characterised by small orders and low margins, often below US$3 per order. To attain viability in this category, e-tailers have to create special promotions and deal in upmarket brands to increase the average per-consumer expenditure. As a result, online pharmacies rely heavily on prescription drug sales to achieve profitability.

Model 5.3: *Online and offline pharmacy profit drivers*

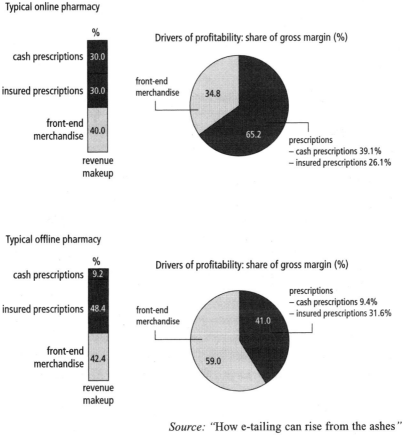

Typical online pharmacy

Typical offline pharmacy

Source: "How e-tailing can rise from the ashes"
(mckinseyquarterly.com, July 2000)

The fact that the online and offline profit drivers lie in two halves of this enterprise's stock creates a synergous relationship between Rite Aid and Drugstore.com's operations. Each partner contributes to the profit of the alliance by focussing on what they're good at.

Books

Large scale is the key to success within this category, which is the main reason Amazon.com, with its annual book revenue rate of US$1.2 billion can show a profit per book sale of US$5. Yet this revenue return means Amazon.com's book business is barely breaking even. Amazon.com's first-mover adavantage has contributed to the online giant's status as one of the world's best-known brands, an asset that has reduced the e-tailer's average acquisition costs to as low as US$19 per consumer (in 1999's fourth quarter). Despite this rare advantage, Amazon.com has yet to show a profit within all its categories. Until its customers spend more per order, Amazon.com won't enjoy great returns.

The following model gives an insight into comparative sales levels by category over the 1998 and 1999 holiday seasons.

Model 5.4: *Christmas orders and sales by category from Amazon.com*

	Orders*		Sales* (US$)	
	1998	**1999**	**1998**	**1999**
Entertainment	3,291	9,354	313,840	1,332,980
Gifts	1,207	8,967	78,040	482,390
Computer products	1,416	5,368	150,420	469,970
Food and wine	306	4,907	27,470	360,820
Consumer goods	1,215	2,699	90,720	313,320
Apparel	845	2,506	67,510	235,570
Home and garden	91	1,096	4,790	84,670

* in thousands

Source: BizRate.com

What's to be Gained in a Clicks-&-Mortar Relationship?

A bricks-&-mortar presence provides dotcoms with the most credible means of entering a market place. A dotcom presence strengthens the local retailer's reputation by adding the cachet of internationalism and innovation. So an appropriate clicks-&-mortar partnership injects major value into the operations of both parties by donating a local presence and a distribution network to the online partner and an international reputation to the offline partner. The combination paves the way for loyal local market growth, through the retail presence, and international branding, via the website. A successful clicks-&-mortar partnership should, after a period defined by its development strategy, increase efficiencies and consumer access for both parties, and gain value for them within these areas: infrastructure, marketing, reputation and brand versatility.

Clicks Join Bricks

Jed Smith came of age at around the same time the Internet was born. As a computer-savvy business student, he firmly believed that e-commerce was the way to go. Similar to the now-famous startup list that Jeff Bezos made before embarking on Amazon.com, Smith made a list of his own. He systematically explored a diverse range of consumer goods best suited to an online commercial environment.

After studying the statistics, he calculated that beauty and health products offered the best margins. And there were other advantages. Health and beauty products were generally small, making them easy to ship; the Internet was uniquely equipped to deliver the wealth of information consumers needed about their prescription drugs; and the pharmaceutical sector had an endless supply of repeat customers with prescriptions to be refilled, soap to be replaced frequently, razor blades that need replenishing, lipsticks that wear down and shampoo that runs out.

The first draft of Smith's online pharmaceutical business plan was ready in December 1997. Conscious of the advantages of being first in the field, he planned to get big fast. He approached venture capitalists Kleiner, Perkins, Caufield & Byers who in turn put the idea to Jeff Bezos who was interested in becoming an investor. Everyone agreed that Smith's notion was worth pursuing.

Kleiner, Perkins, Caufield & Byers helped put together a management team, starting by recruiting the all-important, highly qualified CEO, Peter Neupert. Neupert, in turn, introduced experienced front-end/back-end technicians and designers, pharmacists, editors and merchandising logisticians to categorise and photograph the initial 17,000 items (approximately 14,000 more than the average neighbourhood drugstore) that the online pharmacy would offer its customers. The team even invented category names. For example, if you're looking for vitamins, diet products, or herbs, you'll find them under the "Nutrition and Wellness" button.

Details on prescription drugs are extensive. However it was the prescription-drug side of the site that presented Drugstore.com's greatest challenge. Pharmaceutical benefit managers, who are tied to 80% of Americans through health insurance, refused to deal directly with Drugstore.com. Customers were forced to pay for their prescription drugs in full, and apply separately for the benefits reimbursement.

Peter Neupert set out to overcome this major hurdle. He stepped up negotiations with Rite Aid, a traditional bricks-&-mortar pharmaceutical chain. Rite Aid bought a quarter of Drugstore.com's stock, and General Nutrition Company, a partner of Rite Aid and a supplier of vitamins, bought a further 8%. This strategic partnership now gave Drugstore.com immediate and direct access to the 50 million people who are covered by corporate health insurance plans. Additionally, it gave Drugstore.com's 168,000 customers a further option. They could order their prescription drugs on the Web and then pick them up at any one of Rite Aid's 3,800 retail branches.

The deal was mutually beneficial. Rite Aid wanted to enter the virtual drugstore world, a development too costly to undertake independently and one which it had insufficient expertise to achieve. So Rite Aid's search for an online partner resulted in the chain finding a permanent — and prominent — place on the Drugstore.com site.

The Rite Aid and Drugstore.com partnership achieves perfect synergy: Rite Aid offered Drugstore.com's customers real live pharmacist advice at retail outlets and Drugstore.com offered Rite Aid's customers an efficient website where they could conveniently place their pharmaceutical orders in less time and for less money. This synergy confidently and fluidly established customer trust in both the cyberstore and real-life store.

In June 1999 Forrester Research predicted that start-up Internet pharmaceutical operations would not emerge as the leaders in the field. Rather, they believed that the winner would emerge from a traditional bricks-&-mortar company or a pharmaceutical benefit manager. Drugstore.com, with its strategic partner Rite Aid, is well placed to fulfil Forrester's prediction.

Infrastructure

When Drugstore.com teamed up with Rite Aid, Drugstore.com suddenly gained 3,500 distribution centres around the USA. Rite Aid, on the other hand, gained access to Drugstore.com's online databases and Web presence. This enabled Rite Aid to claim they had national coverage. Now Rite Aid's and Drugstore.com's customers could order and purchase their products online and collect them at their nearest Rite Aid pharmacy. The partnership resulted in customers not having to queue, Drugstore.com not having to establish and man costly warehouses and Rite Aid not having to do all the paperwork. Now the customers typed in their own data, provided their credit card details, and so on, thereby saving the pharmacist time and, consequently, money.

Visit **DualBook.com/cbb/ch5/DrugstoresFuture**
to see how Rite Aid and Drugstore are doing right now.

The cheaper its product and the faster its product delivery, the more value will attend a clicks-&-mortar relationship and the more value the partnership will be able to calculate into its setup costs. Most FMCGs will, therefore, suit a clicks-&-mortar strategy because of their relatively low purchase prices and revenue returns. (The minimum US$70 price point per unit which I discussed in Chapter 1 is a crucial breakeven point from a pure-play's perspective.) However, these factors mean that extra shipment costs (i.e. for items that are difficult to pack and ship) can only be justified in the case of large orders and that quick delivery is not a viable possibility. So a clicks-&-mortar partnership can add value to FMCGs by simulating flexible, efficient and immediate delivery: the consumers themselves take care of distribution by collecting their personal requirements from the bricks partner. Drugs are one example. Their purchase price is low and their delivery time usually needs to be quick.

Brand Handling

The question you must ask yourself is: Will my brand clearly benefit from being exposed both off- and online or would it be more cost-efficient to use resources on other communication channels?

Determining a brand handling strategy means more than working out how many places you can plaster your logo. It's about analysing what values your brand represents and ensuring that these are communicated to the consumer in all situations, via all channels and using all senses. Just think about it. When using the Internet you're chiefly using one sense: sight. You can use your hearing too, but mostly the Net communicates visually. Realising this limitation, offline stores have started to really think about appealing to all the senses, because they can.

The Senses: Offline's Point of Differentiation

Starbucks, the world's biggest coffee shop chain, US-based and now spreading around the world, not only aims to appeal to its customers' collective eye by creating a cozy environment, it also appeals to the olfactory sense and to taste. You know when you're passing by a Starbucks café because you can smell it. The aroma its marketers have created is one of

Starbucks' leading branding points. Having been tempted inside you can sit down and imbibe the total sensory experience: listen to the fountain, smell the coffee, feel the comfortable atmosphere, made all the more so by being occupied by patrons who are there to relax. So the Starbucks brand communicates to all five senses. Do you think it would be possible to move its service online?

Singapore Airlines offers another good example of brand handling that cultivates multisensory appeal. Besides having built its world-famous "Singapore girl" image, the airline connects the whole flying experience with the promises it implies in its advertisements. The flight attendants manifest the serene elegance their commercial representatives suggest; the airline's cabins seem suffused with a certain relaxing aroma, one which also rises from the hot towels the cabin crew distribute frequently. Food flavours and presentation are carefully created with the airline's brand values in mind, as are its inflight announcements which are scripted by an advertising agency. The cabin's décor and the materials used have also been married to the brand's core values which include relaxation, harmony and trust. The Singapore Airlines brand communicates with all five senses, a brand experience that can't be replicated online.

So why is it that major stores like Toys "R" Us, Barnes & Noble and Target have neglected the sensory potential their stores could tap and have focused only on the delivery of their products?

Barnes & Noble enjoyed an 18% increase in total sales through 1999, most of it due to their new cafe concept.

The news is that retailers are now creating brand environments around their products. Barnes & Noble, for example, has been creating a book lovers' club. In the centre of its stores there are now small cafes, oases of comfort and relaxation: easy chairs, lounges, tables and coffee on tap. The store also organises lectures, writing seminars and discussion groups, transforming book buying into a pleasurable adventure. The result? Not only have sales of new books soared, Barnes & Noble enjoyed an 18% increase in total sales through 1999. These increases should be comprehended against an overall increase in book sales in the United States of only 4% in the same year. (Borders, however, saw a sales increase of some 14% in 1999.) Virtual consumers flocked to the Barnes & Noble superstores, not only in search of something to read, but to relax and enjoy themselves in peaceful surroundings with similarly interested people. But the fact is that Barnes & Noble was slow to act on its capacity as an offline retailer to differentiate its business from that of online competitors. It was several years after the appearance of the World Wide Web before Barnes & Noble hit upon the notion of creating an environment which attracted customers by appealing to their five senses and to their sense of community and belonging.

Marketing

The marketing value of a clicks-&-mortar partnership is twofold. For the clicks partner it harnesses trust; for the bricks-&-mortar party it creates wider consumer access. Because of these factors, clicks-&-mortar partnerships increase brand visibility for both partners through wide media exposure.

Because of their long history as part of popular culture, offline media and brands enjoy more public trust than online media and Internet-born brands. We're familiar by now with television, radio and the print media. They've been around for decades. The more time you've been exposed to a certain message, or a channel for it, the more receptive you are to it. On this basis the added marketing value for online companies entering clicks-&-mortar arrangements is likely to be high if they establish a partnerships with solid offline entities, well-known to consumers. This association with the offline partner's established name and the additional exposure that comes with it (in the form of street, broadcast and print advertising) gives the online company increased credibility.

The clicks-&-mortar arrangement gives the offline partner access to a wider customer base and bestows a reputation for innovation upon it. The addition of "innovativeness" to the traditional retailer's solid reputation is positively received by industry experts, the press, the stock market and staff. From a consumer perspective, the value in their local retailer being available online lies in increased accessibility, convenience and efficiency. Online technology makes customised marketing, once a dream for offline advertising, a real possibility for bricks-&-mortar companies. Clicks-&-mortars can look forward to a marketing future in which retailers will talk one to one (see also Chapter 15) with consumers via wireless internet technologies.

Reputation

As I discussed in the preceding chapter, trust is a key determinant in motivating consumer choices. According to a joint study conducted in 2000 by Cheskin Research and Studio Archetype, only 10% of 463 respondents perceived little or no risk when purchasing on the Web. For the rest, issues about the security of personal information and about privacy were mentioned as important concerns and given as reasons for not purchasing via the Net. Twenty-three per cent felt threatened by hackers and 16% were concerned about unauthorised bodies obtaining and abusing their personal information.

This lack of faith in online service was usually misplaced but, as we know, perceptions often subdue objective vision.

More than 80% of Charles Schwab's transactions now occur online. When the company's market research surveys ask consumers how important they consider having a local branch office to be, Charles Schwab maintains that the survey answers indicate the local branch concept to be fairly unimportant to consumers: it scores seventh or eighth on the customer's wish list. Yet every time the company opens a local office it doubles its business in that community. Seventy per cent of accounts are opened face-to-face in a branch office.

> *80% of Charles Schwab's transactions occur online. 70% of all new accounts are opened face to face.*

It's not easy to offer a logical reading of the incongruity this suggests between reported customer perception and documented customer behaviour. But the fact is that the consumer rates trust as a high priority, but perceives a lack of it in their relationship with the Internet. The offline presence is often the starting point in a customer's life cycle with a company. Confidence is created in the real world store, between humans. This trust is crucial in carrying the consumer through the transformation from an offline to an online customer. Herein lies the added value for the online player in establishing an offline ally through a clicks-&-mortar partnership.

It might not be efficient that the majority of first contacts with consumers happen in the bricks-&-mortar store. But the initial real life contact can transform consumers' offline behaviour to online behaviour in the most cost- and time-efficient manner. The costs of transforming an offline consumer to an online consumer via communication channels like broadcast and print media are substantially higher than those occasioned by direct human contact. Personal contact, made possible by the clicks-&-mortar relationship, minimises consumer transformation costs because human contact, between the customer and a retail representative the consumer trusts, is personal, focussed, reassuring and, therefore, persuasive. If the transformation depends on communication channels like television, radio and print media, costs are substantially higher.

Conversely, clicks-&-mortar alliances introduce offline partners to up-to-date consumer data which, in the "old" world, was expensive and time-consuming to capture. A website interface is the most cost-effective means of system-atically capturing consumer information and is an efficient forum in which the initiated consumer-retailer relationship can develop. IBM Global Internet Services studies have

> *There is a cost ratio of 1:50 to capture consumer information via the Net versus offline.*

shown that the cost ratio of capturing consumer information via the Web to capturing consumer data offline is a staggering 1:50.

The role of the bricks-&-mortar representative should, therefore, be clearly defined in the clicks-&-mortar's operating strategy to ensure the customer relationship is handled cost-efficiently and in a manner that adds value to the brand's reputation. Being mindful of the fact that most consumers prefer their first contact with a company to occur offline, the solution is to determine at what stage the consumer is prepared to answer questions online without losing trust in the company and brand. Generally, the 80/20 rule, explained below, would apply.

Eighty per cent of initial transactions occur offline and subsequent transactions move online over time; 20% of first transactions take place online and move offline. The percentage of consumers enacting the transfer from an offline relationship to an online one is dependent on the online partner's real world reputation, on the length of time the consumer-retailer relationship has existed and on the consumer's consequential trust in the brand. For example, the famous jeweller, Tiffany's, has limited real-world outlets and, consequently, weak distribution. Online access makes the famous store accessible from every home and the brand's reputation would encourage consumers to override their cyber fears and buy online if they so desired.

Brand Versatility

Brand versatility is reflected in a company's ability to use its communication channels in a timely, customer-sensitive and intelligent manner in order to maintain the customer's relationship with the brand. Both offline and online brand versatility is measured in its delivery of the right services and the right messages at the right time and through the most appropriate channels.

Brands shouldn't be tied to or dependent on particular channels. They should be independent so that their discrete products can move from channel to channel and meet with the consumer's trust at every manifestation. For example, the Virgin brand embraces everything from airline services to canned drinks. Each product exists independently of the next and gains strength from the umbrella brand. Compare this strategy with that of Coca-Cola. Both brands produce cola, but Coca-Cola is a brand that's tied to its product. The Virgin brand is independent of the cola product which makes it free to operate divergent products through multiple channels, like the mobile phone and Internet service it has established in Singapore. Because Coca-Cola is tied so closely with its chief product, it can't embark fluidly on product extension or Internet strategies. The brand isn't versatile. Virgin, however, boasts a strong Internet presence, much of it clicks-&-mortar driven. Brand versatility enables seamless channel transfers.

So, if your brand is perceived by the consumer as being narrow, as inflexibly representing one product category, now is the time to start expanding your brand's image. Adopt a strategy to increase your brand's versatility so that the doors to other channels are open to it.

Is Clicks-&-Mortar for You?

A clicks-&-mortar relationship doesn't necessarily have to be between an online and an offline partner, or between companies working in the same product category as each other. AOL (America On Line), the Internet giant, and Time Warner, the media group, joined as two media companies with their own established off- and online presences. Yahoo!, the famous Internet search engine, mostly chooses to team up with online players rather than offline partners. Microsoft and Australia's Channel Nine television network created NineMSN which, again, did not represent the marriage of a clicks and a mortar player.

However, most successful clicks-&-mortar partnerships are between an online and an offline partner working in compatible, if not the same, product categories. Some companies handle both the online and offline channels by themselves. But, as is often the case, juggling two divergent disciplines requires intense focus which can distract a company from its broad business responsibilities.

Independence versus Partnership

When considering whether your company should handle its off- or online move internally or by entering a clicks-&-mortar arrangement, you need to consider:

- How much knowledge does the company have inhouse about its product's online/offline markets?
- What are the brand's strengths and is it possible to independently establish a similar position online/offline without incurring major costs and causing internal and external problems?
- How would the brand's move online/offline be viewed by the market place and how would this view affect its reputation?
- What online/offline player would the company, at any price, wish to prevent its competitors teaming up with?

Answering these questions should give your organisation an idea of whether it should make the transition online or offline at all and, if so, whether it should do so alone or in partnership with a team on the other side. The next model summarises and compares these alternatives' advantages.

Model 5.5: *Clicks-&-mortar strategy alternatives*

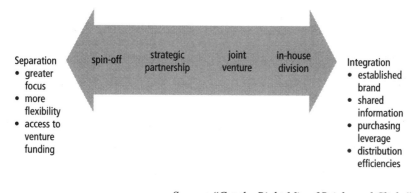

Separation
* greater focus
* more flexibility
* access to venture funding

spin-off | strategic partnership | joint venture | in-house division

Integration
* established brand
* shared information
* purchasing leverage
* distribution efficiencies

Source: "Get the Right Mix of Bricks and Clicks"
(Harvard Business Review, *May-June 2000)*

How closely or loosely should your company integrate its traditional operations with its Internet initiatives? This consideration leads to the next area of self-analysis: determining if the brand's image is sufficiently well-known and favoured to make an impact on the consumer as an online entity. If your online launch is lost amongst the plethora of Internet babies, it'll never get enough consumer attention to reach maturity. The benefit of an online partner brand is that it has already forged its identity as an innovative Net player, so your partnership with it can be introduced with *éclat*. Of course, the partner needs to be a logical one for your bricks-&-mortar product.

Upsides and Downsides
Here are some of the most common wins and losses as reported by existing clicks-&-mortar partnerships:

Not moving online/offline

Negative:
* losing potential market share
* losing market respect
* not being seen as an attractive future partner to team up with in other cases
* losing touch with the market

Positive:
* maintaining focus
* avoiding confusion among customers about your core business
* not risking large sums of money and substantial time investment

Teaming up with external partner (strategic partnership/joint venture)

Negative:

- sharing customer base (and potential revenue) with external partner
- dealing with cultural mismatch
- resolving conflicting objectives
- reconciling conflicting brand perceptions in the market place
- costs of integrating existing systems like computer databases, other soft- and hardware
- experiencing the partner's reflected financial crises and/or loss of respect in the market place
- achieving synergy (seamless co-operation and consistency) between both parties' communications strategies and business operations
- not being in full control of processes

Positive:

- avoiding lack of focus
- saving time
- gaining leverage on partner's existing brand credibility
- gaining leverage on partner's existing market share and access to customers
- creating acceptance in the market place among customers and investors by demonstrating preparedness for and competence in new media and readiness to accommodate consumer preferences (who will deal equally online and offline)
- making investment savings

Independent transition (in-house division)

Negative:

- substantial investment
- losing focus on core business
- lacking internal knowledge
- risking loss of credibility in the market place

Positive:

- controlling the process totally
- brand image consistency, off- and online
- avoiding consumer confusion
- achieving perfect synergy between off- and online operations

Remember the pivotal question: what does the company expect to gain by entering a clicks-&-mortar relationship? For dotcom companies, establishing consumer and market trust might be the main objective. For bricks-&-mortar companies, it might be locking out online competitors. In neither case can the objectives be compared or their achievements easily ascertained or measured. But the goal is that both parties benefit equally from the relationship. To achieve this requires synergy which is discussed in the next chapter. Supervising the development of synergy in all business areas ensures that both parties see benefits from the clicks-&-mortar partnership, and this maintains their motivation to mature the relationship.

Summary

- Offline firms that operate from a store environment, communicate their services via traditional means and which promote themselves via old-world broadcast media are known as "bricks-&-mortars".
- The term "clicks-&-mortar" refers to a combination of off- and online business activity.
- The majority of e-tailers lose money on every transaction for these main reasons: fulfilment costs and inexperience and lack of scale; inexperienced inventory management; high online marketing costs; and online consumer-acquisition costs.
- A well-established bricks-&-mortar player joining a clicks-&-mortar partnership can enable the online partner to break even because of the offline ally's lower fulfilment, marketing and consumer-acquisition/ retention expenses.
- Physical realities mean that the online conduit just isn't practicable for some products and services, fulfilment costs putting many products at a disadvantage.
- Full communication is crucial to achieving the synergies that make for viable clicks-&-mortar deals. Insufficient strategy explanations to staff and inadequate staff involvement will result in an atmosphere of competition between the clicks and the mortar partners, rather than a workplace spirit of co-operation.
- The e-tailing kings and queens will be experienced retailers that are skilled direct marketers. The losers will be pure-plays that fail to build efficient fulfilment, shipping and marketing processes. Clicks-&-mortar partnerships allow inexperienced online retailers to avoid these areas which can be assumed and/or continued competently by the mortar partner.
- Establishing a clicks-&-mortar partnership is costly and time-consuming so it's imperative to ensure that both potential partners are compatible, not only with each other, but with the online and offline environments.
- Any business transition must achieve added value from the customer's perspective. Increased customer loyalty, lower costs, faster response

capabilities, larger selection and improved reputation are among the value gains a brand should expect from entering a clicks-&-mortar alliance.

- A bricks-&-mortar presence provides the most credible means of entering a market place. A dotcom presence strengthens the local reputation by adding the cachet of internationalism and new thinking. The clicks-&-mortar arrangement gives the offline partner access to a wider customer base and bestows a reputation for innovation upon it.

- The cheaper the product and the more efficient, rapid and cheap its fulfilment and delivery, the more value will attend a clicks-&-mortar relationship.

- A website interface is the most cost-effective means of systematically capturing consumer information. And it's an efficient forum for maturing the consumer-retailer relationship to develop.

- Brand versatility is reflected in a company's ability to use its communication channels in a timely, customer-sensitive and intelligent manner. Versatile brands maintain their relationship with both the offline and online customer by delivering the right services and the right messages at the right time and through the most appropriate channels.

- If your brand is perceived by the consumer as being narrow, as inflexibly representing one product category, now is the time to start expanding your brand's image. Adopt a strategy to increase your brand's versatility so that the doors to other channels are open to it.

- A clicks-&-mortar relationship doesn't necessarily have to be between an online and an offline partner, or between companies working in the same product category as each other. However, most successful clicks-&-mortar partnerships are between an online and an offline partner working in compatible, if not the same, product categories.

- The pivotal question in considering a clicks-&-mortar option is: what will the brand gain by entering a clicks-&-mortar relationship?

Action Points:

Making your clicks-&-mortar operating strategy click

By now you've developed a clicks-&-mortar operational strategy that includes goals and alternative revenue model options. It also includes trust-developing, maintenance and monitoring plans and an initial channel strategy. These Action Points are about refining that channel strategy. The elements to consider are:

- product's online compatibility (fulfilment needs, application to the online channel's restricted sensory-appeal repertoire);
- communications (brand handling/marketing, consumer-acquisition/ retention); and
- integration of traditional business with new channel.

Analyse your brand's product category for online compatibility

Product's fulfilment needs: Develop a fulfilment plan (a part of your channel strategy). Consider:

- capturing consumer behavioural and preference data and reflecting this knowledge in the e-commerce and retail outlet channels;
- integrating clicks and bricks orders;
- handling impulse orders and one-to-one delivery;
- handling product returns; and
- handling cross- and upselling and increasing per-customer sales.

Product's suitability to online's restricted sensory repertoire: Can the product be adequately assessed using just two senses (sight and sound)? Develop a brand-handling plan, as part of your channel strategy, to maximize brand awareness across all channels.

Determine your marketing mix

What percentage of revenue will you spend on marketing?

What percentages of the marketing budget will you spend on customer acquisition and retention?

Determine what value gains a clicks-&-mortar will achieve for your consumers (lower price, greater accessibility to the store, larger selection, more product and service information, more flexible service, more entertainment in the shopping experience, access to unique product selections, better guarantees, etc.) and design a communications plan as part of your channel strategy that communicates these value gains.

Assess clicks-&-mortar development options and identify the most suitable to your company's growth.

Consider your company's experience, surveyed consumer preferences and the consumer awareness your brand enjoys. Assess how closely to integrate your existing business with an online stream. As a:

- spin-off?

- strategic partnership?
- joint venture?
- or as an in-house division?

Step 4 Identify a partner

What online partner would you, at any price, wish to prevent your competitor teaming up with? Be prepared to continue this step at the end of the next chapter.

Chapter 6

Operational Synergy

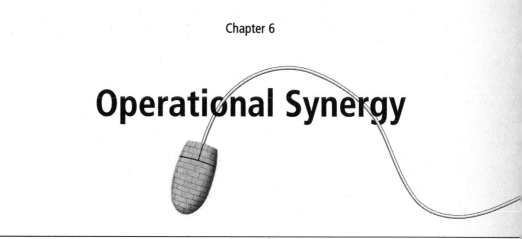

"Synergy" is a term that appears in this book almost as often as "clicks-
&-mortar" and "branding". Successful clicks-&-mortar endeavours are
wholly dependent on highly developed synergy between partners; and
successful branding is the outcome of well-coordinated clicks-&-mortar
partnerships. Synergy is … 2 + 2 =5.

Why 2 + 2 = 5? Because synergy achieves a whole that's worth more than the sum of its parts.

Synergy requires clicks-&-mortar partners to share compatible philosophies, goals, core values and practices. The areas which are crucial to the creation of synergy and in which, therefore, partners must share homogenous views, objectives and strategies are: value gain for consumers, brand handling, channel optimisation, infrastructure, data exchange and consumer maintenance. These areas stand as measures against which offline and online partners can assess their achievements and evaluate the development of operational and philosophical synergies.

> *Synergy achieves a whole that's worth more than the sum of its parts.*

Synergy = Value Gain for Consumers

In a clicks-&-mortar arrangement, it's vital that both the online and offline partner share a cohesive understanding of what the enterprise's values are to the consumer. Does a clicks-&-mortar setup make the brand easier to use than as a purely offline or online service? Faster to use? Cheaper? More convenient? More informative? Offer a larger selection? Does it increase the brand relevance to the consumer by facilitating customisation?

One or more of these points must be apparent to the consumer for there to be increased value for the offline and online partners in forming an alliance as a clicks-&-mortar entity. Often, the dealings associated with the transition online/offline and into a partnership can obfuscate this underlying justification and goal. The only way to make sure all parties don't lose sight of the main goal, to add value to the consumer's relationship with the brand, is to identify those consumer values which the partnership's formation should increase *before* signing and then to track these values' developments during the transformation process.

Identify, Track and Increase Values

Defining and tracking these consumer values isn't simply claiming that the new partnership makes things "easier" or "more convenient" for the customer. You must attach concrete figures to your specified value-goals. How much easier do you mean? What is easier? Is it easier to find the product on the shelves? Easier to conduct transactions?

Testing and Measuring Values

Identify the values that are relevant to your consumers, your product and your brand, and attach goals to them which allow you to measure their progress. At the outset of your clicks-&-mortar setup, you need to allocate a testing period to ascertain whether the relationship is worth pursuing. For example, survey your consumers at the venture's launch for their opinions on the convenience, reliability, and cost-competitiveness of your business. Ask retail customers about their willingness to adopt the online channel, and e-tail consumers about transferring some business to the offline channel. Plan your development strategy within a time frame and conduct the survey again at an appointed review time. Gradually you'll acquire achievement milestones that motivate staff and foster synergy in offline and online goals and values.

The principle of this exercise is to ensure that the original motivations for creating the clicks-&-mortar relationship remain intact and are fulfilled. It also arms the marketing department with clear consumer and investor arguments as to why the relationship is so beneficial; motivates staff in the reconstruction phase by giving them a sense of shared direction; enables the results of everyone's hard work to be clearly documented; and paves the way for new objectives to be set for the maturing relationship between the partner entities.

Coherent internal communications which familiarise all online and offline staff with values and goals are vital. A sense of pride in and ownership of company values will solidify staff morale, foster loyalty to the company and, in the end, assist in translating values into service for customers. These are the ways in which clicks-&-mortars achieve value synergy, a value gain for customers.

The Channel Strategy

Channel Optimisation

This is both about focusing on what channels and activities a company is best at, avoiding the distractions of other channel responsibilities and communicating the brand's values by the most effective means. A bricks-&-mortar company usually hasn't sufficient programming expertise to develop Web pages and design navigation. A dotcom company is usually inexpert in supply-chain management, and is therefore not able to make the most efficient use of real-world infrastructure. But together, each party can reap the benefits of the other's expertise and, therefore, enjoy the advantages of optimising the offline and online channels. When finding a partner and developing joint channel optimisation strategies, define the skills for which each partner is best qualified and assign channel-based roles. This part of channel optimisation helps create the best synergy by maximising efficiencies, minimising costs, and developing seamless cross-channel operations.

Entering a clicks-&-mortar alliance should result in consumer-maintenance cost savings across the partner organisations: lower acquisition costs, lower conversion costs and lower maintenance costs. But these savings depend upon good channel strategy, that is, using each channel to its best advantage and, thereby, optimising the consumer's time spent online or in the store and achieving multichannel synergy.

The bricks-&-mortar channel is today the most efficient means of establishing a relationship between customers and brands. The relationship, forged initially in the company of staff members and other patrons will, ideally, grow into familiarity with the brand, which will mature into trust of it. The bricks-&-mortar channel is also the most appropriate one for deploying complex product demonstrations and other persuasive promotions aimed at convincing customers.

The dotcom channel is ideal when automated responses suffice in a transaction, say in the case of repeat purchases. The process is cost-efficient for both the consumer and the brand. The dotcom channel also allows consumers the freedom to conduct product research at their leisure and pose queries without having to disclose their identity or feel under any pressure to make a purchase.

InternetTV is an appropriate channel for accommodating impulse purchases while **wireless Internet technology** is an even more flexible impulse purchase tool. By going online, via the mobile phone, consumers can respond to on-the-spot offers. They can save time by pre-purchasing products and arranging collection thereby ensuring no waiting time.

Catalogue services are price-driven and allow consumers to access products not necessarily available in their area. This channel suits planned purchases, the time lag between purchase and delivery allowing the consumer time to reflect upon the purchase. This isn't a good channel for cost and product comparisons or trust development, nor is it a practicable one for repeat purchases. However the channel is cost effective for both consumer and brand.

Brand Handling

The Internet has the capacity to eliminate a brand's point of differentiation. This distinction can threaten to intrude upon the brand's offline identity. For example, Toys "R" Us' warehouse-full-of-stuff concept parallels the nature of the Internet. The brand's policy of constant price cutting is reflected in its warehouse-style presentation: gigantic toy stores which devote most of their space to thousands of products, all arranged in four- or five-metre-high shelves with barely any space devoted to entertainment activities like product demonstrations, displays, shows, competitions, and so on. The advent of the Internet dislodged Toys "R" Us from its unique presentation position. The Net makes millions of shelves with millions of products available at a low price. Until the day the Internet began trading, Toys "R" Us was a tremendous success. It still is, but the advantages Toys "R" Us held in its large selections of toys offered at the lowest prices, and accessible worldwide, were robbed by the Net. In short, the Internet eliminated Toys "R" Us' point of differentiation.

An AC Nielsen study (in 1998) concluded that consumers were 67% less likely to drive several miles to reach a hyperstore than they were five years previously if a similar selection, offered at the same price, were available online. Why spend time driving to the nearest Toys "R" Us and walking about in large impersonal warehouse-like buildings without being able to touch or test the products? The Net now offered the time-saving opportunity of buying the same products at comparable prices and with no time constraints: the Net operates twenty-four hours a day. Toys "R" Us is open from 9:00am to 8:00pm.

> *67% of all consumers are less likely to drive several miles to reach a hyperstore than they were five years ago.*

In response, Toys "R" Us had to identify its own advantage over this new competitor. Question: What was the added value for consumers in visiting a Toys "R" Us store compared to making an online visit? Answer: Customers could get hold of products twenty-four hours faster than the online businesses could deliver.

Effective brand handling means developing and communicating your company's values and identity consistently, via all channels and devices. In a clicks-&-mortar relationship, brand handling must be consistent online and offline with the result that the sum of both entities, because of the brand synergy that's achieved, is greater than its parts. Brand synergy is an imperative. It depends on the compatible marriage of the click's and the mortar's cohesive understanding of their brand with the brand's offline and online handling. And brand handling has much to do with channel optimisation strategies.

Dotcom and Retailer Forge a Perfect Fit

Kozmo.com has a deal with Ticketmaster's Online City Search. The deal is that City Search will feature Kozmo.com's home-delivery service on Internet city sites in the markets that Kozmo.com currently serves. This is common online practice. E-tailers pay premium rates to high-traffic portal sites for preferred positions in their shopping malls. The deal Kozmo.com struck with Starbucks Coffee Company in February 2000, however, puts an offline twist on this standard online marketing practice. For the sum of $150 million, to be paid over a five-year period, Starbucks gives Kozmos.com a prominent place in all of the coffee company's US outlets.

The two businesses enjoy a perfect fit with each other. Kozmo.com is a New York-based startup Internet retailer specialising in home delivery. In under an hour, Kozmo.com will deliver convenience items, including movies, food, DVDs, CDs, books, and now Tazo tea and Starbucks coffee products, to the customer's front door — providing they live within Kozmo.com's range of operation. At the time the deal was signed, Kozmo.com operated in six major US cities and had plans for immediate expansion to over 20 other major urban markets. Starbucks, a well-established bricks-&-mortar coffee shop chain, has over 3,000 outlets worldwide.

Starbucks Coffee Company maintains that 90% of their 10 million customers are Internet users. According to Jill Frankel, the director of retail research for Gomez Advisors, Kozmo.com is a company that "offers a value proposition to the lazy, hungry 25-to-30-year-olds in metropolitan areas". In fact Kozmo.com bases their free delivery service, with no minimum order, in areas where Internet usage is known to be higher than average.

Joseph Park, the chief executive and co-founder of Kozmo.com believes that the fit with Starbucks is "a natural one". He estimates that piggy-backing on the trusted Starbucks brand will attract an additional 1.5 million customers to Kozmo.com's delivery service. Kozmo.com will also establish drop boxes in Starbucks stores as a convenience to customers, enabling them to more easily return items like videos. This instore exposure is crucial for Kozmo.com's ambitious expansion plans.

The deal is not entirely one-sided. Howard Schultz, the chairman and CEO of Starbucks Coffee said, "This alliance defines the benefits of a truly integrated clicks-&-mortar strategy for our customers ... a value-enhancing proposition for everybody." Although Starbucks has been selling coffee, tea and accessories online, it hadn't had a significant e-commerce presence. The union with Kozmo.com will alter that, the home delivery partner undertaking to deliver all Starbucks products. Together, they have plans to trial an "e-mmediate" hot beverage delivery service.

If all goes well, Starbucks could very likely invest in Kozmo.com. After all, Kozmo.com has attracted some substantial investors to date, including Amazon.com and Flatiron Partners. But the truth is that the $30 million a year that Kozmo.com will pay Starbucks is more than all the investment they've been paid to date. Time, as always, will tell.

Cross- and upselling These days we're less and less likely to plan purchases when visiting the supermarket or the store. We let the stores inspire us. What happens with this inspiration when shopping online? How can e-tailers ensure that cross- and upselling occurs? Since 1997 Amazon.com has offered its book customers reading suggestions, based on their previous purchasing patterns. The next step is likely to be free samples being sent with the original purchase, just as book clubs have done for decades, with huge success. Such precedents put extra pressure on the e-tailer's struggling order/return processes. E-tailers will, therefore, resist cross- and upselling tactics but this may be the solution to pushing consumers' average online expenditure over the US$100 mark.

Efficient fulfillment comes down to knowing who your customers really are, and this comes down to capturing and controlling relevant consumer data and deploying it appropriately. Since the Internet introduced the capacity for manufacturers to deal directly with customers, consumer profiling data has itself become a commodity. The online grocer store, Peapod.com, for example, generates enough consumer data to market to clients such as Coca-Cola and Kraft Foods.

Consumer Maintenance

Marketing, brand awareness, growing brand loyalty and achieving initial or repeat purchases constitute the duties of consumer maintenance. These tasks, like all other operation necessities, require a synergous application that hopes to add value to the partners' joint business future. Harnessing and maintaining consumer loyalty, and accelerating conversion rates (the speed with which consumers convert their knowledge of a product into a decision to buy it) forms two halves of the consumer maintenance responsibility.

Synergous consumer maintenance should achieve efficiencies and cost reductions in these areas. Assess, for example, whether costs of harnessing consumers rise or fall after consumers are introduced to the clicks-&-mortar relationship? Do the costs of maintaining consumers rise or fall after consumers are introduced to the clicks-&-mortar relationship? Within which categories do cost differences occur? In which channels (offline or online) do cost differences occur? Analyse why they differ.

Your answers to these questions, and your analysis of them, are essential in determining how to optimise your per-customer per-order spending in each channel.

Know Thy Customer — The Key to CVS.com's Success

Case study by Don Peppers and Martha Rogers, Ph.D.

How US pharmacy chain CVS handled its move to clicks-&-mortar last year shows how more and more online companies are realising the importance of understanding their most valuable customers. Once CVS.com saw that its best customers were coming from the ads it was running on specialty medical websites, it refocused its ad budget and boosted customer purchase rates more than 20 times over the broader-based banner ad and portal links figures.

When CVS purchased online pharmacy Soma.com in May 1999 (launched as CVS.com one month later), the first priority was to replace Soma's old web-analysis tools. The click-stream metrics, customer database, and other information it provided were useful, but everything was scattered across the website. CVS.com wanted to be able to use the data to provide reports to its market analysts, and also generate ad hoc reports. But, unlike a lot of companies that upgrade their web-analysis tools, it was in no hurry for return on investment (ROI) — just good information. According to David Zook, strategic alliance manager of CVS.com, "The project was deemed to be of such importance, it was beyond ROI."

CVS.com turned to Quadstone, which specialises in software that understands, predicts, manages, and influences purchasing behaviour, to find out who its customers were, where they were coming from, and what their buying habits were. Almost immediately, CVS.com saw a dichotomy: banner ads on major portal sites were steering a large number of visitors to CVS.com, but they weren't making a lot of purchases, while ads on smaller, medical sites (such as WebMD.com and the Black Health Network) resulted in fewer visitors, but a much higher purchasing rate (more than 20 times more!). Since then, CVS.com has reconfigured its ad budget, placing more emphasis on the specialty sites. "CVS.com was able to go the next step beyond traffic analysis – to real mapping of marketing ability," according to Mark Smith, president of Quadstone.

More good news: CVS.com can now do market-basket analysis to give vendors an idea of what to promote, according to Zook. And, these reports are useful throughout the firm: Drop-off visit rates will alert the design or catalogue group that certain web pages aren't user-friendly, or where the site is distracting the user. Since CVS.com is in the final phases of installing the tools, it's too soon for any real ROI. But, right now there's no argument that CVS.com's CRM initiative is good medicine.

CVS launched its first major online and offline integrated promotion throughout June 2000. Instore customers were handed cards steering them to CVS.com, where they can enter to win a sweepstakes. (Like some other established bricks-&-mortars, CVS is using its offline clout to draw customers to its website.) This convergence of multichannel marketing "is really the first full-scale, full-blown integrated promotion for CVS.com," says Mike Hartman, vice president of marketing at CVS.com. "We absolutely believe that the road to success and profitability is one where the marketing is fully integrated between the stores and the site." Since CVS does more than 3 million transactions per day, Hartman says CVS.com could get unprecedented numbers of new visitors to the site. The question is, will it get them to return?

The Boston Consulting Group study, "Insight into Online Consumer Behavior" (which I mentioned in Chapter 2 in relation to trust and efficiency), showed that 51% of Internet users have purchased goods or services online. Consumers who had a positive first-purchase experience were likely to spend more time and money online, engaging in twelve online transactions and spending $500 in the previous twelve months. The unhappy first-time purchaser spent $140 on four online transactions; 28% stopped shopping online; and 23% stopped purchasing at the site in question. Significantly, 6% of those consumers also stopped patronising the retailer's bricks-&-mortar store. The relationship between off- and online consumer maintenance, therefore, clearly influences the consumer's brand perception and loyalty.

In the Internet world, the term "conversion rate" refers to the speed at which a consumer decides to purchase a product. If a consumer visits a florist's site twice before purchasing flowers, the conversion rate is 50%.

Online conversion rates

The costs of accelerating conversion rates online are substantially lower than those occasioned by encouraging offline purchases. This is because it's cheaper to educate a consumer online. Most of the consumer's questions are FAQs (frequently asked questions) which can be answered automatically. Therefore consumers can do research for themselves, without costly human interaction. Thus, they are prepared when they visit the bricks-&-mortar store: they know what they're looking for and what other questions to ask. This saves offline staff time and consequently saves the organisation money.

Offline conversion rates

At the same time a clicks-&-mortar relationship increases the costs of accelerating conversions for the dotcom company. What is the value, then, for a dotcom company in having offline customers move online? Remember that a dotcom company is likely, in the initial phases of the clicks-&-mortar relationship, to have access to only 20% of potential customers. The costs of harnessing the other 80% via offline communications would be enormous, except for the presence of the offline partner whose contact with the target 80% is already established.

> *A dotcom company is likely, in the initial phases of the clicks-&-mortar relationship, to have access to only 20% of potential customers.*

Data exchange

There's no doubt that the customer information captured from each transaction is one of the most important assets an organisation owns. And, because of this fact, clicks-&-mortars must have data capturing and retrieval systems in place which they can draw upon in unison.

For example, the operational strategy should allow for captured data to prompt appropriate action. This action might be online and/or offline, and directed at an individual, a target group, or it might advise broad promotional or operational decisions. Let's say customers have occasion to explain their book preferences to a clicks-&-mortar bookstore. They might key in their favourites and communicate them via the Net. Now, the business's system should remember this data as well as all the books the customers have bought previously. It should be capable of comparing their profiles with those of other readers who exhibit similar literary tastes. And it should be able to predict what book titles the customers are likely to be interested in. When those customers visit the offline partner they should feel that the knowledge they have already shared with the brand online is known to the same brand offline. When this occurs a positive data exchange synergy has taken place.

To be frank, we won't see this level of synergy any time soon. Such sophisticated data acquisition and exchange systems will cost a lot of money and take a lot of time to develop. In the meantime, it's important to clarify a data capturing and utilisation strategy.

Infrastructure

Just as it's vital to identify what increased consumer values will be achieved by companies entering clicks-&-mortar relationships, it's necessary to identify what infrastructural advantages are to be gained from the transition and to design a strategy to achieve these advances. Smooth, consumer-oriented operations depend on well-coordinated infrastructural deployment, in other words, on infrastructural synergy.

Any merger requires a consolidation process to eliminate duplication and cut costs. Salaries, outsourcing, marketing, consumer loyalty programs, general consumer communications, rent and other fixed store and warehouse costs are likely to be targeted and adjusted.

Integrating two fully functional infrastructure setups can cause substantial problems. It not only forces both parties to evaluate their existing systems and choose elements to retain, it also demands staff retraining to ensure that the newly integrated system is used optimally. In the worst-case scenario none of the existing systems would be retained, either because they're outdated and unable to fulfil the clicks-&-mortar's needs or the partners' two systems are incompatible, because of databases written on different platforms for example.

Consolidation should extract an efficient and smooth working relationship from the newly married operational systems. This contribution to operational synergy has special significance for communications infrastructure.

Typically, infrastructural considerations cover data capturing, data mining, ordering systems, internal communications, external communications, monitoring systems, and so on. Infrastructural consolidation redeeming is an issue that demands its own book. Here we are focusing on clicks, bricks and brands, with an emphasis on brand management, rather than on infrastructural management. So let's consider infrastructural adaptations.

You'd logically assume that both partners would conduct an inventory of their infrastructural processes and communication practices in order to ascertain whether there are any overlaps, omissions, contradictions or incompatibilities in the emissions. How does each partner gather consumer data and which is the most efficient process to retain? Which products are more efficiently shipped to consumers and which are better picked up at the store? Is it just as easy for the consumer to learn about the store policy online as it is for the consumer to pick up the brochure in the store? Are there existing loyalty programs running? And so on.

A healthy infrastructure is dependent on contact with the customer from order to delivery.

The infrastructure behind Drugstore.com and Rite Aid is the backbone of the chain's functionality. The setup handles the process from the minute consumers type in their order on the website to the second they either receive the product on their doorstep or collect it in the Rite Aid store. Between these two points of customer contact a range of processes take place. The typical fulfilment process checks product availability, ascertains whether the customer is already registered, approves credit card details, payment and updates loyalty program records.

The product is then ordered from either the warehouse, another store, or the manufacturer. If the order is to be fulfilled and shipped directly to the customer the product will be picked, packed, labelled and shipped. If not, a message is sent to the retail store asking the store to call, e-mail or fax the customer and alert staff about the order's collection.

If the product is delivered a message must be sent back to the fulfilment address to confirm that the customer has received the product. If the product is picked up in the store a similar notification process will take place. If the product is returned from the receiver for any reason a process must be in place to ensure that non-fulfilled orders are integrated back into the system.

Between 1% and 10% of all products are returned.

The percentage of returned products varies according to product category, product price and demographic area. However a good rule of thumb is that between 1% and 10% of products (mainly pornographic materials) are returned.

The handling of commission is achieved through often complex setups designed to satisfy all parties involved. The split often is determined by who initiated or received the order. But there are often royalty fees also to be put in place.

Advanced systems aim to optimise the customer's future purchase processes, both to generate higher customer loyalty and to cut internal costs. Instead of the customer visiting the store every month to pick up heart pills, for example, it's more cost-efficient to handle the repeat purchase via the Internet. Loyalty point statements, cross- and upselling materials and general promotional information must be sent to the customer via e-mail or mail.

Testing and measuring infrastructural improvements

Attention to these operational areas may have to be prioritised. It would be counterproductive and possibly paralyse the whole organisation to tie up resources in the pursuit of bedding down all these areas at once.

It's also imperative to measure improvement in these fulfilment activities. Clarify the concrete values the clicks-&-mortar partnership aspires to and monitor progress toward infra-synergy. The overall goal is to add value to the consumers' experiences of your company. To ensure that both partners also perceive added value in the clicks-&-mortar transition, concentrate on improvements in key areas like customer satisfaction, delivery time, fulfilment costs per order, marketing costs per order, customer expenditure and repeat purchases. Activities that require joint and co-operative understandings of the common goal provide useful measuring posts for ascertaining progress towards infrastructural synergy:

- joint marketing programs;
- joint branding exercises;
- joint staff training and human resources management;
- centralised purchasing unit;
- single point of data collection and maintenance;
- shared channel development strategy and resources;
- and joint administration.

Visit **DualBook.com/cbb/ch6/InfrastructuralProcess** to learn more about infrastructural processes.

Infrastructural integration is likely to be one of the most expensive steps in a clicks-&-mortar's development strategy. It affects both partners' total operations. This book focuses on the rationales for and against establishing a clicks-&-mortar concept, from a strategic and marketing point of view. To find out where to learn more about integrating infrastructure, a new and untested area, visit the DualBook™ site.

Fulfilment

As I discussed in the previous chapter, efficient handling of fulfilment processes is a survival challenge for e-tailers and for clicks-&-mortars. Acquiring and retaining customers means making product outcomes match brand promises. So fulfilment is a major part of achieving complete customer satisfaction. The fulfilment challenges include efficient order collection, packing and shipping, competent handling of customer inquiries, complaints and product returns. Mishandling the fulfilment process can damage an online brand rapidly.

In theory, fulfilment is simple: you deliver the product when, where and as the consumer wants it delivered, the goal being to deliver goods as quickly and cost-efficiently as possible. It took the traditional mail system decades to establish a solid infrastructure for flat letters. Now the sizes and formats of items being sent are unpredictable and defy standardisation. These irregularities cost unforeseen amounts of money and require the development of new systems and processes to handle them within forty-eight hours. And trends indicate that the consumer expectations are dictating that the forty-eight-hour delivery time be cut to twenty-four. But making all this happen is a matter of complex logistical control. Amazon.com wrote its own fulfilment system, claiming that no equivalent software existed at the time, a fact that indicates how ill-prepared e-tailing was for this vital part of the retailing business.

Model 6.1: *Online's high fulfilment costs*

	superstores	online
Average sale	$US100	$US100
(discount)	−10.00	−20.00
Shipping and handling	−	11.00
Sales tax	7.00	−
Customer pays	97.00	91.00
Cost of sales	67.41	57.60
Shipping and handling	2.88	9.90
Gross profit	26.71	23.50
Operating Expenses		
Rent	0.96	4.55
Labour and store	10.75	−
Website development	−	2.90
Marketing	2.50	17.29
Total	14.21	24.74
Operating profit per order	12.50	−1.24

Source: Thomas Weitzel Partners

Model 6.1 exhibits the fact that online discounts, marketing and fulfillment (shipping to handing) costs inhibit e-tail's achievement of a black bottom line. Existing brand awareness to a street presence, personal collection to retail pricing mean retailing depends less on each sale than e-tailing equivalents.

Central to the e-tailer's fulfilment difficulties is the fact that, unlike bricks-&-mortar retailers whose shipping is conducted in large quantities, truckloads of goods moving from warehouse to retail outlet, the online merchant has to make small shipments to individual households. To solve this problem, WalMart's online venture entered an outsourcing arrangement with Fingerhut, one of the USA's catalogue retailers. Why? Because WalMart quickly realised that their own fulfilment experience, stacking products on pallets and shipping large quantities to stores, had no similarities with the one-to-one delivery setup required by online customers. Additional to the outsourcing solution is one in which customers themselves are obliged to enter all their own order delivery details. *The McKinsey Quarterly* reports that this simple strategy reduces delivery errors to 4%.

Outsourcing

FedEx, since 1997, has invested US$1 billion per year in e-commerce fulfilment systems that support e-tailer outsourcing needs. That amount represents 25% annual growth in the logistics industry. Outsourcing has enabled KB Toys to establish a fulfilment system with a capacity of processing 20 million packages a year and which allows customers to examine KB Toys' backend systems for product availability. This complex system was set up within seven months, an efficiency that was only possible because it was handled by an outside expert.

Outsourcing becomes necessary when over 8,000 packages a day are handled. The rule of thumb is that 10,000 orders a day would support an investment of US$70 million in order-processing systems and one million square feet of warehouse space. Compare these figures with Amazon.com's 400,000 items a day, sold during the 1999 USA holiday season, the company's investment of US$300 million in fulfilment systems and its 3.5-million-square-foot expansion and you get an idea of the volumes required before handling the fulfilment process internally is profitable.

> *10,000 orders a day justifies an investment of US$70 million in order-processing systems.*

Not surprisingly, few e-tailers or clicks-&-mortars have decided to handle the whole fulfilment process themselves. Even Amazon.com co-opts external help to some extent. The benefit of internal fulfilment management is, of course, total control. But the downsides are significant: high salary costs, inflexible scalability, the risk of losing focus on the core business and the huge requisite infrastructural investment.

Handling returns

Retailer return policies have established long-held expectations amongst consumers who are now Internet customers. It's common to have a "return without question" policy that sets a new level of challenge for most e-tailers.

To begin with, few e-tailers design their packaging for easy return. Customers often have to find new packing materials, call to arrange credits and refunds and physically take packages to delivery services. Every step in this process represents a turnoff for the consumer who questions the value of the troublesome online purchase compared with hassle-free offline purchase. *The McKinsey Quarterly* reports that the value of online retailer returns constitutes 11% of revenue. For catalogue sales it's 9%. The cost of processing online returns represents a significant percentage of operation expenses. There's only one answer to this: total online fulfilment costs must decrease to preserve e-tailer profitability.

Integrating clicks and bricks orders

The reality is that integrating the bricks-&-clicks systems takes time, is not fault-free once a uniform system is established and costs a huge amount of money to achieve. Therefore, the most efficient way for clicks-&-mortars to run their fulfilment processes initially is via the offline partner's established order management system. This option makes most sense while the volume of online orders is too low to justify large IT investments.

Integrated systems automatically transmit Internet orders through a processing centre and transfer them to the shipping manifest, occasioning savings of up to 30% (according to *The McKinsey Quarterly*) if the costs of long distance phone calls, data entry, teleserver operations and error corrections are reduced. An integrated system with full ERP (enterprise resource planning) capabilities, for example, can ensure that surges in demand don't retard key fulfilment operations such as data entry, inventory and packing. So far, no bricks-&-mortar retailer has made the transition to total integration and automation of online and offline orders, a fact which indicates the huge challenge this task represents.

The Evolution of a Clicks-&-Mortar Relationship

So far you've examined clicks-&-mortar potential for your company by:

- analysing your consumer's expectations of your brand;
- concluded that a clicks-&-mortar future will add value to your brand;
- considered a suitable online/offline partners; and
- initiated brand-handling, value-adding, infrastructure, loyalty-fostering, consumer-maintenance, channel-handling and data-exchange joint strategies.

Model 6.2: *Clicks-&-mortar maturation*

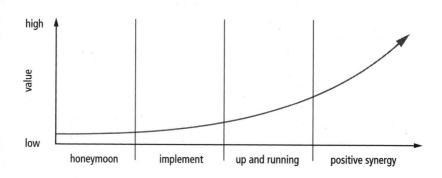

Let's look at the development stages you could expect a maturing clicks-&-mortar partnership to travel through. I call these milestones:

- the honeymoon stage;
- the implementation stage;
- the up-and-running stage; and
- the positive synergy stage.

Brand handling synergy means developing and communicating your company's values and identity consistently.

The Honeymoon Stage

Like many honeymoons, the risk at this stage can be that the expectations of one party in the other are unrealistic, naïve or idealised. The experience of established clicks-&-mortars like Barnes & Noble, Rite Aid and Gap shows that from day one, consumers will expect a seamless branding, co-ordinated operations and consistent messages — in short, synergy — between both entities.

Realistically, synergy won't be achieved for some time. It is, therefore, important to pre-empt expectations and define them realistically. Promise a level of service that both parties can achieve. Misleading promises create badwill among the client population and this in turn ruins the new company's internal goodwill that should be being nurtured. Such a wound is damaging and likely to compromise all future developments.

So any joint press releases, which for some companies are intended to boost share price, should be couched in realistic and responsible terms. For some clicks-&-mortars, a marketing campaign becomes the product of this stage: both entities promoting the relationship with the aim of generating instore and online traffic. Of course, traffic is survival, but it must proceed patiently and contentedly. A measured introduction to the business will keep consumer traffic travelling smoothly. Raising false expectations in order to increase flow will create collisions and jams where ill-will and disappointment occurs.

The Implementation Stage

This stage is the most complex of the merger process. The merger of two companies' legacy systems (their databases, ordering, production, salary and accounting systems, etc.), cultures, brands and client groups is the true test of whether the enterprise will be a long-term success or a flash-in-the-pan marketing spin. Typically, this stage will occupy between six and eighteen months, depending on the level of human, economic and material resources dedicated to the process.

The Up-and-Running Stage

When most systems are up and running — the databases talking the same language, the ordering systems working compatibly and customers being treated uniformly — the big test is near at hand. But the up-and-running stage takes time. It's expensive to introduce new systems, to re-educate existing staff, integrate existing systems and accustom clients to your new business identity and culture. And it takes time. So you can't expect the benefits you predicted to flow from the partnership to be manifested immediately. Cost savings, value adding to the brand, increased revenue and a growing consumer base will emerge over time. Only at this stage will a positive synergy between the clicks and the mortar really reveal itself.

The Positive Synergy Stage

By the time this stage has been reached the emergent business should be handling clients smoothly, whether they're moving online from offline, or offline from online. Cross-selling and upselling across media and cross-promotion of products and services across the organisation should be happening by now. New products and services, the products of the joint effort, should also be introduced. Convenience and availability will prompt new consumers to purchase products for the first time. Consumer-maintenance costs will be reduced across the organisation with consumers engaged in their own online research.

Summary

- Synergy achieves a whole that's worth more than the sum of its parts.
- Synergy requires clicks-&-mortar partners to share compatible philosophies, goals, core values and practices.
- The areas which are crucial to the creation of synergy and in which partners must share homogenous views, objectives and strategies are: brand handling, value gain for consumers, infrastructure, brand loyalty, channel optimisation and data exchange.
- Determining a brand-handling strategy is about analysing what values your brand represents and ensuring that these are communicated to the consumer in all situations, via all channels appealing to all senses.
- Brand handling synergy means developing and communicating your company's values and identity consistently, via all channels and devices. In a clicks-&-mortar relationship, brand handling must be consistent online and offline.
- In a clicks-&-mortar arrangement, it's vital that both the online and offline partner share a cohesive understanding of what the partnership's

value is to the user. Identify values you jointly aim to develop before signing and then track these values' developments during the transformation process.

- At the outset of your clicks-&-mortar setup, allocate a testing period to ascertain whether the relationship is worth pursuing. The principle of this exercise is to ensure that the original motivations for creating the clicks-&-mortar relationship remain intact and are fulfilled. It also arms the marketing department with clear consumer and investor arguments as to why the relationship is so beneficial, motivates staff in the reconstruction phase by giving them a sense of shared direction, enables the results of everyone's hard work to be clearly documented, and paves the way for new objectives to be set for the maturing relationship between the partner entities.

- Clicks-&-mortars achieve value synergy through coherent internal communications which familiarise all online and offline staff with values and goals. A sense of pride in and ownership of company values will solidify staff morale, foster loyalty to the company and, in the end, assist in translating values into service for customers.

- Smooth, consumer-oriented operations depend on well-co-ordinated infrastructural deployment, in other words, on infrastructural synergy.

- Acquiring and retaining customers means making sure product outcomes match brand promises. Fulfilment is a major part of achieving complete customer satisfaction so efficient handling of fulfilment processes is a survival issue for e-tailers and clicks-&-mortars.

- Central to the e-tailer's fulfilment difficulties is the fact that, unlike bricks-&-mortar retailers whose shipping is conducted in large quantities, online merchants are obliged to make small shipments to individual households.

- The most efficient way for clicks-&-mortars to initially run their fulfilment processes is via the offline partner's established order management system.

- The costs of accelerating conversion rates online are substantially lower than those occasioned by encouraging offline purchases because it's cheaper to educate a consumer online. Most of the consumer's questions are FAQs (frequently asked questions) which can be answered automatically.

- A dotcom company is likely, in the initial phases of the clicks-&-mortar relationship, to have access to only 20% of potential customers. The costs of harnessing the other 80% via offline communications would be enormous, except for the presence of the offline partner whose contact with the target 80% is already established.

- Entering a clicks-&-mortar alliance should result in consumer-maintenance cost savings across the partner organisations.
- Good channel strategy is using each channel to its best advantage and, thereby, optimising the consumer's time spent online or in the store.
- The bricks-&-mortar channel is the most efficient means of establishing a relationship between customers and brands.
- The dotcom channel is ideal when automated responses suffice in a transaction, say in the case of repeat purchases.
- WebTV is an appropriate channel for accommodating impulse purchases while wireless Internet technology is an even more flexible impulse purchase tool.
- Catalogue services are price-driven and allow consumers to plan purchases of products not necessarily available in their area.
- Clicks-&-mortars must have data-capturing and retrieval systems in place which they can draw upon in unison.
- A maturing clicks-&-mortar partnership travels through developmental stages.
- The honeymoon stage can suffer from the unrealistic, naïve or idealized expectations of its constituent.
- The implementation stage sees the merger of two companies' legacy systems (their databases, ordering, production, salary and accounting systems, etc.), cultures, brands and client groups.
- The up-and-running stage, when the databases talking the same language, the ordering systems working compatibly and customers being treated uniformly, precedes the cost savings, value adding to the brand, increased revenue and growing consumer base that both partners would hope to achieve through the relationship.
- The positive synergy stage has been reached when the emergent business is handling clients smoothly, online and offline; cross-selling and upselling across channels; cross-promoting products and services; and introducing new products and services jointly.

Action Points

By now you've developed a comprehensive channel strategy as part of your overall clicks-&-mortar strategy. The channel strategy encompasses marketing, fulfilment, infrastructural roles and nominates partner responsibilities in these areas. Your operational strategy defines trust, development and maintenance plans, and revenue model alternatives (i.e. product options etc.).

Determine how you will avoid the most frequently encountered problem areas and ensure:
- Efficient fulfilment handling processes.
- Efficient inventory management.
- Online-compatible product categories that are uncomplicated and cheap to ship.
- A well-established and trusted brand.
- A clear point of service/product differentiation.

How attractive is your product from an e-commerce revenue point of view? Score each of these criteria from 1 to 10, giving higher scores to the criteria that describe your product.

Your most important asset is your customer. Determine what value gains a clicks-&-mortar will achieve for your consumers using the following criteria:
- Lower price.
- Greater accessibility to the store.
- Larger selection.
- More product and service information.
- More flexible service.
- More entertainment in the shopping experience.
- Access to unique product selections.
- Better guarantees.

Realistically assess how efficiently will you handle these fulfilment challenges?
- Capturing consumer data on behaviour and preferences, and subsequently reflecting this knowledge in an automated e-commerce enterprise.
- Integrating clicks-and-bricks orders across the same system.
- Handling impulse orders by managing one to one delivery.
- Handling product returns.
- Handling cross- and upselling and increasing per customer sales.

Using your answers to Step 4's challenges, which fulfilment strategy best suits your company's abilities, consumers, products and preparedness?

1. One hundred per cent outsourcing of the fulfilment process.
2. Partial inhouse fulfilment processes, partial outsourced fulfilment processes.
3. One hundred per cent inhouse execution of the fulfilment process.

Chapter 7

M-commerce

The mobile phone is set to become one of the most important tools in solidifying clicks-&-mortar business. The mobile, or cell phone, has already bridged the gap between retailers and the online world, and has given birth to another buzzword: m-commerce. What influence will m-commerce have over brand-building and how will its offspring, m-tailing, affect clicks-&-mortars, e-tailing and retailing?

Now that we've explored the nature of clicks-&-mortar birth and maturation, let's look at the newest item in the consumer's repertoire of shopping options: m-commerce. Whether you treat m-commerce as a threat or an opportunity will depend on your role in the online market place. Are you a purely offline retailer, an online e-tailer or have you embraced the clicks-&-mortar revolution and entered an online-offline alliance?

By 2003 the majority of Internet access will be via wireless handsets rather than PCs.

According to the Yankee Group, by 2003 more wireless handsets will be accessing the Internet than PCs. That means digital wireless users, worldwide, already out-number Internet users and the former's numbers will double by 2004. Internet-enabled phone users are expected to reach 48 million worldwide by 2002, and 204 million by 2005. Yes, there's some potential in mobile Internet commerce.

The principle of m-commerce is that it gives consumers constant online access, via their mobile phones. Mobile Internet offers user-values like personalisation, localisation, immediacy and convenience. Its service ubiquity simultaneously breeds trust in the technology and dependence on it.

Until now only bits and pieces of the consumer's day have been interactive. M-commerce potentially makes the consumer's whole day interactive. WAP (wireless application protocol) technology gives bricks-&-mortar retailers an interactive communication tool and access to consumers the sector has never had before. Wireless Internet technology is likely to be the mortar between bricks and clicks. The ubiquitous nature of the mobile phone interface will foster impulse-buying behaviour and favour FMCG sales. Read on and learn how.

M-commerce in Operation

Payment is a pivotal necessity in any commercial dealing. To make wireless e-commerce work, consumers as always have to be able to pay for what they buy, usually with a credit card. Naturally, the world's major credit cards are working on wireless strategies. The initial m-commerce focus is in Europe, where the concept of mobile Internet first began and where the networks provide a uniform air interface.

In 1999, MasterCard International created a Global Mobile Commerce Team to focus on the convergence of credit card payments and wireless commerce. Over the following years, this resulted in two major acquisitions of wireless-related payment companies. Visa International teamed up with handset and infrastructure manufacturer, Nokia, in 2000. This was part of a global initiative to introduce payment solutions for wireless e-commerce. The two companies aimed to develop standards for making secure payments via WAP-enabled devices, including the development of a mobile "e-wallet" to allow simple click purchases.

E-wallet technology allows customers to pay for items remotely via the Net, or face-to-face in stores. At the time of writing, Visa and Nokia plan to run a pilot program of the system with the MeritaNordbanken financial institutions in Finland and Sweden.

So wireless payment is becoming a probability. Because of the global proliferation of mobile devices, and because it costs nothing for mobile manufacturers to enable their devices to access m-commerce, it's likely that m-commerce will develop a channel for promoting, communicating, transacting and branding products via a mobile device.

As I discussed earlier in the book, enterprise success depends, among many criteria, on product compatibility with its commercial channel. M-commerce offers no allowances. There are product categories that don't suit wireless shopping. You wouldn't make a "high consideration" purchase, such as a new car or home, from a mobile phone. But you would make impulse-driven FMCG purchases.

One of the most popular mobile Internet sites is BarnesAndNoble.com's m-tail website. The online shop, which supports leading mobile phones as well as Palm Inc. wireless-enabled digital personal assistants, offers books, CDs and other products. A "Wireless Listening Wall" allows shoppers to listen to CD music samples. Site visitors can also send "e-cards" to friends, peruse top-ten book lists or check the shipping status of an order. A number of web travel sites are also testing m-tailing: travel service retailers (airline, car rental companies, hotels) are likely to become m-tailing mainstays.

What's WAP?

One of the most common terms related to m-commerce is WAP (wireless application protocol). WAP is not a generic term for mobile Internet but one of the most common platforms that enables the Internet to be transferred to a wireless format and operated via the mobile phone. WAP is an open platform, a set of rules within which mobile software can be developed. If WAP were not available, we'd end up with systems that couldn't talk together, like VHS, Beta 200 and BetaCam in the old days.

Another platform is iMode, launched by DoCoMo in Japan. The concept was launched in the late nineties. iMode has since claimed more than 15 million subscribers who all use their mobile phones as their primary tool for verbal and written communication. Most Japanese DoCoMo subscribers send between eight and ten written messages a day — to other subscribers for a cost of a couple of yen each. The popularity of the system has affected most retailing in metropolitan Japan. A range of restaurants have now integrated the wireless system with their karaoke music system enabling guests to order their favourite music, and pay for it via their DoCoMo mobile phones. The system also enables the mobile phone to assess the owner's geographical position and display special store and event offers related to the appropriate area. And the service now offers to "warn" the user when a person whose phone number is stored in the user's address book is about to pass you in the street. You'd hate to miss the chance of saying "Hi!" in person! The "warning" is attached to a suggestion about, for example, drinking a coffee together at a nearby coffee shop, which, of course, pays for every such advertisement the system transmits.

And just remember, I'm not describing the future. I'm talking now. Given these facts, the question is how is WAP technology affecting retailing? Is the wireless Internet becoming the mortar that joins the clicks and the bricks?

Let's try and figure out how m-commerce is likely to operate within just two to three years. Of course, this is all speculative, but as we've learnt, being prepared is a commercial survival technique. Survey and understand the market facts, and set sail accordingly. Gear up for the future. In this chapter let's look at being prepared to capitalise on the direction technology might offer brand-building.

M-commerce and the Shopping Experience

So what is wireless Internet communication going to mean for the future of commerce, retail and marketing? Well, let me ask you the question in another way. When you first heard about the Internet (in the form we know it) back in 1995, what consequences did you foresee? Did you consider the impact the Internet would have on consumerism and marketing? The same dramatic change we've witnessed over the past half-decade and more is likely to recur. Imagine combining the ubiquitousness and flexibility of wireless Internet capabilities with online auctioning, chatrooms and customisation functionalities! Wild!

The first phase in the Internet history has pushed retailing beyond its well-established boundaries. The Net's one to one capabilities and twenty-four-hour-a-day accessibility has given consumers a means of influencing product availability, pricing and design. The next phase will see the transfer of such power from the retailer and manufacturer to the consumer even more decidedly. Mobile Internet access gives consumers a tool to negotiate immediately on product price, function and delivery conditions via their mobile phone display.

Predictive Modelling

As if centuries old retailing hasn't had its hands full responding in a half decade to the change the Net has wrought upon the consumer-retailer-manufacturer-distributor relationship, the increased flexibilities brought about by WAP technology introduces startling and major challenges to e-tail's internal culture and capabilities. Will brands retire and products become generic, with the consumer constantly comparing prices worldwide via the mobile phone? Will prices jump up and down like Nasdaq share prices as consumers seek out the best buys? And will the retailer know more about consumer shopping behaviour than consumers know about themselves, seeing that all consumer communications — information requests, purchases and so on — will be channelled through one device: the mobile phone? Prediction could be the retailer's reward for adapting to the flexible consumer environment.

Imagine, for example, walking down the supermarket aisle and passing by the CD rack. What CD should you buy? Let the mobile phone decide. Scan a CD's barcode and the phone will match the CD's contents with your own consumer profile. Basing its analysis on your own and thousands of other profiles, and matching your musical taste to wider consumer profiles, the system could make a

Disney could develop loyalty in its theme parks by creating virtual queues. Using a Disney-supplied mobile device, a customer could reserve a seat hours in advance.

recommendation as to whether or not you should buy the CD. This hypothetical example illustrates the ideal outcome of predictive modelling combined with WAP communications. For more about predictive modelling, see Chapter 13.

As already demonstrated by DoCoMo's capacity to "warn" you that you are about to pass someone you know in the street, geography is a very important factor in an m-commerce environment. Say you're strolling down Market Street in San Francisco and you pass by Barnes & Noble. The data on your mobile phone will automatically connect you with the store. Let's say Barnes & Noble has a particular book on sale, in fact, the book you've been looking for all year. Your mobile phone knows this to be the case and will inform you of the special offer and give you a time frame in which to purchase the book before the offer expires. The time that this offer lasts can be as short as ten minutes.

Online Auctions and Comparison Shopping

It's conceivable that every product you pass in the store of the m-commerce future will be available on auction. So any product you choose will have been surveyed on the Net, making it possible for you to verify its price online and ensure you're aware of the lowest possible cost for the item. M-auctions could sweep every product for sale into a worldwide bidding frenzy. It's likely that, just a decade from now, we won't see fixed prices on any items. Prices will be fluid and determined by an epidemic of WAP-triggered and WAP-communicated consumer demand. A car, which might cost $20,000 in the morning, might cost $21,000 in the evening because the demand for it has risen. The more people purchasing that model, the fewer would be available and the price would go up again.

This flurry of offers and counter offers will be communicated via the mobile phone which, at any time, would update consumers on the state of every product and every service they're interested in around the world. Just as it's possible now to program your mobile phone to show your stock figures and warn you if they fall below a specified point, you'll be able to request any type of consumer item any time. You might only be interested in purchasing a car when it reaches a certain price range. Bidding may never reach your limit so you may never purchase the car. Or your mobile phone might end up transmitting the message you were hoping for: that the price has fallen to meet your bid.

Comparison shopping is a powerful potential m-tailing application. IQorder.com, for example, is betting that shoppers will bring mobile phones into stores for on-the-spot comparisons. The company offers a free shopping service that enables users to compare products and prices in a variety of categories. Users can search for prices by manufacturer, model name, product class, product numbers, keyword and several other ways.

Mobile Internet technology will open the door to true market mechanics which, following the laws of supply and demand, will determine the value of products today, this very minute, as we speak.

M-commerce Means Instant Commerce

With m-commerce just over the horizon the retail environment is likely to be muscled into a corner. It'll have to come out fighting by reviewing its whole pricing structure. Services and products will come to exist in a state of change: prices, products and service levels will vary according to consumer demand. The power of m-commerce is that it will be *instant* commerce. It will give marketers a new means of getting hold of the consumer, right at the most crucial time in the shopping continuum: at the very second the consumer is considering whether to buy or not to buy a certain product, rather than long before such a decision is to be made or after it's a dead issue.

M-commerce will require massive databases. It will need individual digital marketing programs wrapped around each brand and each product under that brand's umbrella, to ensure that every product can learn from, talk, listen and react to each consumer.

Paving the Way to a Mobile Information Society

Case study by Lynne Ankrah, Nokia

In 1990 there were only 6 million mobile phone subscribers worldwide. Most owners of mobile phones were business people and mobile phones were premium products. Within a decade, mobile phones have become mass-market products. No matter where you go, almost everyone seems to have a mobile phone. More than 165 million mobile phones were sold globally in 1998. In 1999, this figure increased to almost 270 million. Nokia predicts that there will be 1 billion mobile phone users in the world by the end of 2002, and by 2003, the annual sales of mobile phones capable of Internet access will exceed the sales of personal computers.

With the onset of digital convergence, a shift is occurring from voice to data. New value added services will be possible with increasing data rates – both circuit and packet switched. The evolution will be a smooth path manifesting itself to the user by a broadening spectrum of new services. Users will be able to utilise personal, location-based mobile information and interactive services and multimedia content. Also many companies are restructuring their business processes to be able to fully exploit the opportunities provided by the emerging new mobile data services.

The distinctive characteristics of the mobile environment which differ from the Internet on PCs are as follows:

- Mobile operators are the new intermediaries.
- Data calls are not free of charge: users pay to access mobile Internet.
- End-user habits differ depending on who is paying the bill.

Common themes received from market research on Wireless Application Protocol (WAP) mobile Internet services suggest that mobile users want services to improve their lives such as traffic information, and suggestions of alternative routes, taxi bookings, or cinema reservations using the mobile internet. The emphasis is very much on "my world", "my local environment" wherever that may be and "my likes". Mobile users also want to control the information they receive themselves. They do not want content providers to second-guess them. Content providers should consider the user's needs when the user is on the move. If they simply translate their current web offering to a mobile service without considering end-user needs they will probably not succeed.

When a retailer is thinking of entering mobile space, regardless of whether they have a physical or Internet presence or both, they need to devise an entry strategy. Clearly, the mobile Internet is in the early stages of development. In many ways it is like history repeating itself in the sense that development of the Internet on personal computers started off in a very similar way with its own glitches that were eventually ironed out. However, in the mobile information society companies that will survive will be those who understand their users' needs and meet their users' expectation.

M-branding

As I've described, m-commerce will change our shopping experience. In doing so it will become a highly effective branding platform. Why? Because it invites and allows the marketer's influence on consumer shopping behaviour right in the midst of the purchase situation — for better and for worse.

Graphic Limitations

One of the biggest challenges m-commerce will face, being reliant on the mobile phone screen, is that of branding via a pure text display. It was a problem that the Internet grappled with before its adaptation to the World Wide Web when, in the absence of graphics, fledgling Web designers had to rely purely on text. When graphics became available later they did so with major constraints. Then graphic display possibilities increased to enable animations, sound and 3D displays. The more tools that became available, the better branding opportunities appeared.

How would you build your brand using a screen smaller than a matchbox and using only one colour?

Back to the branding challenge under discussion. How would you build your brand using a screen smaller than a matchbox? What if you could use only one colour — black — on a green background, you had no scope for graphics and the consumer was paying for every second it took for you to send them a commercial message? That's the new world of m-branding. Now, more than ever, creativity and discipline are needed in the preparation of branding platforms.

Remember the lesson: be prepared. Knowing how fast this next branding revolution could arrive, you'd better be ready. So start preparing for wireless branding now. Consider this anecdote as a great example of preparedness.

Like all tobacco companies in the UK, Silk Cut, in the eighties was faced with an imminent ban on cigarette advertising. Unlike all tobacco companies in the UK, Silk Cut prepared its marketing for the government ban on cigarette commercials. All the cigarette companies knew the ban would come into effect, and they had plenty of time to prepare for the restrictions it imposed. But not many used the time well. So when the day finally arrived Silk Cut was able to continue its marketing campaign where its competitors' marketing hands were tied. Silk Cut manoeuvred around the legislative constraints by eliminating its brand name from all publicity. Silk Cut became recognisable as an image: luxuriously rumpled purple silk with a gaping slash through it. The simple strong image communicated the product's identity wordlessly. Colour and image became the communicators: racing cars in the distinctive purple livery, and the billboard advertisements were just two vehicles that carried the Silk Cut message to the community. And the interesting thing was that no one really realised that the name was gone. *The branding was intact.*

Marlboro was another brand which, through its clothing line, found an escape route into the new advertising reality. The cigarette retained its smokers and communicated with potential smokers by promoting its "Marlboro Country" clothing brand.

So what's the connection with m-commerce and m-branding? Being limited to using a matchbox-sized display, with no colours and no resolution is like running a Silk Cut campaign without being allowed to show your logo or your brand name. It demands creative, disciplined branding planning.

Yes, you can show your logo on the mobile-phone display, but don't forget the consumer is paying for every second you take up on their mobile's screen. So what would you do? Some techniques occur to me, one of which is to work on product placement. Ensure that, whenever it's relevant (on the news, in movies, and so on) your brand is exposed. Another method would be to refine your brand's language: Use phrases that the consumer can recognise as being the voice and speech of your brand. Some brands have already developed recognisable voices through brand phrases. Coca-Cola, for example, has drawn the word "Enjoy" around its identity.

The connection to m-branding is apparent, isn't it? Such a simple word, yet through disciplined brand use, so charged with meaning that its exposure on that tiny mobile display will say a thousand things to the consumer in a split second. Think about Intel Inside's melody and imagine how easy it will be for that brand to broadcast the signature melody via the mobile phone. Both

> *M-branding faces the challenges of being reliant on the mobile phone and being limited to monochrome text display.*

Coca-Cola and Intel have created identifiers around their brands which can, independent of the brands' logos, names and images, remind the consumer about the brand and all it stands for.

But many, many more brands haven't been this inventive. M-branding is all about using very few tools in a very creative way. If you don't have any tools, you need to create them, fast. Because the race for branding real estate on the mobile phone display has already begun. And you need to stake your brand's claim. M-commerce and wireless Internet technology have the potential to advance marketers' access to consumers and consumers' access to market data. Be ready to make the most of it.

The trick is to be consistent and create design and language integration between your brand's messages across all media. It's imperative that the brand's voice is instantly recognisable and that its values are so well understood by the consumer that the little that can be uttered via the mobile phone display expresses the brand's whole story. The brand will need to convey its identity with an articulateness, conciseness and definition that prompts consumer action.

Instant branding

Yet, despite the graphic handicap, a range of marketing challenges and opportunities are likely to appear in the guise of m-commerce, each of them bringing new tools and imperatives to branding-building. M-commerce enables marketers to be in constant contact with consumers, to know where they are any time and to send customized brand messages to them according to their location and profile. Cross- and upselling will be triggered by purchases consumers make and by the profiles that delineate their purchasing behaviour.

Where most other communication channels, like TV and the print media, offer marketing the tools of animation and colour, m-commerce offers the capacity to contact consumers at the very minute a purchase decision is taking place. That's the difference between traditional branding and instant branding and it's the latter's crucial advantage.

Model 7.1 *Media communication tools*

	Mobile Internet	PC Internet	Television	Instore	Print Media
Immediate action stimulation	✓	✓	✗	✓	✗
Animation	✗	✓	✓	✓	✗
Colour	✗	✓	✓	✓	✓
Interactivity	✓	✓	✗	✓	✗
Visuals (sight)	✓	✓	✓	✓	✓
Audio (sound)	✓	✓	✓	✓	✗
Olfactory (smell)	✗	✓	✗	✓	✗
Tactile (touch)	✗	✗	✗	✓	✗
Taste	✗	✗	✗	✓	✗

The capacity to stimulate immediate action is enjoyed only by mobile Internet, PC Internet and instore marketing. The capacity to stimulate immediate individual action is held only by mobile Internet branding. The principle of one to one communication resides in the mobile phone's proximity to the individual, and the marketer's capacity to stimulate the individual's action at the very point of decision-making is the sole preserve of m-commerce marketing.

This valuable potential is squandered without a brand's achievement of the essential commercial asset – e-trust. This essential principle of branding applies to m-commerce as it does in every avenue of marketing. Trust is the goal of brand-building. *Brand = trust.*

The key to establishing trust is adherence to the virtue of consistency. Consistency builds familiarity, reliability and, in the end, renders your brand, ultimately, trustworthy. (Read more about trust in Chapter 4.)

Consistency: The Vital Ingredient

Right now, let's concentrate on ingredients that are peculiar to m-commerce, branding: icons, navigation, tone of voice and logo. These ingredients need to be mixed with that important staple, consistency, a vital and all-encompassing necessity in your communications. As in all brand building, to achieve identity and to start building a relationship with customers a brand must use the same terms, the same icons and the same navigation in every instance. The more elements a consumer can recognize and relate to your brand as its proprietary signals, the more effective your brand building.

Icons

Developing easily recognizable icons for use in all media is imperative and establishing consumer literacy in your icons before commencing an m-branding strategy is an obvious necessity. It enables you to leverage on already-established and understood values, all of which are represented by your brand's icons. But icons appearing for the first time on the mobile phone display will be unrecognisable, meaningless and, therefore, impotent. Graphics are an eloquent and articulate means of communicating your brand's personality to the consumer. If you're icons are legible and the consumer can recognize your brand's graphic style, you're managing strong branding. What two-year-old in nearly any part of the world can't read "McDonald's" for the famous golden arch symbol or for the Ronald McDonald character icon? Your customers should be able to recognize your brand's signature whenever it appears on a WAP device, and it must be consistently used in POS displays, in posters hanging from supermarket ceilings, on the sides of buses, at your website ... on every one of your brand's communications.

Navigation

Easy navigation is a most important requirement on a mobile phone display. The easier your communications are to locate and peruse, the stronger representation your brand enjoys. No one wants to waste time scrolling up and down to find stuff, and don't forget that every second costs the consumer money. Consumers want to be able to locate the information they're after immediately. Navigation on personal equipment must, of course, be consistent with the navigation structure on your brand's website: same prompt and information order, same payment questions, and so on. That's the role of consistency in navigation design.

Tone-of-voice

As copy is just about the only communication tool available to you on the mobile phone's display it's important that you create intelligent, comprehensible, relevant copy around your brand. Text helps define the brand's personality and, in turn, controls the way your brand is perceived, accepted or rejected, by the consumer. Your copy and the tone-of-voice it conveys should reinforce brand values consistently.

Logo

It barely needs mentioning, its importance is so self-evident. But don't neglect your logo. It's shorthand for everything your brand stands for and, in time, could come into a life of its own as a meaningful m-commerce icon. Remember: the consumer is paying for every second of your logo's exposure on the mobile phone, so don't let your brand overstay its welcome. A logo should be exposed on the display when it adds concrete value only and when it leads to action. For example, upon entering a restaurant, the VISA logo might appear on the mobile phone display, confirming that the card is accepted in that establishment.

Sure, focus on m-commerce as an instant branding exercise. That's its chief advantage. It takes place here and now, not tomorrow, not yesterday. This means that everything a brand says to a consumer, everything it wants the consumer to do and every message it tries to convey has to be related to stimulating instant action. Forget everything about messages like "Always Coca-Cola" or other long-term branding messages. They won't change consumers' minds when exposed as m-commerce messages. The m-commerce message must be action-oriented, clear and concise. For example: "35^0C today: enjoy Coke at 50% rrp" might be the message sent, just thirty seconds before the consumer passes by the supermarket. I guarantee this well-timed suggestive selling works. The long branding story belongs to traditional media channels. But consistency underlies all great branding stories. Make sure you use the branding tools outlined on page 152 to develop branding synergy between all your commercial channels.

Model 7.2 *Audio and graphic logos are strong core value communicators.*

	audio	logo	audio and logo
Is cool	61%	80%	73%
Is distinctive	74%	87%	88%
Is a leading brand	70%	89%	86%
Is appealing	70%	79%	77%
Is fun	64%	64%	73%
Is for me	51%	60%	59%
Is energetic	55%	59%	69%
Is friendly	75%	81%	82%
Is entertaining	64%	71%	77%
Is high quality	72%	76%	81%
Is a company I would expect great sound from	66%	76%	80%

Source:Cheskin research and Beatnik Inc., 1999

M-tailing

So, it appears advertising is coming to a wireless phone near you. But, will you want it as a consumer? A couple of startup companies are nearing the launch of wireless advertising. But the technique is, so far, untried. Will the effect be like junk mail bombarding e-mail addresses and letterboxes? How will advertisers get their messages across consumer's mobile phone displays without causing irritation? Despite the question of initial consumer acceptance, market research company, Zawel, expects mobile commerce revenue to account for 3–8% of total operator revenue by 2005, or about US$2 billion in revenue for operators and their partners, opening up gigantic potential for wireless advertising.

M-commerce will take place through m-tailing, m-navigation, m-advice, m-search, etc. But it's likely that m-tailing will dominate the m-commerce arena. Not to be confused with e-tailing, m-tailing is retailing conducted via mobile Internet technology. The ultimate m-tailing vision would see consumers having access to the local store twenty-four hours a day, seven days a week via their mobile phones; trips to the supermarket characterised by mobile phone dialogues between the consumer and the store's advisory services; and all store display materials removed in favour of customised messages read on each consumer's mobile phone display.

M-tailing integrates retailer, e-tailer and mobile Internet technology.

Swedish manufacturer, Ericsson, is betting that wireless m-commerce will permeate all facets of life, from checking the status of food in the refrigerator to checking purchases out at the store. The company is creating a comprehensive set of solutions focusing, not only on handsets, but also on m-commerce services and content. Ericsson believes that soon customers will scan their own purchases using their handsets, automatically checking them out and paid for independently. Already, and separately to the Ericsson initiatives, Safeway stores in Britain have been using palm devices to facilitate shopping and bill payment.

Slowly we're commencing the communication between consumers and brands by using the mobile phone as the interface between them. In the past, dialogue between products and consumers resided in package design and copy. Mobile Internet technology allows products to answer consumer questions and opens the door to a worldwide market. Product information will be communicated in the languages of consumers' choice and be available globally.

Online Coupons and m-POS Communications

Bearing in mind that every retailer and every product will be able to communicate with consumers it's likely that a range of "old" marketing tools, like coupons, will reappear.

Imagine having just purchased drinking-chocolate powder. A message might be sent to you from the store's fridge monitor offering you two litres of milk for the price of one. Or, being a frequent reader of *People Magazine,* you could be sent gossip column headings to remind you that the latest edition is on sale. The system all works via the mobile phone and wireless Internet technology. You'd pay for everything via your phone, which would also give you direct access to your bank account, thus replacing the credit card. When you take up the coupon offers, *the bill would be automatically discounted.*

Most of Korea's public transportation system is already trialling a system that connects the mobile phone to the ticket-purchasing system. Forget about purchasing a ticket using money. Your fare is simply deducted from your transport account when you enter the train with your mobile phone — even if the phone is switched off.

BrightStreet.com already offers online coupons that you can download via a number of channels: WebTV, your mobile phone or the PC. Several other companies, like Nokia, Samson, British Telecommunications, Genie and Sony are working on technologies to enable mobile phone users to receive messages from and send messages to POS materials by pointing their phones at the object of their curiosity and receiving interactive information about it.

CASE: Brightstreet.com

BrightStreet's Online Promotion Drives Customers into Stores

"Two dry-cleaned shirts for the price of one" is printed on the flipside of a movie ticket. A "five-cents-off" offer on a popular brand of dishwasher can be snipped out along the dotted line in a newspaper ad and redeemed at the local supermarket. Specials, free samples and cut-out coupons are an integral part of the retail environment, providing twin hooks for marketers in search of consumer incentive and customer loyalty.

BrightStreet.com has developed the technology to deliver and carefully monitor coupons and promotional incentives online. The company terms its approach "WAM-BAM" (Web Application Meets Bricks And Mortar) and promises to turn web window shoppers into real store consumers. This technology, known as Digital Promotions Backbone, provides marketers with a super-efficient medium for targeting and tracking consumer habits and is able to accurately monitor each stage in the promotional cycle from inception to completion.

The backend technology is licensed directly to websites enabling them to deliver their own branded marketing incentives. Furthermore, it allows them to integrate all their promotional functions while simultaneously driving online and offline sales so that the one complements the other.

Take for example the case of PetSmart, one of BrightStreet's major clients. PetSmart has 493 stores and an online e-commerce site for the American pet's every need. Visitors to the virtual store enter their e-mail addresses and zip codes. They then have access to a variety of coupons which can be printed and redeemed at the real stores. If the promotion determines that a free sample is sent out to a customer, the next time they visit the site the system will recognise them and ask if they would be interested in receiving, say, a 50-cents-off coupon to buy the item, thus extending the promotion to the purchase level.

There are other benefits. The customer database is expanded so consumers can be accurately targeted and notified of any future offers relevant to their needs, while online coupons can be easily updated.

Coupons are big business. Within the first year of operation, BrightStreet.com's prospects looked so ... well, bright, that they attracted a triple-play investment agreement from a powerful coalition of media and marketing interests. With this alliance in place, BrightStreet.com is further able to exploit the world of Internet promotions as another channel through which companies can effectively deliver incentives and special offers. All this helps manufacturers and retailers make the critical transition from offline to Web-based promotions.

New Marketing Plans

What will m-tailing, with its capacity for allowing brands instant, intelligent access to consumers and for allowing consumers instant access to market information, mean for marketing plans?

M-tailing will require marketing plans to work across all channels in synergy. This may demand some off- and online marketing compromises. As I mentioned earlier, some channels are good at telling long branding stories. Others suit concise messages. The trick is to ensure that all brand exposures support each other. A radio commercial might be supported with billboard advertising, which is supported by newspaper advertisements that make the same offers. These offers would be reiterated via the mobile phone display when the consumer is passing a relevant store. The tighter the relationship between the multichannelled messages, the more effective the campaign will be.

According to Nicolas Negroponte, professor and founder of MIT Media Laboratory, the Mobile Internet will become the planet's key communication tool. If this forecast is to be relied upon, it's likely that separate m-commerce strategies will need to be developed for every product. These strategies will tie every product to a massive consumer database and to information about related products with which each consumer shares a history.

Cross-selling and upselling via Wireless Internet

Synergized multichannel marketing strategies will ignite brand chain reactions that, in the old days, we called "upselling" or "cross-selling". Upselling is persuading consumers to purchase a more advanced or more expensive product or service. Cross-selling is encouraging consumers to buy more products within the same category. This marketing discipline was a difficult one to manage in the past, as it required knowledgeable store staff and/or really effective POS materials. In the future, m-commerce will have the potential to be part of consumers' choices at the very second they are made. The consumer's exposure will trigger a call on their mobile: WAP technology will have given brands access to consumers and their profiles enabling marketers to subject customers to upselling, cross-selling marketing onslaughts.

So it's likely that shoppers, while pacing supermarket aisles and perusing the shelves' contents, will find themselves receiving calls on their mobile phones. Activated by the customer's position in the supermarket, the call will be about special instore offers. The calls will not only be activated because the shopper passed by a crucial trigger point, but also because the WAP system will have known that the shopper actually needed the item related to the offer.

For example, the call might be about a Coca-Cola offer. It will have been triggered when the customer entered the beverage aisle and, most importantly, because the WAP system understood that the customer in question was a Coca-Cola drinker.

If you're like me and habitually forget to buy half of the groceries you need every time you go to the store, this could be a welcome marketing move. But for the rest of the world, this might become a challenge for both the consumer and the marketer. The mutual challenge lies in what is potentially a dream tool for both the former and the latter: a tool that has unlimited power to communicate, as well as unlimited capacity to be ignored.

Summary

- By 2003 more wireless handsets will be accessing the Internet than PCs. Internet-enabled phone users are expected to reach 48 million worldwide by 2002, and 204 million by 2005.
- M-commerce revenue is expected to account for 3–8% of total operator revenue by 2005. That's about US$2 billion in revenue for operators and their partners, opening up gigantic potential for wireless advertising.
- The principle of m-commerce is that it gives consumers, at any time, online retail access, via their mobile phones. Mobile Internet technology offers users-values like personalisation, localisation, immediacy and convenience.
- WAP (wireless application protocol) and iMode are two technology platforms that enable data to become accessible via the mobile phone display.
- WAP technology gives bricks-&-mortar retailers an interactive communication tool and access to consumers the sector has never had before.
- Mobile Internet technology gives consumers a tool to negotiate immediately on product price, function and delivery conditions via their mobile phone display.
- It's conceivable that every product will be available through auctions online. Comparison-shopping is likely to become a potentially powerful m-tailing application.
- Mobile Internet technology will open the door to true market mechanics which, following the laws of supply and demand, will determine the value of products right now.
- The power of m-commerce is that it will be *instant* commerce, giving marketers a means of contacting the consumer, right at the most crucial time in the shopping continuum: at the very second the consumer is

considering whether to buy or not to buy a certain product, rather than long before such a decision is to be made or after it's a dead issue.

- M-branding faces the challenges of being reliant on the mobile phone and, consequently, of being limited to monochrome text display; and of the fact that the consumer will be paying for every second of advertising time.
- Brand messages must be consistent across all media: the brand's voice must be recognisable and its values so well understood by the consumer that the little that can be uttered via the mobile phone display expresses the brand's core values and suggests action.
- M-commerce enables marketers to be in constant contact with consumers, to know where they are at any time and to send customised brand messages to them according to their locations and profiles. M-commerce will bring new market motivators to the consumer like flexible pricing, one to one marketing and the potential for instant action.
- WAP technology can trigger upselling and cross-selling through predictive modelling.
- Services and products will exist in a state of change: prices, products and service levels will vary according to consumer demand.
- M-commerce may require marketing plans to comprise off- and online components and ensure that all channels work in synergy. The tighter the relationship between the multichannelled messages, the more effective the campaign will be.
- Developing recognisable icons, easy navigation, intelligent, comprehensible, relevant copy and a meaningful logo is imperative in m-commerce branding where the mobile phone display is the canvas.
- M-tailing integrates retailer, e-tailer and mobile Internet technology.

Action Points

Ascertain your brand's m-commerce future. These steps are intended to be taken after your clicks-&-mortar strategy has been established and executed.

Assess percentage of online sales

If you haven't yet been successful with e-commerce it's unlikely you'll be successful with m-commerce. Success with the first generation of e-commerce is a vital prerequisite to adopting any m-commerce strategies both as a learning exercise and to test whether your consumer group is suited to new commerce services, so before considering whether m-commerce is for your company, it's important that you evaluate how your channel strategy is working. What percentage of your sales take place online, in the retail store and via your catalogue ordering service? How do you believe these figures will change over the next two years?

Assess product compatibilities with the m-commerce environment

If your business belongs in one of the following categories, it's likely your product will suit m-commerce trading.

– Travel, leisure, accommodation and restaurants
– Finance and insurance
– Software
– Information, news services and most communication media
– FMCG retailing
– Mobile phone and telephone services
– Portals and ISP services
– Navigation and recommendation services
– Auction services
– Personal data (health, horoscopes, dentist, etc.)
– Gambling and games
– Translation

If your business doesn't belong to one of the above don't panic. But don't expect to become the Amazon of m-commerce, either. We've learnt from e-commerce that market penetration was almost entirely dependent on the category's adaptability to the online environment. Now, several years after the appearance of e-commerce, less suitable offerings are finding their way onto the Internet. This indicates that products and services outside the above list aren't likely to be successful m-commerce participants before 2004.

If your business fits into one of the above categories, initiate development of an m-commerce strategy. Consider the following questions:

1. Why m-commerce? Do you really believe that this is your path to success?
2. Who constitutes your target m-commerce market?
3. What is your revenue model?
4. Define your point of differentiation. How do you expect to attract your target group, and second, how do you expect to make life difficult for competitors?
5. Is your target market related to your existing clicks-&-mortar clientele? Is your m-commerce service likely cannibalise your existing venture?

6. What synergies do you anticipate your m-commerce venture will achieve between your operating channels and how much do you expect this to increase your revenue?

7. Are your m-commerce concepts likely to conflict with your existing distribution strategy and cause internal conflicts?

8. Conduct a SWOT analysis of your m-commerce concept, and then do the same analysis of your competitor's.

9. How do you propose to leverage on your brand's existing values?

10. What support for the m-commerce concept do you have among your management and distribution partners?

If you still feel comfortable with your m-commerce strategy read on. The next couple of chapters are as relevant to m-commerce strategies as they are to clicks-&-mortars.

Chapter 8

ePsychology

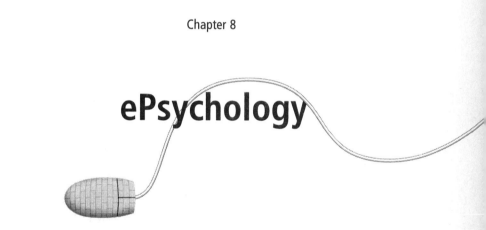

Since the World Wide Web was born in 1994, the Net has undergone steady, though rapid change. It continually addresses the task of becoming more consumer-friendly. Still, the Net lacks a crucial trait: it can't be human.

It's no surprise that the more user-friendly a system, any system, the more it will be used. This lesson is not new to retailers. The past two decades have seen the creation of an increasingly human environment in the retailing industry: multiple aisles of serried shelves squinting under neon light are disappearing in favour of environments that offer demonstrations, entertainment and themed specialty sections. The days of merely stocking shelves with product and providing a cashier near the exit are coming to an end, not because people don't want to shop in hypermarkets, supermarkets and malls any more, but because shopping is being appreciated as a human experience, rather than a necessary procedure. Shopping has assumed the same recreational status as sightseeing.

Shopping: An Experience, Not a Job

So why has this trend taken place? First, because the emergent shopping generation — websters and e-teens (more about them in Chapter 12) — resent boredom, crave variety and is apparently dependent on instant and constant gratification. According to "Future Youth", a study conducted by BBDO Europe, this generation regards boredom as a form of death. Therefore, they seek diversions in every part of life. Shopping aisles replete with row upon row of static products don't do it for them. Merchandise no longer tells its own story, and so now it has to be given context to attract the future shopper.

Retailers can create environments that make contact with emotions, exploit social behaviour and appeal to all the senses.

Second, the rise of e-tailing has forced bricks-&-mortar retailing to rethink its market function. The mistake many retailers still make is to focus on price competitiveness, product selection and delivery terms. It's unlikely that retailers can compete with e-tailers on these fronts. But some retailers have identified their point of differentiation over e-tailing. In the real world, retailers create an environment for consumers which connects with human emotions, exploits social behaviour, and appeals to *all* the senses — not simply those of sight and hearing to which e-tailers are bound.

Knowing the Emotional Balance

Knowing their best capabilities intimately is not only invaluable for e-tailers and retailers, it's going to determine whether businesses survive or not. Rational purchasing decisions are mostly taken online. Offline is where the emotional decisions are taken. This distinction holds advantages for both sales environments. It will become the *raison d'être* of bricks-&-mortar retailing, an essential part of clicks-&-mortar dealings and an indispensable showroom facility for e-tailing.

> *Retailers and e-tailers occupy opposite ends of the rational–emotional balance.*

Retailers use the senses Disney was one of the first to exploit this awareness when they launched their concept stores. They were then followed by the Warner Bros stores. These concept stores aimed to entertain customers and inspire them to buy. Consumers loved the colour, the characters and the overall pizzazz. Their success paved the way for the emergence of concept stores around the world, including theme restaurant concepts like Planet Hollywood and the Hard Rock Café. Common to these concept enterprises is the focus on consumers: they address specific human interests by injecting multi-sensory experiences into the shopping process.

E-tailers orchestrate the senses As sight, hearing and data analysis are the consumer's tools for online decision-making, Internet marketers need to synthesise other sensory appeals. In cyberspace, the rows of products are gone. Touching isn't possible. Smelling and tasting are out of the question. The online marketer's role will be to help the consumer smell with the eye, taste with vision and feel with sight.

In the past, brand control typically covered use of the logo, graphic style, picture quality, typography and the brand's message. These elements are still of prime importance for e-commerce. But the Internet has presented us with new significant influences on brand-building, like the brand "voice". The sound of a brand's website, the tone of voice in the brand's copy and e-mails to consumers, the site's downloading time, its ease and style of navigation, its security policy, its colour scheme, the manner of its call-centre staff … Well orchestrated, these elements can bring out every screen-bound, data-based nuance and value of the brand.

Visit **DualBook.com/cbb/ch8/SenseManagement** for the latest success stories on branding and sense management.

Try Offline, Buy Online

Sony's concept stores in San Francisco and Sydney are good examples of the direction retailing is likely to take over the next couple of years. The stores offer everything Sony offers — computers, flat screens, WebTV terminals, digital recorders and a whole lot more — all available for individual demonstration. The big surprise is that you can't buy anything there. If you want to purchase the product, you test it instore, then you go online and put your money down.

Car dealerships are likely to go the same way. Test driving cars, seeing how the seats and headroom fit you, judging whether the dashboard and the interior suit your style will be a showroom experience. The rest of the transaction will be conducted by e-tailers over the Internet. Of course, there'll be lots to decide on before you pay up: the colour of the car, special features you require, and how to arrange your finance. And all this will be conducted online.

The aim of offline product presentation will be to engage consumers' senses in a purposeful and concerted manner. The more the consumer engages in feeling, smelling, and tasting the products or service, the stronger will be the emotional tie between consumers and brands. And the differences between what the e-tailer and retailer can offer will become more profound.

While the retailer is working on the whole-body experience and emotional discriminations, the e-tailer will be offering factual arguments in favour of products and services. Let's think about it. If you had the chance to taste, smell and feel a product or to simply look at it and review a data sheet on it, I reckon you'd find the actual testing procedure the most persuasive.

The Buying Cycle

To what extent consumers are persuaded by emotional or rational arguments, depends on where they are at in their buying cycle. It's likely that a first-time purchase of a product will happen at a bricks-&-mortar store. A first-time purchase is accompanied by lots of unknowns so, typically, consumers will aim not to add more unfamiliarity to their decision; they'll shop where they know, at least. But the questions consumers might have had about the product before the initial purchase (How does the product taste? What's it feel like? Does it fit? Will it break? Is the colour right?) won't be as relevant when making a repeat purchase. Consumers tend to regard first-time purchases, particularly if they take place offline, as a "trial investment" with risks attached. The trial investment might be related to a product, a whole product category or to a store.

Model 8.1

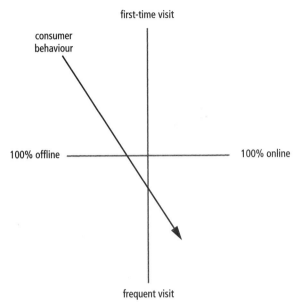

first-time visit

consumer behaviour

100% offline — 100% online

frequent visit

Promoting Appropriate Value Propositions

Retailers and e-tailers have to determine what values they're offering consumers during their buying cycle. Too often retailers attempt to establish value propositions which they've lost before the buyer has even entered the picture. For example, they might focus on price and/or selection rather than communicating the product's application to the consumer's needs.

The retailer's advantage is service, and this will come to define the retailer's particular function. Service will become for the consumer an emotional prerequisite to resolving purchasing decisions. And it will become the retailer's means of retaining a place in the market. To continue the car purchase example I mentioned earlier, the dealers' role will be to analyse customer needs, determine the specifications to best meet those needs, and act as a conduit between the customer and their dream car. You could compare the process with that of buying spectacles today. Opticians conduct standard tests to analyse your vision and come up with a prescription to improve it. Once you have the prescription you can then set about specifying the lenses you need and the style you want. The same process is likely to be the case when purchasing clothing, cosmetics or even furniture. Databases of consumer information will give retailers your prescription.

The e-tailer's advantage will be in repeat sales. E-tailers not only know what the consumer has purchased, they know where the consumer has shopped. And the data are stored in one database offering e-tailers an outstanding marketing tool. Cross- and upselling is hardly possible in the real world unless you know the consumer's purchasing background and have spent a lot of time with the individual. This is not necessary in the digital world, where each individual's purchases can be compared to those of thousands of other customers. The e-tailer's advantage is the intimate knowledge they can gather about consumers' behaviour and their ability to use this information in tactical and predictive marketing strategies.

First-time and Repeat Purchases

Many consumers welcome professional, objective advice to help them make purchasing decisions. It can give them the security, satisfaction and confidence of having chosen well. The cosmetic and skincare company, Clinique, introduced "The Clinique 10-minute Test" in the early eighties. This simple counter-top tool and point of sale promotional device helps consumers determine their skin type, sensitivity and colouring in terms of Clinique's products. The customers and sales clerks use these analyses to select the most suitable Clinique products. The test was introduced in all major shopping

Model 8.2: *Playing on more senses generates repeat purchases*

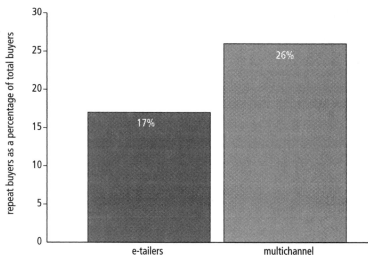

Source: Shop.org Survey, 1998

centres and, during the nineties, became an integral part of Clinique's value proposition — a proposition which held that Clinique would never sell a product without determining that it was perfectly suited the customer's needs.

You can't transfer a model like this to the Internet. You could perhaps replicate the procedure but not the influence of the real-life human contact.

So, the retailer's role will be to support consumers on an emotional level and to convince them why they should purchase a certain product *the first time*. The e-tailer's role will be to establish contact with consumers when they are likely to purchase the already-determined product again.

New Customer and Repeat Customer Costs

It's not surprising to find that the cost of selling a product initially, or just once, to a consumer is substantially higher than the cost of selling the product again. In fact, it costs about ten times more to acquire a customer than to retain a customer. Hence the obvious importance of retaining customers. From the retailer's point of view, the best return-to-outlay ratio occurs at the point in the buying cycle when a product is purchased again. And here's where the clicks-&-mortar advantage appears in the buying cycle. Relationships with consumers are cheaper to maintain online, where there is minimal human interaction and limited infrastructure, than they are offline. So it's preferable to invest in securing initial purchases over the counter, and then ensure that the online partner handles customer retention.

Shopping Behaviour

Shopping behaviour has changed dramatically over the past decade. I'll explain how soon. First let's look at *why* shopping behaviour has changed.

In urban environments, the time we spend at work has increased more than 30%, on average, since the sixties. Rising costs of living and/or increasing lifestyle expectations have sent both partners of married and family households into the workforce. Commuting to and from work is taking longer, the majority of workers moving further and further away from the workplace as cities sprawl and real estate costs soar. These factors conspire to make us time-poor.

Time-poor people rely on tools that help them make quick, efficient decisions. Time-saving machinery and services furnish our households and our local environments. As a result, purchase motivators of past years, like price, become less influential upon consumer decisions, as motivators like convenience and reliability become more relevant.

The other factor influencing changes in shopping behaviour is the Internet. It is an endless mall, which never closes. Customers can purchase products

The purchase motivator of price is no longer as influential upon consumers as decisions based on convenience and reliability.

twenty-four hours a day, seven days a week. Consumers peruse the globe, comparing and selecting, right from their home PC. They can get answers to all their questions — instantly. Consequently, consumer behaviour has acquired a new characteristic — lack of patience.

So lack of time, increased brand and product selections, new shopping channels, easier product comparison and a growing need for general entertainment are all reflected in the consumer's changing shopping behaviour.

Shopping Drivers

The drivers which motivated us in the past — price, selection, brand, geographic proximity, new products — have changed. So what is driving us to shop today? Let's take a look at some key consumer drivers and compare them with those of a decade ago.

Model 8.3: *Two decades of offline shopping drivers*

1991	2001
Price competitiveness	Service
Presentation	Brand selection
Private label brand	Geographic location
Flagship store	New product turnover
New product turnover	In-store entertainment

Only one of the ten-year-old shopping drivers are still relevant for contemporary offline consumers: the role of brands and new product turnover (the rate at which new brands enter the market and disappear again). We can interpret this as meaning that up to 80% of consumer drivers have changed over ten years. But how many retailers have recognised this shift and accommodated it in their planning and promotion? Most stores and supermarkets look very similar now to the way they looked in 1991.

The Offline Shopping Environment

So, shopping behaviour has changed over the past decade. Let's now take a look at the bricks-&-mortar response to this fact by reviewing how store environments, product presentation and consumer management have been changed. All three factors are tightly related. Pleasant environments influence consumer management; contextual product presentation relates to environmental design; consumer management needs dictate environmental and product presentation imperatives. And guess what? Such shopping environments defy online replication.

Environment

As retailers have become more aware that consumers tend to spend more money if they feel comfortable in their environment, they have focused on creating comfortable stores. This takes us back to the chapter's beginning which discussed the evolution of shopping from being a chore into a becoming a

Shopping is now appreciated as a human experience, rather than a necessary chore.

pleasurable experience. No longer is shopping necessarily something we do as a duty; we also do it for recreation and entertainment.

Reflecting this reality, there is a distinct increase in the number of speciality stores. Everything from coffee shops to tie boutiques, cheese stores and delicatessens have become chains. Supermarkets are developing shops-in-shops to gratify the perceived consumer desire for shopping experiences. Starbucks Coffee has dedicated more than 15% of its store space to couches and comfortable corners; Barnes & Noble has created reading corners and coffee nooks where customers can spend time poring over a good book. The aim in all cases is to create shopping environments that remove consumers from everyday stress.

Retailers even stage events in stores to enhance the entertainment experience: book stores and shopping malls organise book signings; throughout 1999 the Diesel store in San Francisco employed a full-time DJ in their flagship store; `LEGO launched "Build the World's Highest LEGO Tower", an event which toured the world's shopping centres over a five-year period; the Danish chain, Illums, organised surfboard-riding-down-escalator competitions to attract and entertain customers. The aim of these events is to create intrigue, excitement, fascination, all of which add interest to the retail environment.

Separate Bricks, Separate Clicks: Barnes & Noble's Online Strategy

When e-commerce was still being born, the notion of selling books online struck many as a preposterous notion. It was argued that of all consumer items, bookstore customers liked to browse amongst real books, touch the paper, smell the ink and finger the unbent spines. Barnes & Noble understood this well. They had become the premier bookseller with chains of superstores all over the United States.

Barnes & Noble stores are designed for comfort. With wooden fixtures, comfortable furniture, coffee lounge service and ample space, their overall ambience invites browsing, relaxing and welcome time out from the world.

Each one of the 490 Barnes & Noble stores carry a comprehensive and authoritative selection of up to 175,000 titles. These literary cafes serve as neighbourhood drop-in centres, where you can pick up a magazine to read while you sip on your latte. The Barnes & Noble bookstores have become a retail phenomenon credited with the awesome statistic of selling one in every eight books sold in the United States.

Barnes & Noble's confidence must have been at an all-time high when Amazon.com started its online bookshop in 1994. But as Amazon.com's early sales figures began circulating, Leonard Riggio, chairman and CEO of Barnes & Noble, and his brother, vice-chairman and chief operating officer, Stephen, were forced to take action. It's reported that they met with Amazon's founder Jeff Bezos, and expressed an interest in buying Amazon, or at least a share in it. Although they couldn't reach an agreement, Steve Riggio is on record as saying, "We have to be a player." In 1997 Barnesandnoble.com was up and running, and so began Barnes & Noble's relentless quest to catch up with Amazon.com.

From the beginning, they decided to keep their online and offline businesses separate. There were immediate advantages in this. As a separate startup company Barnesandnoble.com was unencumbered by the established organisational structure of the traditional business. Barnesandnoble.com would have the flexibility to make quick decisions and would be well placed to be part of the entrepreneurial spirit of the emerging online business landscape. Another consideration was that by creating a separate company they could avoid the costly New York sales tax which would allow them to compete on the same turf as Amazon. Apart from their highly recognised brand, there was almost no cross-fertilisation between Barnes & Noble's off- and online stores.

They invested heavily in their website and undertook the most sophisticated online and offline marketing campaigns to drive traffic to their virtual doors. Their well-known brand was seen in all the right cyberspaces, with a particularly strong presence on AOL. Although still lagging behind Amazon, by 1998 they had narrowed the gap. They subsequently formed a lucrative and powerful alliance with the German publishing giant, Bertelsmann, which increased their already considerable clout from producing to distributing, and from buying to selling. But Amazon continued to enjoy its first-mover advantage, and Barnesandnoble.com still lagged behind in customer numbers and sales levels.

A *Newsweek* study revealed that 82% of Web users have more trust in sites which have established brands. It's unfortunate for Barnes & Noble that it's competing with a Web brand that is so well known that it sets the standard for many e-commerce sites.

Despite all the initial benefits afforded to Barnesandnoble.com, the company has failed to thrive. Barnes & Noble's early decision to separate their off- and online business has not proved to be the best decision. As more e-commerce models emerge, companies are recognising the enormous benefits of integrating virtual and physical operations. Barnes & Noble sacrificed an enormous marketing opportunity by not promoting their website in their stores. Additionally, they have not been able to shake a public perception of being an Amazon imitator.

Barnesandnoble.com is still playing catch-up with a company that has managed to stay one step ahead.

Context Presentations

The concept shift in product presentation has primarily been to place products within a context. Offering the consumer a full picture has come to be valuable. Buying a plate, for example, is easier to visualise when it is part of a table arrangement. Buying a carpet is difficult without seeing it under the table and next to some chairs. It's easier to decide what fridge to buy when you see it actually installed in a kitchen.

We don't buy individual products: we buy products related to other products. Cornflakes are related to milk; fridges are related to other kitchen fittings; carpets are related to walls and windows; and wine is related to food. Telling the whole story adds meaning to products, and helps consumers identify how they apply to their own needs and tastes. Context illuminates product potential.

Consumer Management

Just a decade ago, shopping chains, like the Danish discount chain, Netto, made much of the fact that their queues should be as long as possible. Not before twenty people were in the same line could a new cash register be opened. The rationale behind this policy was that it communicated cut-price operations.

Today, most customers' reaction to this would be irritation. "What a waste of time!" they'd spit as they beat a hasty retreat. Current service policies would aim to reflect an opposite priority more to the effect that time spent by customers in the store should be well spent, enjoyable, inspiring, entertaining, informative and definitely not a waste of time. So Disney World and Disneyland have worked on reducing waiting time by offering people in queues time-stamped tickets that free them from having to stand in line for hours. Remember, this turnaround has happened within just ten years.

As we become more time-poor stress has become an influence upon our shopping behaviour. When somebody asks how things are going at work, you're likely to tell them how busy you are. "Flat out," might be almost as automatic a response as "I'm fine. And you?" It's not often you hear a response like, "Oh, I'm twiddling my thumbs. I've done everything I need to do and a bit more." Probably not.

Model 8.4 *Reasons customers choose stores*

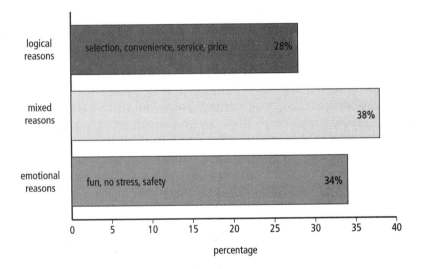

Source: National Retails Federation (USA), "Retailing above the Rim", 1996

How else has service changed to meet the priority shift occasioned by stress? Store planning has changed: aisles have become wide enough to comfortably accommodate two trolleys passing by, and stores have become more spacious. Opening hours have been extended well into the night. These days, you rarely see crowded supermarkets. The rationale behind this? Crowds reflect and create stress. And nobody is interested in adding to their already heavy stress load.

The same can be said for the number of signs and instore promotions, special displays and distracting advertisements. Just ten years ago, a walk down a supermarket aisle was like a stroll through Las Vegas, with colours, neon lighting and signage demanding more attention than the products on sale. Yes, they're still there, but they're low-key, married to the store's layout so that they don't scream at potentially frazzled shoppers. Barnes & Noble's, Starbucks' and Target's signage, for example, is carefully designed to match their stores' interiors.

Noise is another stress-creating factor. There are now carefully designed acoustics to remove any offending noises. Paging systems have been removed, not only in stores, but in airports and at train stations. Only absolutely necessary messages are still publicly broadcast. Public spaces of all types are addressing the need to help reduce patrons' stress levels.

Online Shopping Environments

Making the customer feel at home, helping make decisions simpler, reducing stress factors and creating a harmonious shopping environment is the end goal for online e-tailers as well as offline retailers.

Environment

Consumer stress is present on the Internet, just as it is in the real world. Insecure payment avenues, long delivery time and uncertainties, difficulties in sourcing products and doubts that the product being what it claims to be all contribute to consumer irritation and stress. But an environment to allay this is not easily achieved on the Internet. Yes, easy navigation, attractive graphics and nice images can create some sense of comfort, but a two-dimensional screen can't go much further than conveying a semblance of a new environment. Just like looking at a postcard from Hawaii: it shows you what a great place Maui must be, but it will never communicate the feeling of being there.

Product Presentation

Some people may argue that contextual displays already exist on the Internet. After all, it's possible to create the *look* of a car based on the colours you want it to be, the *look* of a kitchen designed according to your taste and the *look* of clothes you might wear, worn by an everyman/woman for your viewing convenience. But again, these attempts to place products in context, to create a meaningful story around them which has application to the consumer, fail to completely satisfy. They can only appeal to two of our five senses: sight and hearing. Touch, smell and taste are redundant as far as the

Net's capacities are concerned, but they represent three-fifths of the senses we use to make judgments, assess likes and dislikes and ascertain our place in the world.

Consumer Management

There's no doubt that the shopping behaviours manifested by stressed, time-poor, entertainment-needy consumers will define the parameters determining how online companies frame their service policies. Creating enticing and informative online (and offline) environments is now as fundamental as providing shopping trolleys was a decade ago. And the clever shop designer long ago realised that appealing to all five senses rather than sight alone is the alpha and omega of determining which store will have the competitive advantage. Enter the clicks-&-mortar option, for this allows the Internet to pick up where the retailer leaves off: at repeat purchases, and customisation and predictive capabilities.

How to Win Sales and Influence Profit

Let's consolidate the chapter's discussion so far. Shopping is increasingly a recreational experience rather than a chore. It's influenced by consumers' emotional and intellectual assessments of their needs. The online and offline shopping environments can each cater to these polarised influences by recognising their own value propositions, connecting consumers to these at opportune points in their buying cycles, and ensuring ongoing patronage by providing environmental comfort, product context and consumer ease. So, given these understandings, how do they work to influence online and offline profit?

Space Management: An Offline Prerogative

Almost 60% of products consumers buy at the supermarket are not premeditated purchases. "I couldn't help it!" might be heard when a shopper is asked to justify the acquisition of yet another tub of ice cream. And they're probably right.

Supermarkets are able to predict with 90% accuracy what decisions shoppers are likely to make in the aisles of their stores. It's no accident that you have to pass by the vegetables first and a small candy selection last. There's generally a candy display right by the cash register, where you generally spend some time waiting, with the goodies perfectly arranged at kid height. The strategy ensures that sweet treats gain maximum exposure to their most ardent consumers.

This positioning of product represents a well-known and long-used methodology called space management. Space management makes consumers vulnerable to suggestion and has largely been ignored on the Web.

Impulse buying When products are displayed in the most enticing way, it encourages impulse buying. How often do you go to the supermarket for milk and bread and come out with a cartload of groceries? The supermarket's aisles are filled with everyday necessities and tempting luxuries that are irresistible to even the most disciplined shoppers. The full-to-overflowing shelves inspire product purchases. By the time you've reached the cash register, you find yourself paying for a bunch of items you didn't intend to buy.

The grocery store recognized, decades ago, that not only was self-service more efficient, the human's vulnerability to impulse made the arrangement more profitable than old-style service. In pre-supermarket days, an attendant behind the counter fetched the goods on your shopping list and packed them into your basket for you. But the advent of the supermarket heralded new shopping methods that left the consumer free to roam, browse and respond to purchasing suggestions.

Browsing Many e-commerce players forget that one of the most important differentiators between clicks-based e-tailing and the bricks-&-mortar kind is the opportunity the real store gives shoppers to browse. Offline consumers can survey thousands of products without confusion, selecting and purchasing. When consumers try emulating this experience online, by visiting Amazon.com for example, they find that it's not possible to parallel the browse, choose and buy process. Scrolling through hundreds of books doesn't allow for satisfactory perusal. And books are probably the most Internet-compatible of products. The online browsing experience becomes even more confusing if you're trying to buy, say, clothes.

The experience that makes walking from shop to shop an enjoyable pastime, even a passion for some, has not yet been translated to the Internet. In fact, even though the Internet is our most modern communication tool, its sales service hasn't advanced much beyond pre-war practices, when the grocer behind the counter attended to the customer. That's the type of service the Net offers now. It's called "searching" but its function is just as basic as the grocer's was. E-commerce's next priority must be to harness the passion for shopping as a pastime and mould it into an online formula: to create a structure that inspires the user to enjoy Internet shopping, to browse frequently, and to buy extra.

Suggestive selling We are seeing signs of this awareness online. If you're buying a book about computers, for instance, the item might be accompanied by a special offer on software. But the psychology behind shopping is much deeper. At the supermarket, the shelves on your right might carry sauces while those on the left might accommodate cleaning articles. This isn't necessarily a confusing juxtaposition in a real-life supermarket. But imagine buying flowers from a web site and being prompted to pick up a bottle of ketchup. The liaison wouldn't work.

It has taken major brands decades to develop planograms that enable them to control every inch of shelf space. And every inch in establishments like Toys R Us, Marks & Spencer and 7 Eleven is mapped out. Every step you take in the store is planned. Even every minute you spend waiting in the queue. The same planning now needs to be applied to the Internet. E-commerce is faced with the task of connecting products, brands and categories with each other and with the consumer. This is not necessarily a logical science.

Shopping behaviours may be mercurial, but once the blueprint has been drawn up, the true shopping portal will be achieved. A portal that enables e-tailers to cross- and upsell all product categories with each other, without confusing the consumer, and achieving the same 60% of impulse sales that bricks-&-mortar retailers boast.

Retailers' and E-Tailers' Unique Value Propositions

What works well offline can't always be paralleled online, and vice versa. Let's not forget this in the coming years of Internet and shopping development. It's an obvious fact: offline stores can't offer the world's biggest selections or cheapest prices; online stores can't offer sensory experience and human interaction.

It's imperative to stress that retail's future is dependent on how quickly it realises that it can't and shouldn't compete with the Internet on price and selection. Clicks-&-mortar enterprises each have their points of differentiation, and they must identify and act upon these to define their purpose and justify their presence.

Retail's unique value propositions lie in the environmental experience it can build for consumers. Because no matter how efficient e-tailing services become,

> *Retail's future is dependent on how quickly it realises that it can't and shouldn't compete with the Internet on price and selection.*

how large its product selection and low its prices, and no matter how secure the Internet's transaction processes are, sensory gratification, emotional judgments and human interaction will rate high on the consumer's list of experiential preferences. Social connection and satiating the senses are inexorable and indispensable parts of our humanity.

The Real World and the Virtual Consumer

Changing commercial environments and emergent shopping possibilities mean consumers have the choice of operating in two discrete roles: as real-world consumers and as virtual consumers. And then there is the huge majority that floats somewhere in between.

Real-World Consumers

Real-world consumers don't mind flicking through direct-mail catalogues. They prepare shopping lists before they go to the supermarket. They have shopping budgets they adhere to, per day or per week. Real-world consumers are generally loyal to a brand. They are price-driven rather than destination-driven (meaning that a convenient destination won't win their patronage if the product can be purchased more cheaply further away from home). And they probably spare the extra expense of home delivery services.

Real-world consumers are likely to stick with their bricks-&-mortar store longer than their virtual-consumer counterparts. But, once real-world consumers find it suits them to shift their patronage online, they will be loyal to the e-tailer and difficult for the retailer to win back.

Virtual Consumers

Virtual consumers rarely glance at direct-mail catalogues. They have only one-to-three products on their shopping lists when they go to the supermarket because they buy on impulse and according to judgments made on the run. They couldn't tell you what their daily, weekly or even monthly shopping budget is because the expense is hidden in the total spending pattern. They are loyal to only a few brands and shift brands frequently. Their choices are more time-driven than price-driven and they would consider spending extra on services like home delivery to cut down on time consumption. Virtual consumers' shopping patterns vary and are likely to change radically three years from now.

Virtual consumers have probably already tried several e-tailers. This consumer type isn't loyal and is likely to shift between e-tailing and retailing as soon as something goes wrong in either channel. The slightest sense of time wasting will irritate virtual consumers and will trigger reflex decisions to, for example, disconnect from the e-tailer or leave the store.

The Clicks-&-Mortar Opportunity

Clicks-&-mortars should successfully accommodate virtual and real-world consumers. The clicks side of an enterprise will appeal to virtual consumers who, when inclined to do so, can switch their temporary alliance from the Internet operations to the business's retail presence. The retail environment will appeal to real-world consumers who, over time, will move online.

Moving Consumers Online and Offline

Sound easy? The consumer world doesn't divide neatly in half. But, of course, you knew that consumer habits are just about as various as the human personalities that exercise them. The transposition between online and offline will be different for every individual. So clicks-&-mortars will need to design and enact transformation plans for every consumer. The aim of these plans will be to ensure that the clicks-&-mortar setup is a comfortable one for the individual at all times during the purchase process, and to ensure that loyal customers stay loyal regardless of the purchasing environment they enter.

Consult Your Customers

Consulting your consumer base might sound an obvious first step. It's not possible to create a successful clicks-&-mortar strategy without asking your consumers what they want. You might think you know what the real-world or virtual consumer looks like and prefers. But my question is what segments of your business would you eliminate, and what would you keep, in order to attract both consumer types, and avoid frightening one of the two away? And how, at the same time, would you gain leverage from the positive synergies which should result from your well-researched and well-resourced clicks-&-mortar strategy?

Here are some key questions you should put to your consumers before moving online or offline, or entering a clicks-&-mortar partnership. Of course, these questions aren't currently phrased for consumer comprehension but rather to demonstrate the principles they are based on.

Moving from Clicks to Bricks

- What are your three greatest motivations for currently shopping on the site?
- Rank the following in order of importance: price, selection, presentation, customer support, varieties, brand, comparison possibility, access to information, convenience.
- What would make you change from shopping online?
- What was the motivation for you to move from a bricks-&-mortar store to an online one?
- What value do you see in a bricks-&-mortar store?
- Would you see value in a clicks-&-mortar version of your online store?

- What synergies would you expect to see between your store's off- and online presence?
- Would a clicks-&-mortar version of your online store strengthen or weaken your loyalty to it?
- Would you prefer to make a first-time purchase of a product you've never tried before online or offline?
- Would you prefer to watch product demonstrations online or in the store?
- Would you prefer to shop online if your store were also just around the corner?
- Would you prefer to shop offline if the store offered limited selection but instant delivery?
- Would you prefer to shop online if your store were ten minutes' drive away?
- Would a clicks-&-mortar presence increase your loyalty to this store?

Moving from Bricks to Clicks

- Which products that you currently buy instore would you consider buying online?
- What are your three greatest motivations for currently shopping in the store?
- Please rank the following in order of importance: price, selection, presentation, customer support, varieties, brand, comparison possibility, access to information, and instant access to the product/service or convenience.
- What would your motivation be in moving from the bricks-&-mortar store to an online one?
- What value do you see in a Web-based store?
- What values do you see in a clicks-&-mortar version of your store?
- What synergies would you expect to see between your store's off- and online channels?
- What value would you see in a clicks-&-mortar version of your store?
- Would a clicks-&-mortar presence strengthen or weaken your loyalty to it?
- Would you prefer to make a first-time purchase of a product you've never tried before online or offline?
- Would you prefer to watch product demonstrations online or in the store?
- Would you prefer to shop online if you were offered a 10% discount and home delivery in between one to three days (dependent on category)?

- Would you pay for home delivery online if the delivery were immediate?
- Would you prefer to shop online if your store were ten minutes' drive away?
- Would a clicks-&-mortar presence increase your loyalty to this store?

The objective of these questions is to ascertain whether your customers will see a value gain in your retail store moving online, your e-tail business moving offline or your store entering a clicks-&-mortar relationship. Any strategic development needs to be fuelled by the customer's perception of value gain.

Summary

- Shopping is now appreciated as a human experience, rather than a necessary chore.
- The emergent shopping generation resents boredom, craves variety and is apparently dependent on instant and constant gratification. Its members seek diversion in every part of life.
- The rise of e-tailing has forced bricks-&-mortar retailing to rethink its market function by focusing on the use of all senses, especially those of smell, touch and taste.
- In the real world retailers can create an environment that makes contact with human emotions, exploits social behaviour and appeals to all the senses, not simply those of sight and sound to which e-tailers are confined.
- Retailers and e-tailers occupy opposite ends of the rational–emotional balance. Mostly rational purchasing decisions are taken online. Offline is where the emotional decisions are taken.
- While the retailer is working on the whole-body experience and emotional discriminations, the e-tailer will be offering factual arguments in favour of products and services.
- Whether consumers are persuaded by emotional or rational arguments is dependent upon the point they are at in their buying cycle.
- The retailer's advantage is service, which will become for the consumer an emotional prerequisite to purchasing decisions.
- The e-tailer's advantage will be in repeat sales, cross- and upselling.
- The retailer's role will be to support consumers on an emotional level; to convince them why they should purchase a certain product *the first time*. The e-tailer's role will be to establish contact with consumers when they are likely to purchase the already-determined product again.

- It costs more to sell a product initially, or just once, than to sell the product again to the same customer.
- Time-poor people rely on tools that help them make quick, efficient decisions, so purchase motivators of past years, like price, are no longer as influential upon their purchasing decisions as motivators like convenience and reliability.
- Supermarkets are able to predict with 90% accuracy what decisions shoppers are likely to make in the aisles of their stores.
- Changing commercial environments and emergent shopping possibilities mean consumers are finding themselves operating in two discrete roles: as real-world consumers and as virtual consumers.

Action Points

What values can your store offer its customers by adopting another channel? Ask your customers:
- What do they find attractive about the existing store concept?
- What would they like to change?
- What would make them change from offline to online shopping?
- What do they believe they are missing in your existing store?
- Would they increase their loyalty to your store if you added an online presence to it?

If your customers' answers favoured the introduction of an online stream, the next step is to examine what businesses within your product category have achieved a clicks-&-mortar transition. Do you see industry precedents, or would you be the first? If you see examples before you, what can you learn from them? If you see no relevant precedents, ask yourself why. Is it because no other similar businesses saw added value in making the clicks-&-mortar transition? Or is it because you are innovative and/or risk taking?

What is your key motivation for wanting to establish a clicks-&-mortar concept? Rank these points in order of their application to your reasoning:
- Earn more money.
- Increase customer loyalty.
- Retain your existing customer base.
- Get access to a new audience.

- Lock out your competitors.
- Cut operating costs.
- Increase the customer experience options.
- Increase the geographical presence of your operation.

Based on your analysis of why you believe you want to establish a clicks-&-mortar concept (Step 3), determine what your clicks-&-mortar focus should be.

If your primary reasons are to increase revenue, your focus will be on optimising your customers' existing contact with your store. Do they currently require too much of your customer-support time and interact too little with automated processes? Prepare a detailed research paper on what existing processes you should decrease, what processes you should emphasise, what you can introduce to automate the customer-contact processes, and what internal supply chain management tools you can establish to optimise the efficiency of your infrastructural operations. Now ask yourself again, will this concept offer customers any value-gain?

If your priorities are to increase customer loyalty, retain existing customers, lock out competitors and increase the customer's experience options, your focus will be totally different. Cutting costly customer-contact services might save money but the key issue is to ensure optimal customer service, and to see that every point of contact the customer has with the store is well-oiled. So ask your customers to evaluate every customer-contact point yours store runs on. What could the store do better? Would an online option improve the existing relationship? Use the answers to start creating an action plan for your clicks-&-mortar strategy.

If your priority is to broaden your customer base, your next step is to identify the market sectors you are targeting. What is this audience is looking for? What would make them patronise your online concept? Use the answers to start creating an action plan for your clicks-&-mortar strategy.

Nothing is straightforward, and neither is this evaluation and planning process. The above steps are to give you a guide as to the principles of inquiry you should pursue if you're considering entering a clicks-&-mortar partnership. Generally, you will focus on one of the above priority tracks. None of them precludes cutting costs, retaining customers or attracting new customer groups over time. The next step is to determine how your clicks-&-mortar will forge its identity. Your brand will be answering the priority manoeuvres you plan in Step 4. Read on. My focus in Chapter 9 is on how to build your brand in a multichannel environment.

Building eBrands

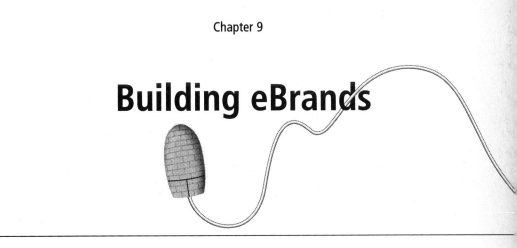

The brand war has just begun again. The battlefield has moved to cyberspace. Online consumerism will impel brands to respond to individual consumer preferences. Brands that receive and address unique preferences and that communicate their values consistently online, offline and in all their parallel operations will be victorious.

This chapter deals with two emerging brand-building issues: the MSP (Me Selling Proposition) and multichannel branding. The relationship between the two is interactivity: online technologies that will collude with consumers' daily lives. The collusion will result in brand-building imperatives that demand both the flexibility to answer individuals' needs and the control to maintain a cohesive brand identity.

The MSP and the Selling Proposition Evolution

The role of brands and of brand-building has changed dramatically over the past thirty years. Why? Because of competition. Today it's almost impossible to develop a product or service, off- or online, without seeing a competitor offering the same within a few days' time. In response, brand-building has moved from its 1930s focus, which concentrated on the brand's unique selling proposition (USP), to what we call the "me selling proposition" (MSP). That progression took place through the development of the "emotional selling proposition" (ESP), the "organisation selling proposition" (OSP), the cult-dependent BSP until the MSP was more recently arrived at. Here's how these strategies work.

Model 9.1: *Evolution of the Selling Proposition*

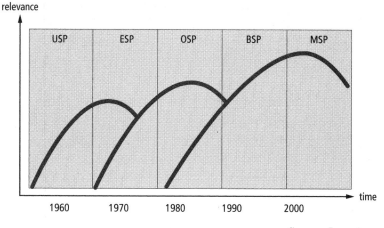

Source: Love Agency

The USP

Only a few products and services are still marketed within this category that promotes a product's unique selling proposition. In fact, I'll bet you can't name three. (Here's a tip: go to the end of the chapter and discover three of the few brands that are still marketed using their USP.) Can you think of one single website concept which hasn't been copied several times on the Net? Selling a product on its unique differences could be dangerous and misguided, because it probably doesn't have any. And basing your marketing on price could be even more ill-advised: not many concepts around the world have managed to survive on this strategy for long.

The ESP

The emotional selling proposition was invented by the advertising industry in the late sixties when it found an increasing number of manufacturers were struggling to position their brand uniquely in the market place. Even though it's logical to select one product instead of another on the basis of price and quality, today's selection of products within almost every category is so large that it confounds the consumer's confidence in establishing choice.

ESPs can be categorised according to the degree of emotional drive their selection demands of the consumer.

Once you've invested the energy in selecting a product or a service and found yourself satisfied with your choice you won't want to have to re-evaluate your choice before your next purchase. This reluctance to go through the mental and emotional expenditure might lead you to simply repeat the purchase and, over time, to the purchase of other products belonging to the same brand. By now emotional judgment overtakes any likelihood of your assessing a product's USP factor: you wouldn't have a clear picture of whether the product you were purchasing was in reality the best or the cheapest or the most appropriate choice for you to make. You have full faith in the first product you purchased, and this experience informs your subsequent choices.

A brand's ESP is called also upon when a product is recommended by others. In this example the emotional motivation might spring from two sources: from the listener's faith in the person making the recommendation and from the reputation of the product itself.

The ESP also calls upon the consumer's self image. Often, without even being aware of it, consumers make brand choices because of how they identify with the image the brand reflects. This point dovetails with the highest degree of emotional judgment attracted by a product's ESP. In this case, consumers' decisions are based purely on the fact that they attach some status to making the purchase. Their choice is determined by a desire for social acknowledgment. The quality of the product and the price has, in such cases, little to do with influencing choice.

Some consumers are more affected by ESP-driven brands than others. But no matter how non-emotional our choices may usually be, we all at some time succumb to the ESPs promoted by brands.

The OSP

Here's an interesting one. The organisation selling proposition appeared in the late eighties and became the key driver in achieving success for a number of companies. It's grounded in the idea of creating a company spirit that's so well-defined it can't help but be communicated through employees to the outside world. You could say that the company's philosophy becomes a part of the product. Its purpose is to infuse the brand with admirable qualities which attract a desire for inclusion from the outside world. Religion is a good example of this principle in operation.

Examples from the commercial world include Nike and The Body Shop. These constructs of the eighties and nineties enjoyed huge success. Both companies ran on philosophies which consumers and society at large admired. This worldwide admiration and the individual's desire to collaborate in the values which inspired it led devotees to become customers. By now these examples have lost the advantages donated by their OSPs and only a few new brands, like Charles Schwab, have the foundation in place for achieving similar recognition. What's that foundation? It's the company culture. In Charles Schwab's case the company founder is still running the organisation. He *is* the brand and his philosophies, around which the organisation is built, motivate the company's operations.

Solid Ethical Bricks: The Body Shop Brand Entwines its Philosophy

Gordon Roddick had a fantasy. He wanted to travel from Brazil to New York by horse. Encouraged by his freedom-loving wife, Anita, he set out in 1976 to follow his dream. She stayed home with the kids and mixed up about twenty-five naturally-based skin and hair products. She packed them in no-nonsense containers and sold them from a small shop she opened in Brighton, a seaside town on England's south coast.

This was the first Body Shop.

With a flair for marketing and a passionate belief in social responsibility, almost immediately Anita Roddick distinguished her shop from every other. She tapped into an expanding niche market. Consumers who were attracted to her nature-based beauty formulae were equally partial to the human, earth and animal rights causes The Body Shop promoted. They signed Friends of the Earth petitions as they bought their banana shampoo. They willingly recycled their patchouli perfume oil bottles for a small rebate. And they happily experimented with eyeliner that had not been tested on animals.

From its humble Brighton beginnings, The Body Shop grew healthily throughout the next couple of decades, while firmly holding onto a socially-responsible corporate agenda. It now operates in forty-seven countries with over 1,500 outlets, spanning twenty-four languages and twelve time zones.

As it grew it forged new paths and found alternative ways of doing business. In the spirit of the slogan "Trade Not Aid" The Body Shop set up sustainable trading relationships with grass-roots communities in over nineteen countries. From Nepal to Calabria villagers are employed squeezing oil from flower petals and nuts, growing seeds and fruit, carving wooden back massagers and weaving baskets. Community trade now accounts for almost 10% of The Body Shop's ingredients and accessory purchases.

The Body Shop websites clearly embody the company's overall philosophy, and colourfully and informatively reflect their belief that people should act locally within a global-thinking framework. The sites are full of philosophy and product information, while at the same time they clearly let the visitor know that they do not currently sell products online. However, online trade is most certainly part of their future plans. Anita Roddick has said, "What is exciting about e-commerce for us when we do it, is that we are such a well-known brand and very little will have to go into the marketing of that."

The BSP

Some brands become such clear identities that they obfuscate their products. This annihilates the product's purpose and turns it into an item chosen through obsession rather than the need for its function. One of the best examples of the brand selling proposition at work is Pokemon. The brand is promoted via an extreme version of its ESP, so extreme that its products' price, quality, benefit, added value and purpose are irrelevant to the consumer. The brand in itself is a brand. At Pokemon's peak *Time* magazine ran a feature story on the phenomenon, featuring one of the Pokemon characters on the front cover. The article resulted in an increase in the magazine's circulation from one week to the next. This wasn't because readers found the article enticing but because the younger generation, kids from six to fifteen years, wanted the magazine's cover for their Pokemon collections. The edition has since become a collector's item among Pokemon fans.

You could refer to the BSP as a CSP (Cult Selling Proposition), because the strategy depends on turning brands into cult items — articles of desire which obsessed consumers are compelled to possess. The lifestyle of these brands is usually one of intense publicity and exposure. And, mostly, their lives are short, perhaps lasting just a few weeks.

The MSP

Finally we arrive at the development of the MSP, the strategy which sees brands no longer belonging to their manufacturers but to the consumer. In these cases the consumer feels clear ownership of the brand, and senses an obligation to protect and develop it. This will probably be one of the most visible brand positioning strategies this century. Why? Because everything brand-building does from now on will be based on consumers' individual needs, their individual preferences and their individual behaviour.

> *The MSP (Me Selling Proposition) is a branding strategy that promotes brands as the property of individual consumers rather than of the products' manufacturers.*

In a way, this development returns us to the eighteenth century when consumers bought ceramic pots carefully handcrafted for them alone and labelled with their own names. Mass production made this an almost irrelevant luxury. But now, technology is making one-off production achievable again. There's a risk that this trend could kill all the USPs, ESPs, OSPs and BSPs enjoyed by other brands.

How much further can you go in attaining products to suit your needs than having items crafted especially for you? What more could the consumer expect? How can mass-production satisfy the consumer when this alternative is feasible? You could conclude that this would be the brand's final destination but there are cases we can reflect upon which counter this.

This is not a happy example, but bear with me. In the late sixties, developing countries were target markets for babies' milk formula. Milk-replacement products became the popular choice over mothers' breast milk in villages from the Ivory Coast to Thailand. The artificial product was perceived as prestigious. To feed babies formula was considered infinitely superior, and something only wealthy people could afford to do. Breast milk, perfectly attuned to a baby's singular development needs, lost its value in the face of the manufactured product's introduction, and also because of the social pressure that was generated in its favour. Peer pressure subdued breast milk's MSP and promoted the artificial variety's BSP.

There is no doubt it will take decades before we'll be able to reset the brand strategy cycle and start all over again. Right now we'll have to focus on the MSP trend because it's this that will affect the way we conceive, establish, operate and profit from clicks-&-mortar development.

Visit **DualBook.com/cbb/ch9/MSPBrandBuilding**
to discover ways to build brands on consumer MSPs.

MSP in action

The MSP will affect the way consumers shop, the way they select products and the way we all behave in commercial environments. It will particularly influence clicks-&-mortar concepts. Not many MSP brands exist yet, but most companies aspire to developing them even though the costs of turning around a manufacturing system and a distribution setup to satisfy the needs of the MSP strategy will be extraordinarily high, possibly exceeding the earnings companies could otherwise hope to achieve over several years.

The MSP strategy will demand the development a highly sophisticated database system, one which is able to capture relevant consumer information and automatically transfer it to the manufacturing process. Manufacturing, in turn, will need to attain new flexibility to enable the production of single items fashioned by individual consumer requirements. Levi's was probably the first international brand to enter the MSP product sector. In 1996 the company launched its custom-made jeans website which consumers could visit to order jeans made to their own measurements and specifications. Estimates suggest the initiative cost Levi's more than US$30 million annually. The project was canned after two years because it caused conflict with existing retail outlets which saw Levi's as a competitor rather than a supplier.

The MSP trend is likely to graduate from being an optional luxury to being a commercially necessity. But it will be a must-have that not all companies will have the financial or technical capacity to adopt. Failure to adopt will probably mean failure to survive. Let's discuss a couple of visionary examples.

Transcending online custom-fitting at brands' websites is the prospect of online custom-fitting at the consumer's very own website. Here's how this might work.

Personal sites would capture data on items of clothing the individual purchases. The database will act as an inventory of clothing owned by the individual for insurance purposes, and for linking let's say to their personal "fashologist". The fashologist would be an online fashion adviser who recommends colours, styles and advises on the most appropriate outfit for various events like job interviews, funerals and parties. The personal database would also link to manufacturers, fabric and accessory suppliers. These personal websites would be the means for consumers to acquire their custom-fitted wardrobe, specially designed and co-ordinated for them as individuals. The clothing would arrive with fashion labels proclaiming the consumer's Web address and would combine with the collection's style to create the individual's own brand. The MSP will be what drives the services that make the wardrobe happen.

Over time, all those sites linked to consumer's own site — the fashologist, manufacturers, fabric and accessory suppliers — would aggregate detailed consumer profiles outlining their clients' tastes. The consumer's personal site would become a mailing target and offer manufacturers permanent consumer survey facilities. The linked databases would reciprocally give consumers access to the latest fashion advice which will be informed by the consumer's own budget and preferences.

The scenario is both appealing and alarming, and probably inevitable. And the most interesting question arising from this is how does the hypothesis affect the retailer's future? If consumer items are headed for customisation, what role will the retailer fulfil?

Interactivity: The Basis of Future Brand-Building

In future brands will have to survive both off- and online. They will need to accommodate individual consumer targets, and be adaptable to an increasingly complex, MSP-informed manner. Let's examine how the future basis of brand-building might operate.

Households and Interactive Channels

At the moment, we're in daily contact with only one or two interactive media. As technology opens household access to multiple interactive channels, consumers will exert MSP imperatives upon brand-building processes. Let's take a look at an interactive day.

Our first task will be to check our emails on the PC. Then, during the trip to work the mobile phone will give us access to wireless Internet technology and will act as our interactive channel until we reach the office. From this point the PC will resume its role as our key point of interactive contact until lunchtime when the mobile phone comes into its own again.

After lunch the PC takes over once more until the end of the day when the trip back home is taken care of by the mobile phone. Once we're home the fridge and microwave will become the focus of interactivity. This is a vision

Model 9.2: *A multichannel interactive day over time. Over a day we change channels several times — all based on a central point of connection. For example, starting with WAP first moving to PC moving to WAP moving to WebTV moving to PlayStation moving to PC...*

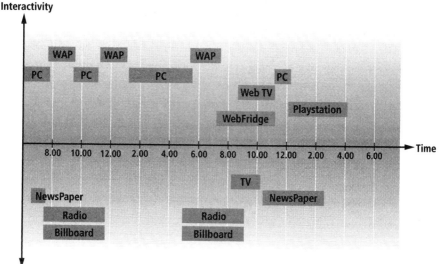

of the household in just a couple of years' time. The refrigerator and the microwave are proposed by many to be the next interactive household computers. The microwave oven will have online access so that it could capture recipes and cooking hints and adjust its cooking times accordingly. The fridge will have a 24/7 link to its owner's mobile phone (via WAP technology) so that the household's food needs are kept apace.

After dinner the WebTV will assume centre stage until the PlayStation is activated. Just before bed we might check our emails again on the PC.

The Bricks-&-Mortar Role in Interactive Consumer Communications

How will the bricks and the clicks in clicks-&-mortar strategies fit into this scenario? To ensure their survival, offline stores will have to fulfil a relevant role in the consumer's interactive flow. Online partners will need to capture primary data, like addresses and phone numbers, as well as detailed consumer profiles. This data would be linked to suppliers whose job it would be to tune production processes to the needs suggested by individual customer databases. GM is among several companies around the world that has spent years preparing for this highly complex manufacturing process. GM expects to be manufacturing cars according to individual requirements, received online, within a few years. Want to know how complex GM's process is? Each vehicle will be subject to up to one million combinations, all directed by consumer preference.

Now let's imagine the counter duties of the e-tailer.

When I visit the store after work, bringing my mobile phone with me, I'll want to know that the products I've purchased online are waiting for me in the store, and that the information I've been feeding to the store's website is informing that store, online and offline. If this is the case I won't have to keep explaining myself. But what I also want is to feel the added value of showing up in the store. If I only feel that I'm acting like a delivery service for myself I'm likely to give up visiting the store and leave that role to a delivery service provider. I have no interest in acting in that role. I want to feel welcome in the store, to enjoy the human interaction, to imbibe another environment before heading home. This puts a lot of demands upon the clicks-&-mortar retailer. They will have to ensure the information flow between the clicks and the bricks is operating smoothly and offering a transparent view of my needs.

This is the basis for future brand-building. It doesn't matter how much you spend on convincing the consumer of the great features of your clicks-&-mortar store if the interactive process fails. If the real-life store doesn't have the right products waiting for the online consumer, or if the retailer has to ask questions that the consumer has already answered online, the product has failed and the brand is incompetent in that consumer's estimation. Brand-building now requires the marketer's full control of every contact the consumer has with the brand.

Building a Multichannel Brand

A multichannel brand is one that can be moved from one media channel to another, and remain intact. Clicks-&-mortar stores will revolve upon multichannel brand strategies which enable their brands to function strongly offline and online. Let's test this assertion.

Model 9.3: *Do you have a channel strategy? And to what degree can your brand survive being transferred from channel to channel?*

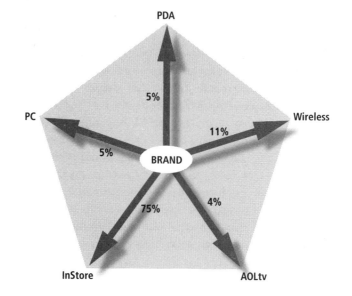

Maintain Your Brand Platform

Assuming that you're familiar with Yahoo!, and assuming that Yahoo! opened a bricks-&-mortar store, what would you imagine this store might look like? Following the image suggested by Yahoo! online I have a clear picture of how the store might look. It would be colourful, making use of Yahoo.com's signature purple and orange. It would communicate fun, craziness and youth; it would be highly interactive meaning there wouldn't just be products lined up on shelves, but shows, events, large television screens with high-quality sound and picture, and interactive kiosks. Every element in the store would be capable of responding immediately to me, to my questions and comments and would be staffed by cool, casual, friendly people with quick wits and open minds. The store's personnel would be multilingual and include Caucasians, Africans, Asians and Indo-Europeans. The ambience would be relaxed and groovy: contemporary music would background a well-planned, easy-to-use layout, which included the surprise of unpredictability and innovation.

What products would offline Yahoo! sell? Would you be surprised if they sold clothes? No. What about stereo equipment? No. Hand-held DVD players, headsets, crazy toys? No. They all sound appropriate.

A multichannel brand can be moved from one media channel to another and remain intact.

But what would you say if offline Yahoo! sold food, wine and paintings? The prospect seems incongruous, doesn't it? What would you say if the store was predominantly grey, the staff were all over fifty, the music was classical, and the lighting neon? I guess you'd be surprised, right? And disappointed. The fact we can make these assumptions without ever having seen a Yahoo! store is a tribute to the brand's strongly-built identity.

Branding is all about building an identity and satisfying expectations of it. If your brand leaves its platform when moving to new channels it can disappoint and, possibly, lose its customers.

LEGO opened its first theme park in 1968 in Billund, Denmark. Since then two other theme parks have opened in England and the United States and there are more to come. The motivation behind the theme park was not that LEGO needed a cash cow. Of course, the company didn't want to lose money through the developments, but the primary motivation was to stimulate kids with exciting and imaginative creations, to appeal to their sense of fantasy and invention. This was to inspire their LEGO play and, as a consequence, provoke their need for more and more of the product. For years rumours abounded that the theme park didn't earn a single dollar. But, it fulfilled its real objective which was to stimulate further LEGO sales.

Now, imagine if the theme parks were dull and uninteresting to children, if queues were long, food poor, the facilities unpleasant, the attractions few and unexciting, the staff crabby and the prices high. How would the theme parks have affected LEGO sales then? Disappointed, disillusioned kids would probably have gone home, packed away their blocks and struck the LEGO brand from their memories.

Translating the Brand Offline and Online

The hypothetical Yahoo! store and the historical LEGO examples should signal to you the importance of maintaining your brand's platform — its values, identity and icons — in all the brand's activities, across all channels.

Clicks-&-mortars are about making a brand work through co-operative and compatible clicks-&-mortar operations. An important basis for this co-operation is that the brand communicates with consumers consistently by expressing the same messages and conveying the same values and identity online, offline and in all the brand's product extensions. There may be room for pleasant surprises but there's no room at all for disappointments.

So, if your store enjoys a reputation for the friendliness of its staff, a relaxed atmosphere, wide aisles, useful signage, informative demonstrations, attractive displays and so on, it's important that all these characteristics are translated onto the Web. This means that your online store would communicate in an equivalent friendly tone of voice, that the site would be simple and uncluttered, the navigation would be easy, the colour palette a direct copy of that used instore, that there'd be informative, attractive product demonstrations, and so on.

Model 9.3 is to help you translate your brand's values from an offline environment to an online one and vice versa. Tick the key values your brand represents and ensure that the key areas are represented in all your channels.

Model 9.3: *Brand translation strategies*

VALUES	TV	Radio	Print	Internet	WAP	Outdoor
Trust						
Innovation						
Consistency						
Harmony						
Differentiation						

Visit **DualBook.com/cbb/ch9/MultichannelStrategies** for the latest on multichannel strategies.

Summary

- The role of brands and of brand-building has changed dramatically over the past thirty years because of increasing competition. The sheer number of products competing in any single category eliminates the likelihood of any one of them retaining unique features.

- Brand-building has moved from its 1930s focus, which concentrated on the brand's unique selling proposition (USP), to the me selling proposition (MSP). That progression took place through the development of the emotional selling proposition (ESP), the organisation selling proposition (OSP), the cult-dependent brand selling proposition (BSP) until the MSP was arrived at.

- The MSP is a branding strategy that promotes brands as the property of individual consumers rather than of the products' manufacturers. It means brand-building is based on consumers' own needs, their own preferences and their own behaviour.

- The MSP trend will affect the way we conceive, establish, operate and profit from clicks-&-mortar development.

- The MSP strategy will demand the development a highly sophisticated database system that's able to capture relevant consumer information and automatically transfer this to the manufacturing process. Manufacturing, in turn, will need to attain new flexibility to enable the production of single items fashioned by individual consumer requirements.

- The MSP trend is likely to graduate from being an optional luxury to being a commercially necessary manufacturing stream.

- Brand-building now requires the marketer's full control of every contact the consumer has with the brand, *the basis for future brand-building being interactivity.*

- A multichannel brand is one that can be moved from one media channel to another and remain intact. Clicks-&-mortar stores will revolve upon multichannel brand strategies which enable their brands to live strongly offline and online.

- Branding is all about building an identity and satisfying expectations of it. If your brand leaves its platform when moving to new channels it can disappoint and, possibly, lose its customers.

Action Points

Consider what values your brand stands for in a multichannel environment. No brand can succeed with an unfocused set of values. So select five key values. Each of the five values will have to be reflected in all your channels. But often one channel is better at reflecting a particular value than another. Review your channel list and dedicate each of the values to each of the channels. Compose an action list for achieving each of the values in each of the channels. Seeing your brand's going online, how will you adapt your brand's core and identifying values for various local markets?

In chapter 4 you described the trust-generating values your brand was planned to reflect in each of its new channels. In chapter 8 you justified why it made sense for you to introduce your brand to a multichannel environment and began planning clicks-&-mortar strategy to achieve this. Pull out your list from chapter 8 and add an extra column which will cover the values you believe your brand will have to stand for in a multichannel environment. Think about the Yahoo! example. Is your brand fun? Exciting? Different? Provocative? Stylish? Authoritative?

Your values list is probably too long. No brand can succeed with an unfocused set of values. So select five key values. Think in terms of what you'd like to hear customers reply if you asked them to describe your brand in five words. Now prioritise the five values.

Each of the five values will have to be reflected in all your channels. But often one channel is better at reflecting certain values than others. Review your channel list and dedicate each of the values to each of the channels. Let's say one of your values is "informative". The website might be the key channel to express this value most meaningfully. The website can accommodate in-depth product analysis, customers testimonials, recommendations from industry experts and comparisons with competitor products.

Just as you did in Chapter 4, when you added actions to achieve trust-building features, you need to compose an action list for achieving each of the values under each of the channels. Have you nominated "fun" as a key value? If so, the best channel for its expression might be the store. And if that's the case, your action plan for your brand attaining its goal might be to run events and entertainments in the store. If your prescribed channel was online, you might plan to tell fun stories on your site. Think in these terms: What will make the customer think your brand deserves a reputation for "fun" after having been in contact with it?

You're now well on the way to controlling your brand within a clicks-&-mortar strategy. Seeing your brand's going online, you'll now have to consider its presentation to other cultures in disparate countries? How will you adapt your brand's core and identifying values for various local markets? Let's consider this after you've read the next chapter.

---

3 USP products are: SteadyCam, Campari and Viagra. However this might very well change when the patents of these products expire.

Chapter 10

The Master Key to Globalisation

The Web makes your online brand accessible worldwide the day it's born. Can local branding exist any longer? The Net introduces opportunities for brand-building and places question marks on past brand-building practice. For, despite the fact that online brands are globally accessible, they aren't recognised or relevant in all markets. So, is localisation extinct after all and is there any such thing as globalisation?

Going international with your brand can be like starting from scratch. Successful national brands establish their images over time, images that relate to their original market. It's not possible to introduce the locally successful brand to the international market without reassessing the brand's platform. How should online brands address other local markets in order to harness their international potential?

Global is Local

The current generation of brands — Yahoo!, Amazon, AOL and eBay, for example — are characterised by being able to communicate with their users worldwide and simultaneously. They've educated new consumer segments, activated new needs, and created new brand platforms with global application. But globalisation is elusive. Yahoo!, for example, was considered a global entity until it entered Japan. This ostensibly global brand then had to adjust itself dramatically to survive in the Japanese market. Yahoo! Japan managed to regain control only by teaming up with an appropriate local partner who could ensure that the brand received the right market exposure.

The fact is that human preferences cannot be the same everywhere. No brand has yet established a global presence by being uniform all over the world. Right now, we're witnessing the first phase in a long adjustment process that will take decades to achieve, one that will see people's needs and behaviours becoming increasingly similar across demographic boundaries. The dream of a truly global brand could yet become a reality, but uniform international brand-building cannot exist.

A global strategy today is, in reality, a local plan for each and every market. If you're under the illusion that global means one voice and one opinion, you'll have to adjust your view of worldwide branding. The more of the globe our media embraces, the more local accents surface, the more they are exposed to mutual influences, and the quicker cultural identity and voice changes. What was local a decade ago may have disappeared in five years' time, replaced by a new, internationally informed reality.

> *A global brand-building strategy is, in reality, a local plan for every market.*

Local is Place More Than People

Almost everyone around the world is familiar with pizza, fried rice, sushi and stroganoff. Mother's Day has crossed into most markets to become a commercially-driven family event. The same music is played all over the world. No matter where we live, we have ready access to each other's opinions, fashions, ideas, and responses to events, both national and international.

"Local" is increasingly tied to geography rather than ethnic culture. Geographic orientation imposes the often immutable constraints of distance, climate, season, demography and infrastructure upon markets. Meanwhile, cultural differentiation is dissolving as traditions meet and are absorbed by one another, as well as the demands of commerce.

Internet companies wanting to go international have to be well prepared. And that is likely to mean teaming up with local bricks-&-mortar players to achieve local penetration and acceptance into local markets. Credibility and trust becoming more and more expensive with each passing day. The Internet has made worldwide brand-building possible, but don't let this fool you. Net users are human beings. They don't suddenly adopt a universally-held preference by mindlessly upgrading to a newer version.

The Universal Brand

Is there really such a thing? The question is this: if a brand achieves an ostensibly uniform identity all over the world, is it recognised by consumers from country to country in the same fashion? Would respondents to a market survey in Moscow identify the same key values in a brand that respondents in Sydney did? In short, no. Our ideas and perceptions are inextricably related to the culture in which we live and/or with which we identify.

There's a catch-22 at work here. In order to be accessible to consumers the brand must be locally recognisable. However, this can limit the brand and its very localisation limits its access to the world's demographic pool.

At the same time, marketers perceive a consumer preference for the same service, same experience, same product, same warranties all over the world, while venture capitalists insist that brands can't afford to be local any more, that they must become global (with the same logo, same identity, same customer base and same product worldwide) from the day they are born.

What is Global?

Two issues are raised by this theory. Where is the freedom to localise brand-building, so vital to growing brand identity? And how does this rationale ever confirm itself? Global branding can only be held by people on the move. There are sedentary consumer groups to whom global uniformity means nothing and to whom local *is* the world. The question that follows both these issues is: can truly international brands, brands that stand for the same values worldwide, really exist?

Sure, Coca-Cola might spring to mind. It boasts international recognition, but is its image perceived by all consumers in the same fashion? No. Recognition is not the same as understanding. Ask Eastern European consumers what they perceive of the product, then go to the United States and ask the same question. The values attributed by each national group to the brand will be different. But, in any case, Coca-Cola was born over 100 years ago and raised in a Web-less world where nations could hardly claim to be connected. So it's not a brand which exists within the parameters of the current globalisation argument.

What are the implications of the simple human fact that cultural difference is very likely to impact on a brand's global ambitions? Any user anywhere in the world has the same access to the same information via the Net, and any international brand's website will be subject to the simultaneous scrutiny of consumers from Norway to New Guinea. Building a global online brand should be easier than building an offline international brand. But everything indicates that the reverse is the case. Why is this and what can we learn from it?

The Online Global Challenge

As the Internet grows the ease with which you used to be able to create an online presence is disappearing. Creating a voice on the Net that's as loud and clear as Yahoo!'s or Amazon.com's isn't possible today without a stupendous marketing budget. Online real estate has inflated dramatically, exceeding real-world real estate valuation increases. Consider this. In 2000, BBDO estimated that it cost around US$300 million in the first year to establish an online brand in the United States. Today, dotcom startups spend an average of $US24 million in their first year. You could buy a lot of land and build a lot of stores for that money.

Building an online global brand is more costly than building an offline, bricks-&-mortar international brand.

In addition to this massive investment, the fundamental challenge, and the one which makes developing an online global brand more difficult than establishing an offline international brand, is that an online brand is bound by the Net to giving consumers global access to the one marketing position. As I have briefly discussed, a single marketing position can't be as efficacious in all cultures: international brands are promoted using different promotional strategies from market to market, from state to state, country to country, culture to culture. For example, the brand Diesel is a respected, interesting but not outrageously trendy fashion label in the United States. In Israel Diesel is the hottest brand you could imagine. And in Italy Diesel is identified as a dull, boring low-price brand.

Cross-cultural communication makes ethnocentric messages irrelevant to all but the culture from which they spring and this causes some dramatic branding challenges.

The leading feminine hygiene protection product, Libra (www. libragirl.com.au), launched its Internet presence out of Australia in 1997. The concept was successful in that market, so Libra tested it in Denmark as well. The result surprised everyone. What women loved in Australia was deemed boring and old-fashioned in Northern Europe. The background culture which had informed the site didn't coalesce with the Northern European market's sensibilities.

In Australian schools, girls usually wear school uniforms, are frowned upon for wearing makeup and generally dissuaded from individual display. The same is the case for boys in most Australian schools. The point is that these rules, enforced in varying degrees, display institutional authority which ostensibly promotes equality but which in fact discourages individuality. Danish children are schooled and brought up in an environment that takes social lives, developed at a young age, for granted and which expects mature expression and clear thinking in all matters. So the Libra site wasn't direct enough for Danish girls and young women. It was boring and didn't satisfy the open-minded culture that informed their perceptions.

The Swedish-based company, Mölnlycke, the Libra site's owners, identified an opportunity to save a lot of resources by using the same site in several markets. The result was, however, that almost 90% of the site's content and creative concept had to be reworked for each market. Even the style had to vary according to the culturally-informed taste of each market.

Even though the Web makes every site globally accessible, it doesn't mean that every site is internationally legible. So, localisation is becoming recognised as an inescapable necessity for cultivating international brand recognition. In short, localisation is the key to global branding.

> *The Web makes every site globally accessible, but it doesn't make every site internationally comprehensible.*

Localisation: The Key to Global Branding

A crisis weathered by Coca-Cola provides a good illustration of this. In 1999, in Belgium, several hundred children became ill after drinking Coke. Besides a local ban on Coca-Cola being imposed by the government, existing stock was removed from all supermarket shelves.

A local accident shouldn't require global explanation, but it should most definitely be addressed locally. Thousands of people in the accident area visited the local Coca-Cola website daily to get updated information on the situation. These updates were almost entirely irrelevant to consumers anywhere else in the world, but essential to Belgian consumers. In this instance, using the Internet as a global forum could have done more harm than good to the brand. But affected consumers expect the courtesy of having the problem handled locally, and to feel that their particular position is being recognised and treated in a sensitive and culturally appropriate fashion. Global treatment of the problem, airing the issues associated with it around the world, could be viewed as arrogant.

Local markets will forever be affected by local events and trends. Marketers need to be sensitive to this and address branding and communication accordingly. That's why Libra had to change its site content for the Northern European markets, even though the identical target group in Australia responded positively to the original content.

Global Assumptions Make an Ass of You and Me

Some years ago I worked with LEGO to create the world's first online advent calendar. An advent calendar an illustrated calendar for December which includes twenty-four small doors, for the first to the twenty-fourth of the month, which you can open day by day to reveal little surprise pictures.

The concept was the product of naivety rather than a well thought-out strategy.

We quickly discovered that an online advent calendar offered many unforeseen and, in retrospect, obvious technical difficulties. For a start, the world's time zones meant that Australian visitors to the site, for example, would be there almost twenty-four hours earlier than west coast USA visitors. Where should the central time zone have been and would that have meant mean for kids waking up in Australia and being denied the fun of opening the last little door on Christmas eve? Then a deeper problem surfaced.

Europeans are familiar with Christmas. For predominantly-Christian countries, Christmas is a tradition that's part of community and individual life. It's not a phenomenon which you have to mention in diplomatic terms to avoid religious offence. The launch of the LEGO advent calendar resulted in thousands of e-mails of complaint, mainly from Jewish site visitors, demanding to know why LEGO was suddenly supporting Christmas. Many writers were furious and some cases threatened to boycott LEGO products.

I'm sure you're reading this and thinking, "Yeah. Well of course that would happen." But because LEGO is a Danish product, and Christmas is a natural part of Danish family life, we didn't question the notion. This example is a good indication of how wrong things can go when you presume to use the Internet globally. Can you ever help but reflect local values?

What is Localisation?

It should be obvious from the examples I've cited that localisation means more than merely translating a site's language. It requires adaptations that reflect the environmental realities, cultural mindset and personality traits of the market. Tone of voice, content and graphics all need adjusting to address the local user meaningfully.

> *Localisation is more than just translating a site's language.*

It's ironic that the world's first global medium, the Internet, will have to be used in a more locally responsive manner than any other medium that has preceded it. When Gillette conducted its worldwide "the-best-a-man-can-get" television campaign, for example, all the marketers had to do was change the emblem on the man's shirt, which read "U.S. Army", to locally relevant slogans. A parallel situation on the Internet would be require adaptation of content, voice and packaging.

The global marketplace is not composed of generic sub-markets. All local markets are exposed to their own situations and consumers expect an understanding of these realities to be reflected in a company's website. Consumers resent and feel alienated by impersonal, unfocused information that seems to be shaped by the same clutter that produces the rest of the world's information cookies.

Dialogue Don't expect to simply talk to consumers. In the future, your brand will have to talk, learn, listen and respond to your customers, in order to have a meaningful dialogue with them. If you're not properly informed, and therefore ill-prepared to interact with consumers, they'll drop your brand like the proverbial hot cake.

For example, the LEGO group decided not to give children or adults the opportunity for e-mail dialogue when the company launched its site in 1995. To emphasise that people should not expect to receive any replies from LEGO, all return e-mails were addressed blindalley@lego.com. The result was thousands of frustrated LEGO fans sending e-mails to their favourite brand, but failing to elicit any response. Fortunately the situation was controllable and the decision was quickly reversed. Today consumers may not give the brand a chance to rectify the damage such a disastrous decision would cause.

Brand identity While your brand's dialogue must be locally relevant and comprehensible, it must still accommodate global loyalties. An essential part of localisation is gaining leverage from the millions of dollars spent on worldwide brand marketing. Most international brands are exposed through global media channels like CNN, CNBC, MTV and BBC world. This exposure creates a basic brand model upon which local marketing is built. So your brand needs to fulfil the promises it vociferates globally and communicate them in locally-sensitive terms.

Coca-Cola and McDonald's both offer excellent examples of global branding made relevant through localised communications. In Melbourne Australia, devotion to the AFL (Australian Football League) is fanatical. Loyalties to teams can be generations old and newcomers to town quickly find themselves swept into the football current. The game is truly loved and every spectator has expert analysis to offer on any game or player.

Coca-Cola has found its way, not only on to billboards at grounds all over town, but into the crowds themselves. At the main ground, the MCG (Melbourne Cricket Ground), quarter-and half-time commentary and analysis is solicited from crowd members. Their interview is live, displayed on the giant screens visible from anywhere in the stadium, and met with appropriate encouragement from the 90,000-plus crowd. The vox populi subjects are chosen from amongst those in the crowd who have a Coca-Cola "buddy" in their possession.

McDonald's participates in the AFL by sponsoring mini-games that are staged in the oval at half-time. Children's teams spend the twenty-minute interval emulating their grown-up idols, running around in red and yellow McDonald's outfits emblazoned with the famous logo.

While a brand's logo should normally remain intact at all costs, there are occasions on which this key identifier may need to change. Take for example the original Carlsberg beer logo. This was a swastika inscribed with a twelve-point star. The swastika was the inspiration of Carl Jacobsen, the son of the founder of Carlsberg beer. Carl was a man fascinated by antiquities and who no doubt wished to pass on the original meaning of good luck and long life which the swastika symbolised in cultures as far apart in time and geography as Ancient Rome and Hindu India. Needless to say that during the Nazi occupation of Denmark during the Second World War, the swastika's original symbolism was completely corrupted by the German military's embrace of it, and thus was immediately removed from the Carlsberg logo. The swastika remains a universally shunned symbol in the western world.

Localisation that gets to the heart of cultures fuses with the background knowledge universally held by consumers of a brand to create market-to-market brand synergy.

The Bricks-&-Mortar Factor: Getting Close to Your Customer

In relationships, we all need to feel understood and needed. The brand-consumer relationship has parallels in this respect. If you address local markets in generic terms, individual consumers will find the message irrelevant or incomprehensible at best and culturally insensitive and arrogant at worst. Failure to localise brands risks disenfranchising consumers from them. Physical presence, in the form of bricks-&-mortar stores, is one way of instilling local brand awareness within a community and of avoiding harmful dislocations between your messages and their intended audiences.

McDonald's again provides an admirable example of localised branding instore. The chain evinces its awareness of the importance of local adaptation in the menus it offers from country to country. McDonald's sells wine in its French restaurants, beer in its Danish ones, an Oz burger in Australia and a NZ burger in New Zealand. And, back in 1963 McDonald's introduced Ronald McDonald to the world.

Ronald is a mobile promotional identity. The Ronald persona has become a vehicle for articulating the McDonald's brand within communities. He opens hospitals, collects money for charities, runs drawing competitions, and celebrates Christmas and birthdays. Ronald McDonald is an icon which can be applied to every single McDonald's restaurant. It can operate locally, responding to community issues, without creating trouble for the brand in other communities and territories. Can you imagine what problems Ronald McDonald could create if he suddenly attained a global voice via the Internet? He'd be uttering the same things in the Israeli market as he would be in Sweden. Apart from the fact that the utterances would be so irrelevant as to be incapable of communicating anything effectively, their cultural inappropriateness could cause irreparable offence.

The Local Bricks-&-Mortar Role in Global Brand-Building

Having established the fact that localisation is the key to globalisation, the brand-building role for clicks-&-mortars is logical. While the clicks part of the partnership concentrates on locally-advised content, language and concepts thorough local domains, the bricks-&-mortar stores are the brand's local voice and presence. The store can respond to local events and create community hype by developing a relationship with the local press and the district's households.

The best way, therefore, for a dotcom brand to establish a locally-informed market presence is through a bricks-&-mortar identity. The store is the brand's interface with the local environment. This is not to say that purely online brands can't hope to succeed in markets that are foreign to their origins. But it is to say that a bricks-&-mortar presence introduces brands within a local context. Being surrounded by what is familiar to local consumers, brands achieve acceptance more readily than if they are introduced into a market entirely on their own.

Visit **DualBook.com/cbb/ch10/InteractiveGlobalBranding** for the latest on interactive global branding.

What role can the bricks-&-mortar partners of clicks-&-mortar companies perform in the pursuit of the global market? Real-world stores can attune brands to local realities, issues and environments. To succeed in this role without compromising the brand's core and global values, bricks-&-mortars should consider these four Cs in terms of consistency, the necessary common denominator in them all:

- core values
- communication
- corporate culture
- country culture

Core values and communication deal with the bricks-&-mortar's interface with the consumer. Corporate culture and country culture address the brand's connection with its employees.

Harmonious balance between these operating principles and their consistent treatment within the retail environment is imperative to the creation of an unambiguous global presence.

Consistency

Consistency is the essence of international brand-building. As I've discussed in detail in Chapters 5, 6 and 7, brand-building, especially via a clicks-&-mortar strategy, has to be articulated through clear and consistently applied values, language and iconography. No matter where your consumers are in the world, no matter what communication channels they receive your message through — the store, the website, mobile phone, AOLtv, television commercials, press advertisements or staff — your brand's values must be consistent and recognisable. Any inconsistency will break the value chain.

While the bricks-&-mortar presence can ease an international brand into a local market, the Internet can connect local brands to the global arena, as long as they are built on platforms which are

Consistency is at the root of communications and brand-building success.

both universally legible and which don't frustrate or refute various and divergent local-level values. An offline brand that has been disjointedly established all over the world risks an impotent introduction to the Net's audience. A brand that's been created haphazardly, with no co-ordinating value base, can't easily find a universal message to apply to the web consumer.

Model 10.1: *Global and local synergy*

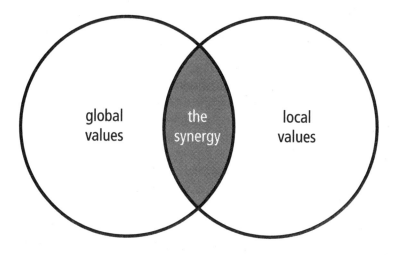

The Disney Corporation's values which have always focused on family, fun, entertainment and fantasy, are perceptible in all markets. Yet the Disney brand accommodates local values and conditions without compromising itself. Donald Duck is known as Anders And in Denmark and Calle Anka in Sweden. Disney characters dress according to the demands of some markets, they utter locally meaningful catch phrases and convey locally inspired opinions and ideas. Donald Duck celebrates Christmas in Northern Europe but doesn't mention it in Israel.

Consistency is part of location as well as brand values. It should ensure customers can predict where they might find your bricks-&-mortar. Typically, for example, 7-Eleven stores are located on corners; there's always a Starbucks Coffee or McDonald's store close to a city's central station. Geographic placement becomes part of the brand and is important for consumers in unfamiliar territory, being the only means of finding their way to your brand.

Average marketing expenditure for offline stores has increased more than 100% over the last eight years according to AC Nielsen (1999). Therefore, consistency is as important as it has ever been. Changing a message too often or communicating it inconsistently increases marketing expenditure and decreases marketing effectiveness. Consistency is branding's overarching imperative and a necessary part of the Four Cs.

Core values

A brand's global platform is made up of values that have universal relevance. These core values determine a brand's reputation and recognisability. Status and style, safety and service are examples of values with universal relevance to consumers, and so they can be communicated consistently to markets all over the world. Apple Computer and BMW are examples of brands that thrive on the certainty of safety and service being consumer priorities. Gucci and Louis Vuitton are examples of international brands which successfully apply their status and style core values in all their markets. (But if you take a close look at the Louis Vuitton stores you'll realise that their interiors appeal more to Japanese and Asian customers rather than Europeans. This is hardly surprisingly when you consider the fact that the majority of Louis Vuitton customers are from Japan.)

In all these cases the store expresses the brand's core values by making contact with as many of the senses as possible: sight, hearing, smell, taste and touch. Herein lies the crucial bricks-&-mortar role in global brand-building.

The outlets of internationally known brands are designed to reflect the brand's core values and they include slight adjustments from market to market to reflect local conditions. McDonald's on Paris's beautiful Champs Elysee adopts the Parisian practice of placing café chairs on the sidewalk and operates from a façade which sympathetically matches the magnificent houses that surround it. Even the famous "golden arches" have made a concession to the locale by appearing in gold rather than yellow.

Starbucks Coffee in Sydney's Elizabeth Street pays homage to the city's informal yet stylish personality, its inhabitants' predilection for casual dining and its climate by occupying a glass-surrounded store that looks onto leafy Hyde Park. Yet Starbucks' signature elements which distinguish the brand from its competitors are present: the green, black and white colours, the recognisable counter, the same cups, the familiar aroma and a similar coffee selection.

Do these local adaptations damage the brand? No way. They nurture it. They help brands achieve a relevant presence without alienating the locals or confusing foreign visitors. Such an achievement is almost impossible via global media. Only the bricks-&-mortar store, where the brand lives at street level, can develop a local relationship with the brand that is necessary for its growth as a global brand.

Communication

Consistency is at the root of communication success: every pronouncement must concur with the next. But surmounting consistency is the question of controversy which is, in fact, a measure of how your brand handles issues of cultural sensitivity.

Just how controversial a brand is, is necessarily defined by its audience's tolerances and sensibilities. Benetton is notorious for its controversial campaigns. One of its most controversial ads involved a dying AIDS patient. It was banned in the UK but hardly noticed in Denmark. Another advertisement portraying a nun kissing a black man was banned in Italy at the Vatican's insistence, but barely raised an eyebrow in Sweden.

Model 10.2: *Local values allow heightened controversy*

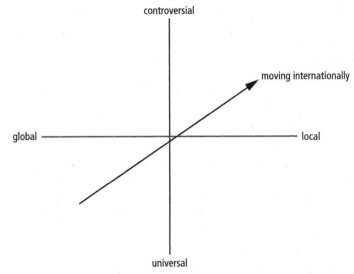

So what can be dangerously controversial globally might be perceived as merely representing a strong opinion locally. Strong opinions aren't as polarising as controversial ones. At the local level you can predict consumer responses more easily than you can at an international level because you're dealing with a more homogeneous set of community attitudes. A bricks-&-mortar campaign for Orange.com was orchestrated in San Francisco in 1999. The campaign offered car paint jobs to hundreds of students and the result was a preponderance in that city of vehicles in the signature orange colour. Perfect for San Francisco, but quite unsuitable in predominantly Catholic Dublin where the colour is associated with an order which consists of

Unionist Protestants who have been warring with Catholics since King William of Orange's war in Ireland in 1689.

One to one communication via the Net can focus on the most local of issues while communicating a brand's core, global values. For example, an oil company might, in global terms, express commitment to environmentally responsible behaviour; at a national level the company would communicate its support for parochial conservation management; and at a one to one level it could communicate its interest in specific neighbourhood environmental campaigns. The local bricks-&-mortar presence reflects the overall brand strategy. The concept is simple. The closer you are to the consumer the more direct you can afford to be. The brand's voice can speak in its most controversial tones in the bricks-&-mortar store. As long as the core values of the brand are being underlined, patronage of local issues will buttress the brand's global identity.

One international voice can no longer exist. You might claim that brands like MTV and CNN have demonstrated that global communication is possible. But even such a well-defined market segment as the MTV generation is different from country to country.

MTV recognised this fact, ascertaining that one station wasn't enough for the world. The United Kingdom, Northern Europe, Asia, Scandinavia, the United States and Argentina all needed their own versions of MTV if the brand was going to communicate effectively. "Provocative" is a key MTV concept and its manifestations vary around the world where levels of provocation vary from market to market. Some markets happily accommodate cutting-edge visuals and commentary (people on the street expressing uncensored views; liberal video images, and so on), American MTV adopts a relatively conservative interpretation of the provocative personality. Asian MTV focuses on a softer version of the key concept and places an emphasis on Asian-derived music.

The MTV experience shows that global brands aren't necessarily "global" just because they exist in most countries and use the same logo. A brand is truly global only when it has matured uniformly worldwide and communicates the same message to its market internationally and simultaneously.

Tell me. What do you think creates the strongest bond between the consumer and the brand? A pure Net presence? Or a clicks-&-mortar presence that can inject the brand's voice into the community and have its message spread at street level?

Corporate culture should be cultivated and communicated through effective and thorough internal training and external communication. Often a bricks-&-mortar employee will work far away from the brand's birthplace, the distance being physical and/or cultural. So all employees must be well-versed in the brand's core values: what motivations lie behind its formation, the direction the brand is taking and the company's vision for the brand's future. These parameters are typically created by a brand's founders and maintained by the company's management. They're what drives the brand on a global level. Employees need guidance to feel part of the brand and to feel respect for their brand's identity. Ensure employees really understand the importance of how their contribution fits into larger picture, and what the whole story is around their brand. The term "story branding" is based on the idea that every product needs a story to prompt the consumer's involvement with it. The thing is, such knowledge encourages employee involvement with the brand, and includes their role as an important part of the story.

For instance, at home I have a salt and pepper set designed by Arne Jacobsen. It's nice, but not something you would spend hours talking to your guests about. However, there is a story behind the set that you would find fascinating if you were at my table. You see, almost fifty years ago the designer had dinner with one of his business partners. The business partner admired this salt and pepper set Jacobsen had designed. The business partner was so fascinated by the design that he asked his partner to design a whole hotel around the salt and pepper set. And so he did. It took Arne about twenty years but the hotel he designed became an icon in Copenhagen. Not only was the hotel specially designed to match the salt and pepper, so were the plates, the cutlery, the curtains, the beds and, well, everything you could name that a hotel would need. The chairs were also inspired by the design and the "egg chair" was later to become part of the Museum of Modern Art's collection in New York. The whole environment had been spun from a simple salt and pepper set.

What is your perception of this salt and pepper now? Does it mean something more to you? Strong branding is all about creating a story or, if a story already exists, making it spin off the product and the brand. And a healthy corporate culture includes the whole team in a common understanding of their brand's values, identity, goals and story.

Country culture As part of developing a cohesive corporate culture, a brand's headquarters should design communication and training strategies that can accommodate local freedoms in culturally disparate workplaces.

As I've indicated, corporate culture and its adaptability to local conditions relates to employees identifying with their brand. Having respect for their brand, their employer and their own part in the big picture is conducive to a good workplace morale. Corporate culture is adopted and communicated by staff. Ethnic culture should be recognised and used as a filter for the adaptation of a brand's core values to local market needs. It's unrealistic and unproductive to focus on headquarters' processes and opinions. Such cultural insensitivity blinds the brand to its local role and can result in alienating it from that market.

Clicks-&-Mortar Globalisation Strategies

Global branding is a matter of creating awareness of and trust in the relationship between brands and new markets. The only shortcut to this market position is through the leverage gained from partnerships with already existing, trusted brands.

There are five ways to create a global brand. They all necessitate clicks-&-mortar co-operation:

- Pure global branding.
- Global branding combined with national branding.
- National branding supported with a national clicks-&-mortar strategy.
- Pure national branding.
- National clicks-&-mortar strategy.

Most global clicks-&-mortar growth plans will combine a number of these approaches. I want to help you gain a clear focus on which strategy will serve as the backbone of your clicks-&-mortar globalisation plan.

Pure Global Branding

Few brands can afford this extremely expensive approach. The exceptions are brands that already have a global presence like Coca-Cola, Mercedes-Benz, IBM and Ford. Such brands are pioneers in their fields and have never lost the edge their FMA gives them.

Around 1995 it cost approximately US$500 million to establish a brand's worldwide presence — worldwide being defined as encompassing twenty countries or more. At the time of writing, it costs an estimated US$1.2 billion in just the first year. These estimates cover only the marketing expenditure and don't include the costs of establishing a physical presence in each market. The fact is that FMA is no longer a phenomenon which is easily achieved. With more than three billion pages on the Internet there is always someone who has done the same thing, thereby adding to the already onerous communication challenge.

We're probably going to keep seeing brands attempting to establish a worldwide presence from scratch. But they will become fewer and will be backed by established bricks-&-mortar brands. We'll probably also see the appearance of brands that collude with each other to establish a mutual global presence. These will be leading world brands which team up to create new global presences, like AOL-Time Warner and regional brands like Star Alliance and One World. These manoeuvres require substantial branding and financial support. Star Alliance wouldn't achieve fruition, for example, if it weren't composed of well-known and well-respected airline brands. Over time it's likely that Star Alliance will become the main brand name while the airlines' individual brands will become secondary and meaningful only to their local markets.

Global Branding Combined with National Branding

Combining global and national advertising strategies might not be as effective as the purely international strategy outlined above, but the method is cheaper and, therefore, more practicable.

When a message is spread across countries within a short time, practicalities demand that the strategy focus on a hierarchy of markets. Most of the resources would be dedicated to what are identified as "tier one" countries. Then, once a solid presence has been established in these markets, the strategy can move into the next phase and focus on tier two and three countries. The benefit of combining global and, subsequently, local communication is that global visibility becomes a door-opener onto local markets. Even though eBay, for instance, could be seen as an FMA brand, it capitalised on its global reputation before entering local markets. eBay's success in the USA is a key reason for ready consumer acceptance of the brand into local markets. Here's the trust factor at work (see Chapter 4), as it always is when any measure of business success is to be explained. eBay entered local markets with a heritage of trust bestowed by millions of American consumers and this helped to guarantee the brand and recommend it to other markets.

Countries as brands

This last point diverts me to an interesting and often overlooked factor which has played a part in brands achieving global acceptance. Countries can be seen as brands, with their reputation often have meaning in consumer terms. If I mention Switzerland, you might associate qualities of detail and exactitude with it. Germany might mean first-class engineering. Italy might resonate with the romance of lifestyle, quality fashion and food. But what if I mention Finland?

Apart from the fact that Nokia originated in Finland you'd probably have problems ascribing values to your concept of the country. Why? Because local brands create national reputations, and those reputations create global brands. Finland was not well-known for its communications technology, in fact Nokia originally manufactured chainsaws. Had the phone system hailed from Japan, the US, Switzerland or Germany it would possibly have had an easier brand-building task. The manufacturing and consumer values we associate with these countries match the product and, therefore, justify consumer trust in it.

Yahoo! is misconceived as being the world's first portal. It wasn't. Several others appeared on the Internet much earlier but never found a voice. Jerry Yang and David Filo, Yahoo!'s founders, were both working on their doctorates in the Computer Systems Laboratory at Stanford University in 1994 when they began compiling a guide to World Wide Web sites that they found interesting — just at the time when the Internet market's large volume created the opportunity of momentum, the brand grew rapidly and fast became a worldwide presence.

Häagen-Dazs, the ice-cream brand, was created upon the supposition that it was from Denmark. Denmark was perceived as enjoying a high quality of life, good quality food and a cold clear environment that cohered with the profile the ice-cream brand wanted to achieve. The name Häagen-Dazs was invented and presumed by North American consumers to be a Northern European brand. Of course, the supposed heritage was fictional. The brand had nothing to do with Denmark, and if you asked Danes about the name they would probably wonder if it wasn't Dutch because of its strange pronunciation.

I'm not saying that fabricating a false background is the way to achieve global branding success. I am saying that national reputations can have a powerful effect on the speed at which a brand earns credibility, and this factor has to be taken into consideration when creating a brand-building growth plan.

 Visit **DualBook.com/cbb/ch10/Country**
and read the latest news on how perceived country of origin can affect your brand.

National Branding Supported With a National Clicks-&-Mortar Strategy

This strategy can be approached by a partnership, comprising an existing, respected and well-known bricks-&-mortar player and a new online business, or by an online company making an independent foray into the clicks-&-mortar adventure.

For an international brand wanting to enter a new territory, teaming up with a bricks-&-mortar business already respected in that market is the quickest way of securing the trust of that local consumer group. The trust reflected upon the newcomer by the existing offline partner is of priceless benefit because it's entering that long and hard-fought battle for consumer trust at an advanced level. Obviously, the more the offline player is respected in the local market, the easier it is for the newly formed partnership to gain the clicks-&-mortar consumers' trust. Once this is established the clicks-&-mortar can embark upon the brand-building process.

The trick to a mutually beneficial clicks-&-mortar relationship is to find compatible partners (See Chapter 6). For the incoming international brand, it's essential to analyse the offline brand's established values and be sure that its local reputation and market fits the global brand's platform.

When Starbucks Coffee expanded across the Atlantic from the United States, it moved into several hundred existing Seattle Coffee Company stores in inner London. Starbucks Coffee didn't gain leverage from the Seattle Coffee brand at all. It took all its advantages from the existing stores' geographic positions. Starbucks Coffee inherited a loyal clientele, used to popping around the corner for a coffee. The coffee now sold by Starbucks Coffee is almost the same as the product formerly sold at these establishments, but the label has changed. Overnight, Starbucks Coffee became the most prominent coffee chain in England.

Pure National Branding

For all those who've succeeded with this approach, as many have failed. The two most common players in this clicks-&-mortar scenario are:

1. One hundred per cent locally-owned subsidiaries of foreign companies, not backed by any local partnerships; and
2. Fifty/fifty joint ventures backed, both financially and promotionally, by a local partner (who need not be a potential clicks-&-mortar player).

One hundred per cent locally owned subsidiaries of foreign companies
Fewer and fewer companies are attempting this game. It's expensive and risky. Yahoo! adopted this approach in most of its markets. The strategy has ensured that the company doesn't have to share revenue or equity with any partners. But you have to remember that Yahoo.com was unusual — an FMA brand which not only managed to be the first in its home country but which was often the first in every country it moved into. Wherever they were pipped at the post, Yahoo.com benefited from the international reputation that preceded it. In this respect, Yahoo.com's global brand-building experience also reflected the global-branding-combined-with-national-branding approach that I discussed earlier.

Fifty/fifty joint ventures These are the models most commonly adopted to establish a global presence. Many brands — including Alta Vista which teamed up with Yellow Pages in Australia; Excite@home, which teamed up with British Telecom in the UK; AOL which teamed up with Bertelsmann in Europe until it merged with Time Warner; and Lycos, which teamed up with Comundo in Spain — have found respected players in key markets and used them as entry points to those markets. Apart from being well-respected, these partners also offered additional financial value to a potential partnership and had local media contacts and distribution access.

It appears that this strategy is attractive to most international-bound companies. However, over 1999 and 2000, there was a change in the partner-selecting process. Prior to 1999, joint ventures were created as a way of increasing the stock value of participating companies. The joint venture arrangement justified a company's claims to be international and gave it the kudos of association with other attractive brands. Now joint ventures tend to come together in the interests of mutually beneficial and compatible infrastructure or objectives. Finding synergies in partnerships has come to be more valuable in the long term than short-term stock gains and so has directed partnering choices.

National Clicks-&-Mortar Strategy

In 1999, 72% of offline marketing money was spent on below-the-line promotion: instore promotions, coupons and events. Over the previous two decades, the retail industry found that this was the most effective means of pushing sales. With this in mind, it makes sense that future clicks-&-mortar players will be driven from a grass roots level, heavily promoted instore and gaining leverage from the local retail partner's visibility and reputation. For most clicks-&-mortars this strategy will mean solid growth and the establishment of a strong dual reputation. In short, this is just what most Internet sites are looking for today with their GBFOD tactic (grow big fast or die). This acronym will have to be adjusted to include the adverb "solidly".

In simple terms uniform international brand-building cannot exist. What does exist is the lesson that the best way to express a brand's voice is through a local bricks-&-mortar presence. The result is that more and more brands are likely to opt for a clicks-&-mortar strategy. The clicks partner introduces the international facet to local versions of a brand, and gives local brands access to global markets. The bricks build a brand solidly from community level up.

Summary

- Uniform international brand-building cannot exist. The fact is that human preferences cannot be the same everywhere.
- A global brand-building strategy is in reality a local plan for every market.
- The more of the globe our media embraces, the more local accents surface, the more they are exposed to mutual influence and the quicker cultural identity changes. What was local a decade ago may disappear in five years' time, replaced by new, internationally informed realities. This means that the concept of "local" is becoming tied to geography rather than ethnic culture.
- Building an online global brand is more costly than building an offline, bricks-&-mortar international brand. In addition to the massive investment required, the online brand is bound to giving consumers the world over access to the one marketing position. A single marketing position can't be efficacious in all cultures. And you risk alienating and/or offending markets when you presume to use the Internet globally.
- Consumers' ideas and perceptions are inextricably related to the culture in which they live and/or with which they identify.
- Even though the Web makes every site globally accessible, it doesn't mean that every site is internationally legible. So, localisation is becoming recognised as an inescapable necessity for cultivating international brand recognition.
- Localisation means more than merely translating a site's language. It requires adaptations that reflect the environmental realities, cultural mindset and personality traits of the market. Voice, content and graphics all need adjustment to address the local user meaningfully, while retaining the brand's core values and global loyalties.
- It's ironic that the world's first global medium, the Internet, will have to be used in a more locally responsive manner than any other medium that has preceded it.
- Don't expect to simply talk to consumers. In the future, your brand will have to talk, learn, listen and respond to your customers, in order to have a meaningful dialogue with them. If you're not properly informed, and therefore ill-prepared to interact with consumers, they'll drop your brand like the proverbial hot cake.
- Brands must fulfil the promises they vociferate globally and communicate them in locally-sensitive terms. Localisation that gets to the heart of cultures fuses with the background knowledge universally

held by consumers of a brand and creates market-to-market brand synergy.

- Physical presence, in the form of bricks-&-mortar stores, is one way of instilling local brand awareness within a community and of avoiding harmful dislocations between your messages and their intended audiences.

- Localisation is the key to globalisation so the brand-building role for clicks-&-mortars is logical. The best way for a dotcom brand to establish a locally-informed market presence is through a bricks-&-mortar identity. The store is the brand's interface with the local environment.

- Real-world stores attune brands to local realities. To succeed in this role without compromising the brand's core and global values, bricks-&-mortars should consider core values, communication, corporate and country culture and consistency. A harmonious balance between these operating principles and their consistent treatment within the retail environment is imperative to the creation of an unambiguous global presence.

- An essential part of localisation is gaining leverage from the millions of dollars spent on worldwide brand marketing so while the brand's dialogue must be locally relevant and comprehensible, it still needs to accommodate global loyalties to avoid confusion.

- A brand's global platform is made up of values that have universal relevance. These core values determine a brand's reputation and recognisability and are starting points for building local communication.

- Consistency is at the root of communications and brand-building success: every pronouncement must concur with the next and the brand articulated through clear and consistently applied values, language and iconography.

- While the bricks-&-mortar presence eases an international brand into a local market, the Internet connects local brands to the global arena, as long as they are built on platforms which are both universally legible and which don't frustrate or refute various and divergent local-level values.

- Global branding is a matter of creating awareness of, trust in and a relationship between brands and new markets. The only shortcut to this market position is through the leverage gained from partnerships with already existing, trusted brands.

- Corporate culture should be cultivated and communicated through effective and thorough internal training and external communication.

Employees should be well-versed in the brand's core values: what motivations lie behind its birth, the direction the brand is moving and the company's vision for the brand's future.

• Ensure employees understand the importance of their contribution, how it fits into larger objectives and what the whole story is around their brand. A healthy corporate culture includes the whole team in a common understanding of their brand's values, identity, goals and story.

Action Points

Do you have plans for expanding your brand into foreign markets? Your answer will depend on your ambitions, the potential of your product or services to adapt to new cultures, your investment capacity and international competition.

Identify the values you'd like your brand to carry from market to market. What is the essence of your brand that you believe is most universally applicable and which value will differentiate your brand in disparate local markets? Is the product easy to use? Is it uniquely designed? Is it very functional? Of the best quality? Describe the essence of your brand, using a selected key value, in one sentence.

It's no coincidence that most international brands have chosen a local partner to achieve an instant local presence. The stronger the partner's brand in the local market, the more successful your brand's entrée to that environment will be. Do you see your international strategy as being dependent on a:
– Global branding approach;
– Global branding approach combined with national branding:
– National branding supported with a national clicks-&-mortar strategy;
– Pure national branding; or a
– National clicks-&-mortar strategy?

Select one of these five options and create a SWOT (strengths, weaknesses, opportunities and threats) analysis of your decision.

Your next step is now to consider your approach in terms of these four areas:
– Core values;
– Communication;

- Corporate culture; and
- Country culture.

What core values would you like your brand to stand for? Keep the sentence that describes the essence of your brand in mind. What will characterise your international communication strategy? What characterises your unique tone of voice? How willing are you to let the corporate culture behind your brand adapt to local prerogatives?

How much will the essence of your brand be able to reflect the host country's culture? Can your brand's product selection change? Will you accede to a local partner's marketing advice?

Hopefully you had problems resolving Step 3's questions. It's almost impossible to make even hypothetical evaluations without surveying local markets for their opinion and perceptions about your brand and its introduction to them. You can't get around the fact that you have to be prepared to test your assumptions in new markets. Do your brand's expressed values work in the market? Is your partner successfully guiding your brand's introduction? Your brand's introduction to a new market should be accompanied by the appointment of a local person who is cognisant of the market's values and culture, who acts as your adviser on such matters, and whose perceptions can be relied upon when a new brand initiative is being considered for the market.

If your decision at Step 2 was to introduce your brand to local markets internationally by yourself, you may have changed your mind by now. A clicks-&-mortar strategy is how most companies have succeeded in markets foreign to their brands' origins. If you maintain that this needn't be your strategy, I'll challenge you one more time in Chapter 11.

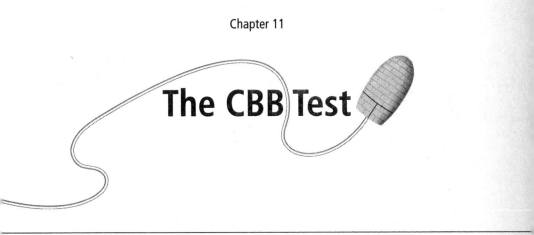

The CBB Test

The clicks, bricks & brand trend is as obvious as it is inevitable. It amounts to this: an online strategy is only successful with the help of an offline partner, and equally, an offline business won't survive without a healthy online mate. But before identifying and harnessing a suitable online partner, way before designing and executing an online strategy, how does an offline business assess its clicks-&-mortar suitability?

So, a clicks-&-mortar outcome is on the cards. The questions you need to ask yourself are, "How do I analyse my business's potential as a clicks-&-mortar partner? How do I identify a suitable online partner? How will I achieve synergy with that partner?" This chapter deals with the first of these questions. Chapter 14 helps you to select a suitable clicks-&-mortar partner and Chapter 6 discusses synergy.

This chapter also introduces the Clicks, Bricks and Brands Test (CBB) for offline retailers considering entering a clicks-&-mortar relationship. It analyses four criteria to determine how well your company and brand will coalesce with online media:

- Product attributes
- Consumer behaviour
- Product familiarity
- Channel conflict

Product attributes
Is the product suited to online distribution? This part of the test focuses on the relevance and use of our five senses in relation to your product.

Consumer behaviour
What traits (buying habits, lifestyle, taste, income, ambitions) characterise your consumer group? This part of the test focuses on your existing customer types, their likely conversion rates (that is, how likely your customer is to purchase your product after being exposed to it) and their concerns about online trust and privacy.

Product familiarity
How familiar are consumers with your product, product category and brand? How ready are they to purchase the same product online? How dependent are they on physical contact with the product? In this part of the test we focus on the 80/20 rule of repeat purchases described in Chapter 5: that 80% of consumers will make their initial purchase of a product offline while 20% will prefer to visit the online store initially. In time, some offline consumers will make repeat purchases online while 20% of that 80% offline group will still prefer to shop offline.

Channel conflict
What competition do you have? What distribution deals are you involved in? How will they hinder the establishment of an online distribution channel? In this part of the test we focus on analysing the competition in your product

category to ascertain the advantages an online presence will give you, and we assess your existing distribution deals, employee and investor attitudes to see how they could conflict with new online deals.

The outcome of the CBB Test depends upon a well-judged balance between all your answers. Your product might be very suited to the online environment, but if consumers couldn't tolerate the prospect of dealing with you in cyberspace there's not a lot of point forcing an immovable issue. Think of the old adage: "You can lead a horse to water…"

Product Attributes

In Chapter 8 I examined the retailer's advantage in having access to all five of the consumer's senses. One of the easiest ways to determine whether your product suits online media is to focus on which senses the product appeals to. Products which primarily appeal to smell, touch and taste will obviously be less suited to online communication than products which are more accessible to sight and sound.

Sight and hearing are able to adequately inform us about most products. A brand's reputation, a product's familiarity and its price mostly sublimate the need for information to be supplied through the other senses.

Brand

As discussed in Chapter 8, brand and the guarantees of its reputation can compensate for a product's physical absence. Recommendation and/or personal experience can replace the security of physical inspection with confidence in a brand's reputed quality.

Consumers have come to know heavily branded and long-established products, over decades, and products packed to prevent inspection all dismiss sensory evaluation. Kellogg's and Campbells, for example, have taught the consumer to confidently understand what's inside the tin or box by reading their labels' illustrations and copy. In fact, we've been educated to taste, smell and feel with our eyes. Perception tests conducted by BBDO in Denmark on snack-food package design revealed that wrappers carrying a number of snack illustrations encourage up to 80% of consumers to think that those packs contain greater quantities than similar-sized packs with fewer illustrations.

The conclusion is that grocery packaging limits the consumer's full sensory assessment of it. So, the criteria for choice is comparison with similar products, or direct experience with the product or brand in question. Such criteria are easily accommodated online. You can make a similar evaluation for all product categories. How distant from the senses can a product be and still enjoy the consumer's evaluation. Items like socks, handkerchiefs and shirts are often sold in packaging. Again, the manufacturer has educated consumers to divorce themselves from sensory dependence and make purchase decisions by analysis, comparison and perception.

As suppliers and distributors reflect upon the challenges of the electronic age they will need to re-examine the ways in which products are presented to the consumer. As discussed in Chapter 8 stores of the future will be emotional and sensory adventure facilities that exploit product and consumer proximity to each other in order to promote brands. To amplify the experience, barriers that interfere with product and customer communication will be removed. There will be no boxes, wrapping or packaging in order to maximise contact between products and consumers.

The Window Test

While sensory appraisal indicates the distance a product can afford to be from a potential purchaser, the window test indicates what products attain added value by being displayed. If a product, distanced from a customer's senses of smell, touch and taste, can still attract purchase because of its visual appeal (its window suitability), brand reputation or previous purchase recommendation, it's likely to be suited to life online.

Product Familiarity

Closely related to the consumer's brand knowledge and product reputation, product familiarity depends on the consumer's personal experience of a product. Having purchased it once and been satisfied, a consumer's decision to make the purchase a second time doesn't depend on applying any of the senses again. So, repeat purchases can be handled suitably online seeing consumers are already familiar with what they are purchasing.

Cost

Since a personal introduction to each consumer is not possible, over the past fifty years broadcast and print media have been responsible for informing consumers about products. Not only has advertising introduced products, it has familiarised consumers with assessing product suitability at a distance from the real article. The price of a product alone can determine whether a consumer is willing to purchase it. Very few of us would buy a car without test-driving it, nor would we be likely to purchase a house or furniture without having seen the real-life article. The conclusion? Cheaper products and FMCGs are likely to suit online purchase, though their low per-unit cost often makes them logistically unviable. (See also Chapters 1 and 2.)

From Clicks to Bricks: Amazon.com Builds in the Real World

When Amazon.com began their Internet bookshop, their vision was as big and as wide as the river they named themselves after. Jeff Bezos, the dynamic founder, had a business plan that was so broad in its scope that it would profoundly affect the way the world did business.

For the first time ever in the retail environment, an expensive storefront on the right side of the street was unnecessary. All that was required was a room with a good supply of power, and computer programmers and designers who could build a place in cyberspace that would attract the customer and enhance the process of discovery. They rose to the challenge of making a book site engaging. They religiously adhered to the Bezos's golden rule of customer needs: selection, convenience and price. Amazon planned to be the earth's largest bookstore with a fraction of the overhead costs that their physical rivals were bound by. This way they could afford to pour all their resources into refining their clicks and creating a community of well-serviced customers.

When Amazon.com opened its virtual doors to do business in July 1995, they had more than a million titles listed on their database, a few chairs to sit on, and a 400 square foot warehouse — which was just about the right size to garage two cars. This was not perceived as a problem because books would only be there long enough to fill the orders on hand. They would physically leave as soon as they arrived.

During the first week of operation, Amazon.com took $12,438 worth of orders, but could only fill $846 worth of books. The second week's orders totalled $14,792. The company was quite simply unprepared for the volume. They had no packing tables, they had no storage shelves, they didn't even have a photocopy machine. No one was hired specifically to do the packing and everyone pitched in on their hands and knees, and wrapped the orders on the floor.

As they hastily hammered packing tables together and scoured garage sales for desks, the orders kept coming. In the first month of business they shipped books to 45 countries and 50 states. Not surprisingly they soon outgrew their 400 square feet of warehouse space and moved to larger premises. Books were still being turned around as quickly as they arrived from the distributors, and the customer base was building at a rapid pace. Amazon.com was becoming one of the Web's first household names.

CASE STUDY: Amazon.com

Servicing the community of customers remained its primary focus. Amazon.com realised that if a customer saw the latest John Grisham in their local bookshop before receiving their Amazon copy they would lose their edge. In order to address this quandary, they began stocking the top-ten bestsellers. This quickly became the top 25, and in no time at all, the top 250. By the end of 1996, Amazon had chalked up $16 million in sales, were employing 150 people and, understandably, had way outgrown their warehouse space yet again. They subsequently leased 93,000 square feet of warehouse space in Seattle and Wilmington, Delaware and now held an inventory of over 200,000 best-selling books.

Amazon went through a new metamorphosis. It was now diversifying. The company added music and videos, electronic goods, auctions, tools, toys and homewares to their virtual stocklist. During the busy 1998 Christmas season they shipped over 7.5 million items. In less than three years they had built one of the Internet's most powerful brands.

But in spite of all the record-breaking, chart-busting growth that they had achieved, the company continued to bleed money. They remained dependent on expensive delivery options and needed to move towards more economical distribution solutions.

Amazon.com's business plan was forced to undergo a whole new incarnation as the Web's number one e-tailer came to the conclusion that they had to invest heavily in bricks. Shareholders with high expectations demanded that the necessary logistical decisions be made to stem the losses. Most importantly, Amazon decided to keep their distribution in-house. They had to decide on locations — bearing in mind a million things, including market proximity, state sales tax and staffing requirements. They had to decide on picking and packing systems.

With the help of outside expertise and key executive appointments, $300 million was allocated to build nine distribution centres (two in Europe) with a combined floor space exceeding three million square feet. They opted to write their own warehouse management software, although still relying on United Parcel Service and US Mail for their deliveries. By 2000, 70% of Amazon.com's employees were working on the physical side of the business.

Like many start-up Internet companies, Amazon has made it up as it goes along. But in the ridiculously short space of five years, it has attracted more than 20 million customers with repeat business that far outstrips its established rivals. If it can now turn its astonishing e-tail vision into e-profits, it will undoubtedly survive as earth's biggest virtual department store, a trader which began its online life in books. The jury is still out. Whatever the case, Amazon.com has earned a prominent and permanent place in the history of the Internet.

Consumer Behaviour

Clicks-&-mortars can analyse the consumer as one of two types: the virtual and the physical. Let's examine these types' divergent behaviours against discrete criteria so that we can grasp an understanding of consumers' key attitudes to trust and privacy, willingness to transfer from the offline environment to an online one, and familiarity with the online medium.

This way of categorising consumers is not based on the demographic criteria used by research centres and advertising agencies some years ago. Such criteria included geographic location, sex, age, income and education. But the results delineated only this empirical information. They didn't speak of behavioural characteristics which could be used to predict shopping habits. You might find people sharing the same demographic profile whose behaviours are dissimilar to each other. One individual might be an innovative user of new media while another fitting precisely the same demographic criteria might be intimidated by new technology and fearful of anything unfamiliar.

It's very important that you determine which of the two groups your consumers generally belong. If the virtual shopper generally characterises your target market, you need to understand which of the four sub-groups described below best describes your consumer group. Your determination of customer type will indicate your possible online suitability.

Comparative characteristics: the physical and the virtual consumer As described in Chapter 8, the physical consumer flicks through catalogues, prepares a shopping list before entering the supermarket, has a budget to adhere to, is generally brand loyal, price-driven rather than convenience-driven, and doesn't use home-delivery services, no matter how inconvenient personal shopping might be.

The virtual consumer rarely glances at catalogues, has only a few products nominated on a shopping list, selects items according to impulse, has no strict budget, is loyal to some brands but shifts readily amongst products, is time-driven, convenience-driven and changes shopping patterns regularly. Virtual consumers are individualistic, more independent than physical consumers (they're less compelled by external pressures, like loyalty for example, when making purchasing decisions) and more ready to use online media for information collection and purchases.

Interestingly, virtual consumers defy characterisation by religion, nationality or income. They can be found in almost every part of the world and are completely at ease with international media, global brands and an understanding of lifestyles across cultures. The virtual consumer is open to change, capable of adjusting personal behaviour in the interests of efficiency, and willing to embrace online consumerism.

While physical consumers often select purchases on the basis of habit and are influenced by mass-marketing and mass-consumption trends, virtual consumers adopt an individual and self-informed approach to consumption. The buying habits of virtual consumers are dominated by their paucity of spare time and attention. As a result, they are often willing to pay premium prices in order to save on both.

Virtual consumers grumble about there being too few hours in the day to satisfy all the demands made upon them. A study by the American Management Association showed that almost half of all middle managers claim they have more work to do than they have time in which to do it. Finding ways to cut down on time consumption is, therefore, one of the most effective ways of snaring the attention of this consumer group. Hence their attraction to the time-saving potential of online shopping.

Research agency, AC Nielsen, conducted a study which organised consumers into categories. Five of these accommodate virtual consumer types:

- *Virtual social shoppers* enjoy visiting stores. They take pleasure in shopping, an opportunity to get out of the house and meet people. Some stores have identified this type amongst their target market. In response they stay open late and encourage shoppers to meet and socialise.
- *Virtual experimenters* are happy to try new things and were the first consumers make online purchases. This category is strongly represented in the generation of young adults who have grown up with the Internet and e-commerce. These people have already established their online comfort levels.
- *Virtual convenience shoppers* are time poor and find shopping a chore. Busy parents typically represent them and they are ready to try online shopping if it saves time and doesn't cost any extra.
- *Virtual value shoppers* will respond to any market initiative which appears to offer the best combination of product quality, value and service. If the same product can be more easily obtained electronically, at the same or lower price than offline and with similar or better levels of service, they will be quick to adopt the new facility.
- *Virtual ethical shoppers* are a minority who put ethics ahead of all other shopping motivations and who cannot be overlooked. Their decision-making is unlikely to be influenced by a product being sold online or offline. They will buy in either environment as long as the business is honest and politically correct.

Trust and Privacy

The physical distance between the consumer and the product which exists in online trading not only affects the consumer's perception of the product, but also of the service being provided. Dealing with intangible products and unseen service providers still requires many consumers to take a leap of faith. Issues of trust and privacy concern consumers in varying degrees, and must be respected and addressed if you're inviting them to follow you online.

Physical distance between consumers and products necessitated by online trading affects the consumer's perception of both the product, and the service being provided.

Your first reaction might be that trust and privacy are important issues to most of us. But it's wise to focus on understanding the particular areas of concern your customers may have. Some consumers will resist purchasing online as they mistrust the security of their credit card number floating in cyberspace. Others mistrust new and unfamiliar technologies and sceptically doubt whether any orders they place in the virtual store will ever arrive. So, offline retailers making the move online have to move the trust offline customers have and duplicate it in every online sphere of operation.

Moving your trust online It's one achievement to create trust. It's another to move that established trust from one media to another. Here are some rules to guide you through this process:

- *Keep communications style and content consistent*: The messages you've been sending from your bricks-&-mortar store have to remain the same online. Retain the same policies and conditions, use the same language, graphic design and icons, make the same special offers and give the same guarantees. Any differences in your service or image will be picked up by consumers (you can be sure of that) and provoke feelings of doubt and insecurity in them.
- *Be honest*: State upfront what benefits and disadvantages there are for consumers in using the online store compared with using the bricks-&-mortar store. Introduce your customers to the comparative advantages by explaining, for example, "If you're in a hurry, visit our regular store where you'll pick up what you need immediately. But, if time's on your side, and you can wait for our reliable 48-hour delivery service, why not visit our online store, where you'll save time by not having to drive and park, line up at the cash register and load the car …"

- *Inject additional trust-builders online*: Set up special guarantees, rules and guidelines that build the online user's confidence in the service they can expect from the online store. For example, establish no-questions-asked return policies and 100% insurance on all products shipped. As the direct marketing experience has taught us, particularly book club marketing, customers seldom return products (up to 10% of products are returned). But the notion of that option being available instils confidence in consumers who feel they can then trust the service they're being offered.

- *Team up with the best*: If you feel you can't deliver the same quality of product, service, backup or consumer know-how online as you do in your bricks-&-mortar store, team up with partners who can help you. The quality of your online service will have to exceed offline customers' expectations to win and keep them there. Remember, 24% of dissatisfied first-time online consumers not only fail to return to the online store, they never go back to the bricks-&-mortar store either (Forrester Research, June 2000).

Willingness to Adopt Online Shopping Practices

Conversion rates describe the speed with which a consumer converts an awareness of a product into a decision to buy it. By extension, online conversion rates refer to the number of visits a consumer makes to a site before purchasing from it. For example, flowers enjoy a higher conversion rate than books. Of all first-time visitors to an online florist, 50% will make a purchase. Research by AC Nielsen, conducted in July 2000, shows that more product categories are likely to join the online list by 2004, including major items like cars, houses and furniture.

Apart from the varying conversion rates experienced by different product categories, trust levels influence adoption rates. Early online adopters often trust, or are more willing to try new products. They are also willing to take the risk of entering an unfamiliar transaction process.

Amazon.com's Jeff Bezos focused on potential consumer conversion rates before any figures were available. The figures in the table below have remained almost unchanged since conversion rates were first scrutinised.

Familiarity With the Online Medium

If consumers are already regular users of interactive media they are obviously more likely to transfer to an online environment. If you know your consumer group rarely uses interactive media, you should accommodate this aware-ness in your online development strategy and investment.

That said, almost all consumer groups are Internet users, including seniors (consumers sixty years and over) and low-income families. This fact invites another question: via what other interactive channels can a brand expect to target its consumers in the

> *Regular users of interactive media will enter the online trading environment comfortably.*

future? For example, the Chinese market is expected to become a dominant wireless audience, with its massive population having access to the Internet via mobile phones. Wireless Internet technology is expanding the online store's product repertoire as flexibility and mobility make FMCGs, train tickets, you name it, procurable online. Your product and target group assessments will need to refer to your channel strategy. Your target group might be online but via which channel and what are the limitations of that medium?

Product Familiarity

The third criterion to consider in the CBB Test is how familiar consumers will be with your product by the time you take it online. Will consumers generally be making first-time purchases, second-time purchases or repeat purchases following their long-established habits? Is your brand a well-known one with a long-established reputation?

If a customer is purchasing your product for the first time, the consumer's selection processes will be counting on the judgment of all five senses. Of course, this isn't relevant in all product categories, where some of our senses are superfluous to our understanding of the product. Let's take books as an example. Do you remember the first book purchase you ever made? It's likely that much of your energy was spent on examining the cover, the book's weight and size, its price, title, author and contents. (Not necessarily in that order.) The second time you made a book purchase you possibly concentrated on the author, the title, the contents and the price. Your conscientious-ness may have decreased, but it's doubtful that on any occasion the taste of a book has persuaded you to buy it.

> *For the first-time purchase of a product consumers will rely on all five senses to aid their selection.*

So, analyse what percentage of your online customers will be purchasing your product for the first time? What percentage will be making a repeat purchase? In other words, how familiar is the consumer with your product and the product category to which it belongs? Ascertain these issues and ask yourself, based on your offline experience, how likely is the consumer to be satisfied with the purchase and to carry on making repeat purchases?

80% of consumers' shopping baskets get filled with replenishment items.

Typically, consumers are familiar with and have confidence in basic food, drink and clothing products. An Indiana University research study (1999) shows that 80% of consumers' shopping baskets were filled with replenishment items. This figure reflects the rule I will describe in Chapter 15: 20% of everything we purchase goes through a thorough evaluation process the first time it's selected, but from then on, it will belong to the 80% of repeat purchases that are made without much further evaluation.

Brand

Building consumer familiarity and confidence is an important hurdle in any market place, whether physical or virtual. Consumer familiarity with a product is connected with brand familiarity. The world's top ten brands, nominated in the model below, have won the trust of their consumers. This confidence would be reflected in the consumers' willingness to consider purchasing the product within the virtual environment.

So, a brand's good reputation justifies moving its product sales online. Consumers who are familiar with and trust a brand are no longer dependent on its physical presence to purchase it. As I've discussed throughout this book, especially in Chapter 4, the way most e-tailers establish and maintain their credibility is via their partnerships with well-established brands. The more known brands they have on their virtual shelves the more the consumer is likely to trust and purchase from the online store.

An established brand enjoys a depth and breadth of consumer franchise that cuts across ages, demographics and consumer types. It builds a commitment and loyalty that urges consumers to pay more for it and to go out of their way to get it. Its perceived value and reliability are highly persuasive motivators. It's hard to see how virtual purchasing, once the online and distribution infrastructure is in place, will present any barrier to consumers buying established brands online.

Companies that have built their brands over time are in an excellent position to take advantage of future changes in shopping habits. As consumers become more familiar with online shopping there will be an even greater premium attached to established reputation. For reluctant online consumers learning to navigate their way through cyberspace, the easiest purchases to make will be of brand names they recognise and trust.

Discriminating between products online, where the only points of distinction are price, appearance and a short product description (if any), will call upon the trust factor. So well-established offline brands that already carry the extra value of reputation have a distinct advantage over their lesser-known competitors.

And this is the reason behind the massive increase in the cost of establishing online brands between 1995 and 2000. In a period of five years the investment required inflated 500%. Association with a well-established offline brand is the key to survival online. There is a positive correlation between strong, recognised brand values and success on the Internet.

Leveraging on your brand The terms "brand extension" and "line extension" are synonymous. They refer to the practice of establishing new products under an established brand's umbrella to gain leverage from the brand's familiar values and good repute. The Shell Oil Company employed this tactic when it launched the Shell Select chain of convenience stores (see Chapter 2). This strategy makes the most of marketing dollars already invested in the brand. The potential risk of brand extension is that if one product fails it could tear down the whole brand family.

A disparate range of products shelter under the Virgin umbrella. Yet they are managed in such a way as to lead independent careers. Sir Richard Branson's personal image reflects innovation, energy, provocativeness and success upon his brand. He isn't necessarily related to a particular product or service as he was a long time ago. He has become a symbol for hundreds of companies which share the values his leadership has cultivated. Unless this remarkable personality's reputation suffers in some way, the products that reside under the Virgin brand will exist in safe independence. The demise of one won't affect another nor will it damage the overarching brand name's reputation.

Microsoft offers another example of this principle. Even though the organisation represents more than fifty brand names, its key brand is still Microsoft. In every communication from the group www.microsoft is the key URL, not www.powerpoint or www.word. Why? Because identity would be dissipated if a new URL appeared with every product. The key focus remains consistently on the core brand — Microsoft. Dependent brand names can't wrest communication control from that entity.

Five-dimensional branding A study conducted by Cheskin Research in February 2000 shows that by offering the consumer a multi-sensory experience of your product you're likely to establish your brand faster and more solidly than if the new product can only be evaluated by the consumer at a distance, using sight and, perhaps hearing. Take for example the Versace brand. Gianni Versace created not only a solid fashion brand, he went further by designing homewares, perfumes and has even opened the world's first Palazzo Versace hotel in Queensland, Australia. The hotel is based on the Versace philosophy: everything from the flooring, to the furniture, the toothbrushes and towels, dinnerware and even the food has been thoroughly controlled by the Italian Versace designer team. The result is that the Versace brand has created and controlled brand extensions that bring a five-dimensional experience of the brand to the consumer, each dimension having appeal to each of the senses.

Another Cheskin Research Study, refer back to Model 7.2, conducted for Beatnik, a sound studio company founded by Thomas Dolby, focused on the value of sound in the brand-building process. The study tested brands like Intel and NBC and concluded that short — five- to fifteen-second — signature melodies, and the effective use of audio alone can equal the impact on consumers of visual branding instruments, like logos. Similar studies by Kellogg's in Denmark on taste, smell and touch show that these senses can be as influential as hearing in influencing consumer choice and brand recognition. The sense of smell was shown to be particularly influential on consumer product choices.

Knowing that a five-dimensional brand, which appeals to all our senses, can delineate a brand identity more solidly than brands which depend simply on sight, should suggest ways to expose brands across interactive and offline channels.

Channel Conflict

If you're a retailer considering the move online, in addition to assessing whether your products are suited to online trading and how willing your consumers are to engage in Internet transactions, you'll also have to consider the political implications, internal and external, of your potential transition. And you'll have to weigh the costs of managing these conflicts against the long-term gains you expect to realise from online investment.

Many brands have struggled with the dilemma of establishing and handling their online presence without offending their existing retail network. For example, until now most car manufacturers have been dependent on their external dealerships for their consumer contact and sales. This relationship of dependence introduces political and diplomatic difficulties when the time comes to have to reduce or remove existing offline dealerships in favour of the online dealership.

The pressure on offline car dealers increased when online car websites, like Autobytel.com, launched websites based on bulk purchase of cars. These sites deal directly with manufacturers and importers. As the volumes of such online dealerships has risen, manufacturers have been more or less forced to join them, dramatically disrupting the whole dealer network and threatening to reduce the revenue of traditional car dealerships. In so doing, car manufacturers are cannibalising their own distribution platform. The next step is for consumers to purchase cars directly from the manufacturer, avoiding overheads and inefficient misunderstandings. This direct dealing will mean that consumers can order customised vehicles. You'll not only be able to specify colour, you'll be able to invent your own colour. Additionally, you'll be able to design interior features and specify inclusions.

The car industry isn't the only industry that's struggling with potential internal conflicts. The medical industry and pharmacies, the music industry, the clothing, toy and sportswear industries also have to deal with conflicts occasioned by channel strategies. So, should retailers abandon the offline sector and sell directly to the consumer via the Net, or should they retain a toehold on traditional retailing and share the revenue between their e-tail and retail identities? The latter option slows down the delivery process but keeps the existing distribution network happy.

As you may have concluded by now, the answer is not to be found in an arbitrary choice. It is to be found in examining and evaluating what roles could happily co-exist for both the retail and e-tail parties. There's no doubt that, in most cases, a combination of the online and offline representation is the most advantageous solution. The CBB Test, which is at the end of this chapter, will help you analyse the best options for your offline company.

Internal Conflict and its Effects on Competitiveness

Involving all parties in planning processes is the most successful way of ensuring general acceptance of change. Involvement means seeking all parties' views on, in this case, a company's reinvention as a clicks-&-mortar entity, and discussing each party's new role. Remember that up to 80% of revenue will still be earnt by the bricks-&-mortar, a point which should signal the importance of retaining existing infrastructure as far as possible. The predictions from most research companies indicate that over the next half-decade, a maximum of 20% of revenue will derive from the online presence.

Typically, you can categorise the political issues that arise from major business decisions into three categories: distribution conflicts, shareholder and board conflicts, and employee conflicts. Consider these in light of the pressure such conflicts will place on your competitiveness. Your strategy will have to determine how to create a solid online stream without creating enemies among your existing distribution channels. The more the existing distribution channels are involved in the process, the more likely they will be to accept and co-operate with the online development. This isn't to say, however, that you should weaken your strategic thinking and tactical manoeuvres by getting bogged down in committee consultations.

Visit **DualBook.com/cbb/ch11/DistributionConflicts** for hints on handling distribution conflicts.

Shareholder and board conflict Investor and stakeholder attitudes in bricks-&-mortar businesses are notoriously conservative. Online investment requires substantial and long-term investment which shouldn't be expected to achieve returns for years. Along with this clear understanding, investors and board members must fully appreciate that conflict resolutions are likely to engage parties throughout the organisation for some time. So consider the costs of investor conflict against the potential gains of online business. How much more profitable will an online revenue stream make the company? When will the online development begin earning money? Will the online business cannibalise existing revenue channels? How many new customers will the online business attract? How will existing offline customers respond to the online business?

Employee conflict All workplace change can engender insecurity and provoke insecurity amongst staff members. Many staff will feel threatened by the Internet as a new part of their employer company's business mix, particularly if they don't have a personal relationship with new media or use the Net. It's imperative to canvass and resolve employee concerns and to harness staff support before any strategy for change is executed. Far too often clicks-&-mortars fail because their online and offline staff work separately, unco-operatively and, ultimately, dysfunctionally. All staff, operations and communications need to share the synergy I spoke of in Chapter 6. They need to understand the whole company story and to appreciate the importance of their role in the organisation.

The key concerns of an employee would be: How will the online transition affect my role? Will anyone be retrenched? Will this new business take over the bricks-&-mortar role? What retraining will I need, and will retraining be available to me?

Evaluating Your Brand's CBB Potential

So, are you ready for the test? Answer each of the questions below by circling the number along the band that approximates your position between the question's two extremes of possibility. Then add up your points. The table at the end of this chapter will help give you an idea of your brand's CBB potential.

The retail and e-tail markets change minute by minute. So you should carry out this test regularly to help you review your position of advantage or disadvantage. Most Internet players change their strategy several times over a year in response to emerging market circumstances. For a bricks-&-mortar business that moves online, this approach will offer new and unfamiliar challenges. But remember: you will be operating in the online marketplace and the strategic responses you're used to making will not necessarily work in cyberspace.

The CBB Test

Product Attributes

1. How dependent are your product's sales on the consumer using all five senses to evaluate their buying decision?

0	1	2	3	4	5	6	7	8	9	10

very dependent on all five senses   **not dependent at all**

User Behaviour

2. How motivated would your existing consumer target group be to purchase your product online?

0	1	2	3	4	5	6	7	8	9	10

not motivated at all   **very motivated**

3. Can you identify a virtual consumer group within your target market and how motivated would this sub-group be to purchase your product online?

0	1	2	3	4	5	6	7	8	9	10

not motivated at all   **very motivated**

Product Familiarity

4. Do consumers, without prompting, name your brand as a leader in its category?

0	1	2	3	4	5	6	7	8	9	10
never										often

5. What proportion of your target consumers has purchased your product at least once?

0	1	2	3	4	5	6	7	8	9	10
none										a high proportion

6. What proportion of your target consumers are regular purchasers of your product?

0	1	2	3	4	5	6	7	8	9	10
none										a high proportion

7. What proportion of your consumer group is typically very satisfied with your product?

0	1	2	3	4	5	6	7	8	9	10
none										a high proportion

8. Do your consumers trust your product?

0	1	2	3	4	5	6	7	8	9	10
no										yes

9. Would your users say that there is no need to check out the product before purchasing it a second time?

0	1	2	3	4	5	6	7	8	9	10
no										yes

10. What proportion of your consumer group fully intend to repurchase your product?

0	1	2	3	4	5	6	7	8	9	10
none										a high proportion

11. Do your consumers see clear differences between your product and those of your competitors?

0	1	2	3	4	5	6	7	8	9	10
no										yes

12. Has your brand established clear brand symbols which distinguish it from those of your competitors?

0	1	2	3	4	5	6	7	8	9	10

no   **yes**

13. How well respected is your brand in the marketplace?

0	1	2	3	4	5	6	7	8	9	10

not respected   **highly respected**

Conflict and Competition

14. How likely do you believe it is that your brand will become one of the three online market leaders in its product category within two years?

0	1	2	3	4	5	6	7	8	9	10

unlikely   **highly likely**

15. How great do you feel your existing Internet competition is?

0	1	2	3	4	5	6	7	8	9	10

minimal   **a major threat**

16. How much conflict do you believe your online presence and a clear e-commerce focus will cause between you and your existing dealer and distribution network?

0	1	2	3	4	5	6	7	8	9	10

much conflict   **none at all**

17. How much disruption do you believe your new online presence will cause within your organisation in the short term? (Consider resource allocation, employee attitudes to the development, retraining requirements and counselling.)

0	1	2	3	4	5	6	7	8	9	10

much disruption   **none at all**

18 How tightly controlled is your company by contractual arrangements with manufacturers? Do any of your supplier deals preclude online sales by retail parties, and therefore preclude a clicks-&-mortar setup?

0	1	2	3	4	5	6	7	8	9	10

highly controlled   **flexibly controlled**

Score your CBB Test results.

18 to 45 points: very high risk
It looks like you'd face substantial problems by creating a clicks-&-mortar strategy. Why are you considering the idea? Pressure to do so from senior management and the board? A request from customers? I'm not saying that you shouldn't consider going ahead but, based on the analysis your score reveals, you would need a unique reason for embarking upon what would be high-risk clicks-&-mortar strategy.

46 to 90 points: high risk
You'll face problems creating a clicks-&-mortar. I suggest you read Chapters 4 to 8 again and follow the action points at the end of each of them. This might clarify if it's worth you going ahead.

91 to 135 points: low risk
It looks like your motivation for creating a clicks-&-mortar strategy hasn't come out of the blue. Your score indicates that your brand and business has potential for the strategy, but this is no guarantee of success. You'll have to examine a range of other factors before you proceed. I suggest that you spend some more time with chapters 3 to 8 and pay particular attention to all the action points.

136 to 180 points: minimum risk
There's no question that the risks you face in adopting a clicks-&-mortar strategy are limited. Your first step should be to revisit all the action points in all chapters before embarking on your strategy's creation. Your attention to the action points will help you compose a rationale in favour of the strategy's adoption which you can use in future dialogue with your management and board.

Summary

- The CBB Test analyses four criteria to determine how well a company and brand will coalesce with online media: product attributes, consumer behaviour, product familiarity, and conflict and competition.

- Product attributes: Is the product suited to online distribution? How relevant are the five senses in comprehending the product?

- Consumer behaviour: What traits characterise the consumer group? What are their likely conversion rates and what are their concerns about online trust and privacy?

- Product familiarity: How familiar are consumers with the product, product category and brand?

- Conflict and competition: What advantages will an online presence give a company over its competition and what are the costs of distribution, employee and investor conflicts?

- The physical distance between the consumer and the product which online trading necessitates not only affects the consumer's perception of the product, but also of the service being provided. Dealing with intangible products and unseen service providers still requires many consumers to take a leap of faith. Issues of trust and privacy concern consumers in varying degrees and must be respected and addressed if you are inviting them to follow you online.

- Inject additional trust-builders online: special guarantees, rules and guidelines that build the online user's confidence in the service they can expect from the online store.

- If you feel you can't deliver the same quality of product, service, backup or consumer know-how online as you do in your bricks-&-mortar store, team up with partners who can help you. Your service quality online will have to exceed offline customers' expectations to win and keep them there.

- If consumers are already regular users of interactive media they will enter the online environment comfortably. If consumers rarely use interactive media, their inexperience and reticence should be accommodated in any online development strategy and investment.

- If a customer is purchasing a product for the first time, the consumer's selection processes will be counting on the judgment of all five senses.

- A brand's good reputation justifies moving its product online. Companies that have built their brands over time are in an excellent position to take advantage of future changes in shopping habits. As consumers become more familiar with online shopping there will be an even greater premium attached to established reputation.

Chapter 12

The Websters

The pivotal difference between what was and what will be resides in one concept: interactivity. The next generation is populated by, let's call them websters, e-teens to whom interactivity is an incontrovertible modus operandi. They belong to a generation born with the Internet for whom mobile Internet technologies will be as necessary to their households as the video recorder was to their parents'. How will websters influence the future of clicks-&-mortar industry?

They are born and bred with interactive technology. They were online long before they started school and they probably spend more time online than they do in the classroom. Websters are the 4-I generation: they expect everything to be instant, interactive, involving and interesting. If your brand doesn't fulfil these criteria, it's likely never to capture the Webster sector — ever!

Why this chapter? Because we need to assess the emerging consumer trends of the next generation — the kids who've been born in the shadow of the Internet. The questions their parents' generation asked —What is a browser? How do I use ICQ (the online chatroom run by AOL)? How do I avoid a virus? — simply aren't part of the e-teens' lexicon. They're familiar with the online mindset from infancy. This is a generation that will determine what will and won't work in the brand-building future. But interestingly enough they are also the generation that, according to an AC Nielsen study (July 2000), prefers, in 45% of cases, to shop at a clicks-&-mortar site rather than at a pure Net site.

> *In 45% of cases Websters prefer to shop at a clicks-&-mortar site rather than a pure Net site.*

The Pokémon phenomenon is a vignette of the Webster's online/offline position. Most toy brands have introduced interactive toys. There's LEGO Mindstorms, Disney Blast, Sony's PlayStation and Mattel's CD-Barbies, for example. But when Nintendo did the unexpected and introduced an offline toy, Pokémon cards, within a few weeks the offline product was outstripping sales of interactive gadgets. The Harry Potter craze followed closely, putting books rather than Game Boys into kids' hands.

What does this teach us? Right when we were thinking that everything has to be online to succeed, the new generation displays offline preferences. Does the fact that kids love collecting and swapping Pokémon cards and getting lost in Harry's adventures indicate that they're already over online mania? Of course, new toys and crazes often enjoy remarkable initial popularity. But it appears that we're facing a future that recognises the desirability of an off- and online balance. Both environments have their strengths, and getting the best from each of them means using them for what they each do best. As websters are showing us, online fun needs offline balance and a clicks-&-mortar future offers branding its best survival strategy.

A Symbiotic Relationship Between KB Toys and KBkids.com

Since 1922, in one form or another, KB Toys has operated exclusively as a mortar-based retailer catering to the highly price-sensitive toy market.

Rather than begin building their virtual store from scratch, KB chose to invest US$80 million in a joint venture with BrainPlay, an existing Internet startup company with a sophisticated technical base and a management team well placed to deal with the challenges of the e-commerce environment. BrainPlay and KB Toys chose to operate their joint venture under the name KBkids.com. By dropping the more limiting word "toy", and replacing it with the more generic "kids", the company allowed itself greater flexibility and opportunity to e-tail all kinds of children's products.

On one level KBkids.com and KB Toys operate quite independently from each other. They have separate management teams and are in separate locations. There's a 2,000-mile space between them. But the clicks and the mortar stores constitute a well-integrated operation. With over 1,300 retail stores, KB Toys is a highly recognised brand that's earned consumer trust and loyalty. Each KB Toys store carries in-house displays and advertising that promotes the virtual store. KBkids.com returns the favour with a "What's happening in the stores" column on their home page.

Kbkids.com and KB Toys have also developed a well-integrated customer service. The real stores serve as local depots for returns and complaints, the website driving customers from the virtual store into the real store for this service.

In addition to this seamless off- and online service and well co-ordinated cross-promotion, Kbkids.com enjoys the extraordinary advantage of being able to capitalise on the established relationships developed over many years between KB Toys and toy manufacturers. Conversely, the website's achievement in building extra business has given KB Toys the advantage of greater buying power and the resultant ability to negotiate exclusives and special deals.

KBkids.com offers a model of balance between integration and separation of the online and offline channels.

Learnt Interactivity

The pivotal difference between what was and what will be in the consumer and marketing worlds resides in one concept: interactivity. Unfortunately, most education systems around the world don't yet embrace this all-pervading concept. Education in junior and senior years is still, in the main, informed by a passive view of information acquisition. Yet almost all toys on the market today are interactive: they can engage in a continuous two-way information transfer with the user, familiarising young people with interactive processes from an early age.

In 2000, PlayStation was the most popular interactive game station in the world. In late 2000 LEGO introduced the world's first film studio for kids. Neatly supported by Steven Spielberg, the LEGO film studio is a place for young filmmakers to mount their own productions, create animations, film and edit their work. The next generation of the Furby is now on its way, not only talking, but interacting, communicating with other Furbies. And it has a memory similar to Sony's Digital Dog, Aibo, introduced in early 1999. The dog has a "memory stick" (a disc) which stores its learnings. It records data on individuals' behaviour and "learns" to respond differently to each playmate. The memory stick gives it a virtual life to remember, including its master's preferences and habits. The stick can be exchanged with your best friend's Sony dog so that you could borrow other dogs for an hour or two's play.

And then there was the iMode telephone craze which turned Japan upside-down throughout 1999 and 2000 and changed the way most kids understand wireless communication. Created by DoCoMo, a subsidiary of NTT in Japan, iMode now has about 15 million users all captivated by images, characters, written messages, games and icons the technology allows you to send your iMode phone-owning friends. There's more on iMode technology in Chapter 7.

Amusing yet serious stuff. The serious edge to these toys is that they habituate children to technology and its interactive premise, and teach them an understanding of the value of personalisation.

CASE STUDY: DoCoMo

Mobile Clicks: Japan's Unwired Future

The world may now be a global village, but access to the Web is handier and easier in Japan, which also constitutes the world's second biggest mobile phone market.

In 1999 NTT DoCoMo, the largest phone operator in Japan, with 30 million voice subscribers, launched iMode, a Web-based information service. By pressing the "i" button on their mobile phones, iMode subscribers are instantly logged onto DoCoMo's gateway server to the Internet. The access is continuous, and the user only pays for the information they retrieve.

The response to this service has been nothing short of startling. In the first year, 5.5 million users signed up for iMobile packages. Drawn from a vast cross-section of the population, working-class people, business people, teenagers and housewives, chose to bypass expensive ISPs and clunky PCs with their dial-up connections, and embraced the small screens that would give them access to the World Wide Web via their unwired *keitai* (mobile phones).

Initially the service offered little more than the most rudimentary sites. But now there's a whole generation of content providers who are fully conversant with cHTML (Compact Hypertext Markup Language), a simpler format for speedier delivery to mobile phones. Commenting on wireless content, Nigel Rudstrom, vice president of Nokia Mobile Communications, says, "The applications provided so far are only the tip of the iceberg".

Demographics have played a major role in Japan's wireless revolution, a place with a massive concentration of mobile phones. Thirty million users in the Tokyo area alone ensure an unwired future that takes e-commerce one step further into the realms of m-commerce where the challenge is to capture the consumer on the move. The essence of mobile commerce lies in the short spaces of time m-tailers have in which to interest consumers and secure sales: the brief intervals in which commuters are waiting for trains, for example; or the minutes teenagers spend waiting to meet friends.

Weather reports and music purchases aside, the prospects of direct-link advertising are overwhelming. The path from seller to consumer has never been as direct. Magnus Nervé at Nippon Ericsson says, "For the first time in history, companies can have direct access to people's pockets".

The unwired revolution in Japan is heralding a new way of using the Net. Mobile phones already outnumber fixed-line phones in Japan. Shortly unwired Web users will outnumber wired users.

DoCoMo has a very high-profile brand, and is now the largest Japanese ISP. In October 1999 it entered a joint venture with Microsoft which was christened Mobimagic. In November 2000 it acquired a major stake in AT&T and teamed up with AOL USA creating a new local joint venture. Mobimagic will bring the Windows operating system to the mobile network. It's entirely possible that together these two companies will set the standard for the global m-future.

Visit **DualBook.com/cbb/ch12/WirelessClicksAndMortar** for more on the wireless clicks-&-mortar trend spreading across Asia.

Websters Online

The Internet is the first medium that television has ever shared at-home viewing time with. AC Nielsen reports that 25% of prime television viewing time, from 7:30pm to 9:00pm, has been usurped by Internet surfing and 55%

of teenagers (thirteen to eighteen year olds) prefer surfing the Net to watching television.

Model 12.1: *Websters' Internet Attitudes. Percentage who agree that the Internet is …*

	Total	Males	Females	Ages 13–14	Ages 15–19
Sample Sizes	*2759*	*539*	*2220*	*1118*	*1641*
	%	%	%	%	%
Fun	80	82	80	85	77
Where the future is headed	79	82	78	78	79
Important connection to my friends	74	67	75	74	73
Creative	74	73	74	77	71
Gives me freedom	69	72	69	67	70
Better than watching TV	55	58	55	56	55
A cool place to be	52	57	51	57	48
Better than going to the mall	19	33	15	17	20
Becoming boring	17	15	17	15	18
A place to make money	11	25	8	12	11

Source: Teens and the Future of the Web,
Cheskin Research and Able Minds, August 1999

Today's teens and kids (five to twelve year olds) are leading a communication and entertainment revolution. They are the first generation to embrace the Internet as an everyday tool, regarding online shopping as the norm, expecting to conduct much research for school assignments on the Net and maintaining friendships via e-mail.

> *Importantly for clicks-&-mortar businesses, websters are the first generation to have begun their consumer-lives with online shopping as a part of everyday life.*

The Internet has taken the age-old concept of pen pals a step further, allowing for instant communication across cultural and geographic boundaries. Jupiter Research claims that almost 70% of teenagers go online to read and write e-mails, and 50% will typically head for a chatroom during an Internet session. A survey conducted in Northern Europe by AIM Nielsen in 1999 shows that 15% of the teenagers interviewed ask new friends for their e-mail addresses rather than their phone numbers, and participants cited that 7% of contact with friends is via e-mail and other Internet tools.

Model 12.2: *Websters' Time Online*

	Total	Males	Females	Ages 13–14	Ages 15–19
Sample Sizes	*2759*	*539*	*2220*	*1118*	*1641*
			hours per week		
Email friends	4.3	3.6	4.4	4.3	4.3
Surf	3.7	3.8	3.6	3.7	3.6
Hang out in chat room	3.2	3.2	3.2	3.4	3.0
Listen to music	3.2	3.2	3.2	3.3	3.1
Other	2.7	2.8	2.7	3.0	2.6
Play games	2.6	3.1	2.4	2.7	2.4
Download music	2.4	2.5	2.3	2.4	2.3
Homework	2.3	2.2	2.4	2.3	2.3
Read magazines	2.0	1.7	2.1	2.1	1.9
Create/redesign website	1.9	2.0	1.9	2.0	1.9

Source: Teens and the Future of the Web,
Cheskin Research and Able Minds, August 1999

Although the Internet offers websters a valuable research and communication tool, it exposes them to disadvantages that past generations haven't experienced. For instance, there are currently more than 8,000 websites offering homework and examination support. Students can purchase exam papers and finished essays, paying on a sliding scale, depending on what marks they expect. Although teachers may have suspicions, it's difficult to prove student Internet fraud beyond a doubt.

Education: Is It Preparing Kids for the Real and Virtual Aspects of Their Lives?

As Jack Winebaum, former president of Disney Online, observed, "The kids we know are changing and so is our world. A seven-year-old school boy was overheard asking, 'Where can I click in my book to get more information?'"

Computers are influencing children's skills and learning patterns. For example, LEGO conducted research on a group of children in 1996, and found that gross motor skills such as those used in juggling, had been replaced by a new set of skills including accelerated reaction speeds, advanced understanding of 3D environments, and quicker but superficial comprehension of large amounts of data.

Websters are fast icon readers, trained in the art of recognising branding as well as programming instructions and facile web navigators, but they lack patience and creativity.

But are education systems preparing for a globally networked society? It seems that education hasn't adapted to the reality that a huge amount of the world's information is at the Internet user's fingertips. Our education systems need to incorporate information technology into the curriculum from junior to senior levels, not only to teach children IT skills, but to ensure young adults are prepared for the networked work environment as well as having an intricate understanding of Internet as one of many communication tools. The Internet must be used an educational tool and its management must form part of curricula.

At higher educational levels, there are problems in fine-tuning technology training. The rapid rate of change in the information technology industry means that courses struggle to communicate developments and leave students with obsolete and redundant skills.

Webster Consumers

Jupiter Research forecasts the number of websters online will double to more than sixteen million by 2002. Importantly for clicks-&-mortar businesses, teenagers will be the first generation to begin their consumer-lives with online shopping as a natural and expected part of everyday life.

Webster Buying Power

The teen market has substantial buying power. Teenage Research Unlimited, a Chicago-based research firm, estimates that today's thirty-one million teenagers spent $141 billion in 1998, up almost $20 billion from 1997. In a few years, they'll constitute the adult households that propel and sustain company growth, and clicks-&-mortar stores are likely to be their preferred shopping providers. Jupiter Research estimates that teens will start spending more of that cash online, forecasting that Webster Net shopping in the United States will grow nineteen-fold and reach $1.2 billion by 2002, with music being the most popular purchase choice. Children in the USA will account for US$100 million of e-commerce's dollars.

Jupiter Research data, unveiled at the IT Expo Digital Kids '99, showed that marketers are actively targeting teens and children for digital transactions, and that teens and children are spending more time and money online. According to a Jupiter/NFO Consumer Survey from 2000, of the 600 teens and kids interviewed, 67% of teens and 37% of kids that use the Internet indicated they had researched or purchased products online. This growing direct involvement in e-commerce will open opportunities for marketers that will be troublesome for parents.

As the Webster market is a lucrative growth sector for online spending, and because the Internet is becoming more and more integrated into the family home, parents will need to closely monitor how their children use it. Over one year, parental concern regarding child-targeted advertising more than doubled, from 17% in 1998 to 45% in 1999. Despite the lucrative revenue opportunity that child-targeted advertising represents, engaging kids in online spending is a challenging

24% of Websters don't trust the Internet.

proposition. Online players that are looking to target these younger consumers risk alienating parents, creating a negative brand image (i.e., one that appears to exploit minors) and fostering greedy customers.

Fortunately, kids are sceptical about what to believe and what not to believe on the Internet. A 1999 Time/CNN study on teenagers between thirteen and seventeen years of age, showed that only 13% of kids trusted the Internet a "great deal" while 24% didn't trust the Net at all.

The Webster Personality Profile

A Cheskin study conducted in August 1999 interviewed 2,759 teens between the ages of thirteen and nineteen. It concluded, unsurprisingly, that teens are not all the same. A rich understanding of teenage communities, individual and group relationships, behaviours, attitudes and cliques, will help clicks-&-mortars identify and anticipate Webster consumption trends.

The same cliques and peer groups that populate high schools are alive and well on the Net. There are five distinct teen segments identified in the study as: the explorers, the visibles, the status quos, the non-teens and the isolators.

Explorers are characterised by a high degree of creativity and independence. They're more likely than the other teen segments to differ from the norm, but not through dysfunctional behaviour or adult-emulating behaviour. This segment constitutes approximately 10% of the teenage population, but it's highly influential within teen culture primarily because of its counterculture appearance and behaviour. These teens are passionately committed to issues and controversies. They build their self-identity and public image around their principles, but are prone to rapidly and repeatedly change their social priorities.

Visibles tend to be the most noticeable members of a teen population, due to their looks, their personalities or their athletic abilities. Until recently, this segment represented the largest percentage of the teen population, but it has declined significantly in recent years and is now believed to represent approximately 30% of teenagers. The teens in this segment are popular and well-known, although not all their peers like them. They are commonly referred to as the "cool kids" and they grow up to account for about 20% of the total population.

Status quos display traditional values of moderation and pride in achievement. Mainstream acceptance is important to them. The status quo segment has increased in recent years and they now represent roughly 38% of the teen population. The segment represents about 35% of the total population.

Non-teens are most unlike the typical teenager, usually because of their lack of social skills, indifference to teen culture and style and/or their intense interest in academic pursuits. The non-teens tend to behave like adults and exhibit a preference for adult or parental environments. They are estimated to include roughly 22% of the teen population.

Isolators are teens who are alienated from both their peers and adults by their disruptive or dysfunctional behaviour. They are particularly hostile towards adult and societal expectations. This group accounts for approximately 5-10% of the teen population. Although the isolator segment is predominantly male, the Cheskin study indicates that females are becoming more numerous within this group. Isolators are the teens that are most commonly associated with societal problems. These teenagers tend to come from abusive homes, have low self-esteem and experience continual problems with authority.

Model 12.3: *Teen Acceptance Trend Curve*

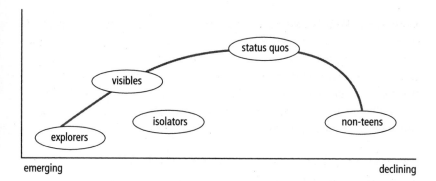

Source: Teens and the Future of the Web, *Cheskin Research and Able Minds, August 1999*

Webster Attitudes to Online Communication

The same Cheskin study revealed the following interesting observations:

The future of the web lies in social interaction. Just as in the real world when they're on the Web teens focus on social activities. In addition to using the Internet as a tool for information gathering, e-commerce and schoolwork, teens also view the Net as means of keeping in touch with their friends. This automatic resort to online interaction could hold significant implications for the future of clicks-&-mortar concepts. For example clicks-&-mortar stores might find a role as meeting places for people with mutual interests. Barnes & Noble have already installed relaxing, comfortably furnished corners where customers can sit and read. But what about toy stores, fashion stores and car dealerships? Imagine the potential for these stores to become contact centres for target markets. The role of the bricks-&-mortar store in the clicks-&-mortar future could be in combining social activities with e-commerce.

Online advertising needs a coherent and authoritative voice to attract teens. While a significant percentage of websters click on banner ads, most find Internet advertising annoying and uninformative. Today's teenage generation is acutely aware of, sceptical about, and consequently immune to marketing hype. This finding should alert marketers to an apparent need to rethink their Internet advertising approach. The maturing consumer generation demands authoritative, consistent information from both clicks and bricks players.

Surfing the Web is better than watching TV A majority of teens (55%) stated a preference for Internet surfing over watching television. Rather than passively being fed a daily dose of entertainment, websters are looking for and creating more interactive entertainment opportunities on the Internet. Websters like the interactivity and expect it in the real world, in the form of interactive events, shows, instore surprises, multimedia stores, constantly changing store entertainments, and so on.

Websters value privacy and freedom on the web Loss of privacy on the Internet is one of the websters' biggest fears. However, where adults equate Web privacy with e-commerce payment and personal information security issues, teens view privacy on the Web in much the same way they do in the real world: as loss of dignity and personal freedom. They consider the Internet a place that gives them freedom. Clicks-&-mortar brands which communicate a respect for freedom are well-regarded by the teenage market.

Teens are the next online entrepreneurs 43% of websters have their own websites and many of them (29% according to the Cheskin Research report) intend to start an online business in the near future. Around half of the teenagers surveyed felt that the Internet was a critical component of their future.

Clicks-&-Mortars and Webster Consumers

Since 55% of teens consider the Internet a critical part of their future, what should online e-tailing and offline retailing expect from them in the future?

Online Teen Personality and Expectations

What characterises websters' attitudes to the web and online consumerism? This is the first interactive generation. Until now children have been used to receiving information passively, from one source at a time. Interactive environments provide multiple information sources which engage the user in continuous two-way information transfers.

The webster personality is underscored by the expectations and responses it has learnt from interactive environments: expectations of immediate satisfaction, of having every query or demand answered without delay. Websters expect ongoing version upgrades in all things; they expect simple navigation to help them locate what they're after with ease; they have very high expectations of service and product performance; they have a demanding curiosity that expects immediate answers; and they want constant entertainment and diversion. Their responses are a product of the skills and weaknesses they've learnt from the interactive environment: they're fast icon readers, trained in the art of recognising branding as well as programming instructions; they're facile web navigators; they lack patience and creativity; and they're inclined to be materialistic, having been accustomed to the concept that everything is available for sale.

Websters have ultra-high expectations of service and product performance; they expect answers now; and they expect to be entertained and diverted constantly.

So, to win over the webster consumer, retailing, like every other facet of everyday life, will need to adapt to interactive expectations. Assuming that this two-way modus operandi describes the communications future, consider how much of today's one-way entertainment tools will have to change: movies, radio, television, theme parks, toys, books, theatre and sports. And, of course, shopping. I'll discuss the interactive shopping experience later in this chapter and in Chapter 15.

Websters *want* and they want *now* Overall, parents generally accede to their children's demands when shopping. But it doesn't stop there. Continuing the shopping context, today's generation of kids are characterised by a presumption that everything and everyone should respond to their demands: the products, the shelves, the brands and the websites. If they have a question they expect a qualified answer, pronto. If they have a complaint, and websters have a well-cultivated sense of their consumer and social rights, they wouldn't waste time resolving their dissatisfaction with the store, they'd just go elsewhere. Yes, they're an unforgiving consumer group. They rarely exhibit patience: more than a couple of seconds is an unacceptable eternity. I'm describing an observable trend rather than measured behavioural characteristics. Technology has fostered this "now" mindset and my question is, how will these traits affect the way retail is conducted?

Websters network Websters conduct much of their social interaction via their mobile phones or PCs. They're not only connected to their local friends; they're connected to friends all over the world. And, please note. I use the word "friends" advisedly. These are personalities kids know and trust. They're not just acquaintances you might encounter at the park or mall. They listen to each other and find soul mates in cyberspace as well as in real life. These connections give websters access to intelligence, including product information, from diverse sources. The implication for retailing is that websters are educated consumers. They research product specifications and have an expectation of value.

Websters lack creativity Toy manufacturers observed long ago that kids' fantasy lives are changing. Websters' parents primarily entertained themselves, playing together on the street or in the woods, much as previous generations of children had done. But websters are bored by two minutes of gadget-free, activity-free time. Toy manufacturers refer to the e-kids' recourse to prepared, packaged play as "pre-programmed fantasy", and the industry has had to do some fancy footwork and quick thinking to keep up with the demands of their consumer base.

LEGO learnt this in 1987 when interactive pocket games from Japan crashed their holiday season sales. But the warning wasn't clear enough, because in 1996 the LEGO Group's fifty-year history of constantly increasing sales reached a turning point. Even though LEGO had several years of interactive development behind it, the group's sales decreased, an unprecedented event. It wasn't until late 2000 that the LEGO Group's sales began showing a slow increase. Between 1995 and 2000 LEGO responded to the apparent change in children's preferences by altering the size of the famous blocks. The LEGO you buy today comes in sets which contain a smaller number of larger blocks rather than a larger number of smaller blocks. In the past you needed lots and lots of the smaller blocks to make the model depicted on the box. Now you only need a few blocks to make the model. Why? Because Websters don't have the patience to build the helicopter, space station or castle out of the many smaller blocks. More alarmingly, they appear to lack the creativity to build something of their own invention from scratch. That's the pre-programmed fantasy principle in operation.

Websters need entertainment Every element in the future consumer's shopping experience will have to be part of a bigger picture. Even the most pedestrian of products will need an exciting store context to survive. If not, the webster generation will find the product irrelevant. So be prepared to hear more about theme stores, theme departments, theme employees, theme weeks, theme days and even theme hours. Websters couldn't be expected to go to a store and put up with the same entertainment they received on their last visit. Websters are possibly the most demanding consumer generation in history. They want to be diverted, to feel special and to be remembered.

Websters are icon readers Being used to responding to visual prompts on PC screens and mobile phone displays, websters are fast icon, logo and illustration readers. Websters' icon-literacy means that offline stores will have to develop visual language skills and use the iconography they develop consistently.

Websters want added value Being cognisant of the threat posed by diminishing personal shopping visits, an increasing number of offline retailers are working to transform the shopping experience and reclaim some of the glamour they offered shoppers a century ago. The message is that, for Websters, there has to be tangible added value in visiting a real world store, like instore entertainment for example. Big selections, competitive prices and high quality are not reason enough for Websters to visit a store. Websters deal with these criteria every day at online stores. To survive the websters, retailers will have to find their niches and drive them to their extremes.

Websters choose brands Brands dominate e-teen product choices. Today kids shop in a brand jungle which hardly existed fifteen years ago. Generic toys have been branded: building blocks are LEGO; games are Nintendo;

space is Star Wars; even lollipops are Chupa Chups. Branding awareness influences kids' shopping behaviour: their shopping inspirations and their consumer aspirations are directed by an acquisitive attitude to brands. And brand awareness goes hand-in-hand with the icon literacy I discussed earlier.

Model 12.4: *Top Webster Web Sites*

The Internet is of a social nature for teens. Not surprisingly Yahoo! and Hotmail top the list of their favourite websites.

Females	**Males**
1. yahoo.com	1. yahoo.com
2. hotmail.com	2. hotmail.com
3. cyberteens.com	3. cyberteens.com
4. mtv.com	4. starwars.com
5. seventeen.com	5. wwf.com
6. gurl.com	6. angelfire.com
7. bolt.com	7. zone.com
8. teen.com	8. mtv.com
9. nsync.com	9. espn.com
10. teenmag.com	10. ebay.com

Source: Teens and the Future of the Web,
Cheskin Research and Able Minds, August 1999

The Interactive Shopping Experience

The future consumer will need to clearly perceive benefit, an added value, from visiting the offline store. In the shopping environment of the future, products will be demonstrated in context. This demonstration role will be the purpose of the real-world store. It won't be there to sell. In fifteen years' time there won't be cash registers in most stores. Their *raison d'être* will be to inspire purchases, made via the Net either from the store using the customer's mobile phone, or from the customer's home PC.

As a result, retailers will concentrate intensely on presentation, image and architecture. Long shelves full of products, aisle after aisle, won't be part of the store's future layout. Products in context will be the focus — displays will illustrate how products are used, and how they'll look in the consumer's home. The crucial fact will be that the contextual displays will show consumers how products are relevant to them.

Presentation and Context

Retail stores will need to be inspiring, creative, fun and original to fulfil their role of stimulating purchases. Remember, the websters of today are the consumers of tomorrow. They generally won't have fantasy lives of their own, or much creative ability in which to invest their imaginative impulses. So clicks-&-mortar stores will need to communicate product information through contextual displays that explicitly demonstrate how the product is relevant to the customer. If a retailer doesn't hit the right chord, their competitor may, so customers will be lassoed by making them see product potential.

Not only will product display, presentation and demonstrations have to tell the product's story by giving it a clear context, products themselves will need to be a part of product chain reactions. You can already see this in action. When buying your first Pokémon set of cards you automatically need another one or two. Then you need a Pokémon folder to keep your cards in. Then there is the Pokémon film to see, the poster about the film, the figurines you saw on the poster, the outfits the figurines are wearing …

When a story starts for a Webster, it has to continue. Isolated products that don't have their context explained, won't be relevant to the future consumer. To be visible, products will have to either be the result of a preceding product or lead to a new one. This will be possible with the advent of one to one e-tailing, soon to be a reality and discussed in Chapter 15. Cross-selling and upselling will be based on what individual consumers purchased minutes, days or weeks ago. All this data on consumer behaviour will be available online.

> *When a story starts for a Webster, it has to continue.*

But the most important reason for every product having to be part of a chain reaction is because the familiarity that context creates will foster loyalty. Loyalty, as we know, is inextricably related to trust. Trust, as we know, is the retailer's and e-tailer's most precious acquisition. In the future, no one will be able to afford to shift their customer focus constantly. Retaining a constant consumer group will be a survival tactic, and that will only happen when retailers understand their users and their needs. Additionally, consumers will need to feel part of the product's story for it to have any relevance to them.

Brand and Story

All this leads me to the story. Integrating your offline store and all your other concept's sites (the website, the mobile Internet phone, WebTV, etc.) will be crucial to achieving clicks-&-mortar synergy. (See also Chapter 6.) Let me give you an example. Do you recall the movie *The Game* starring

Michael Douglas? While it was screening in cinemas a website was built to promote the movie. The movie was about a guy who became a part of a game. The game turned into reality and suddenly the guy couldn't see where the game ended and real life began. So the site was established to reflect the movie's theme. When you visited the site you would be asked to sign up, just as Michael Douglas did in the movie. Then you would hear nothing until, one day, you received a strangely personal question from an anonymous contact. The game then became part of your reality.

Future stores will have to adopt this thoroughly themed approach. Today we would perhaps refer to the principle as escapism, and there might still be some relevance in the word. After all, visiting stores will become a pastime for the future shopper, an escape, a recreational experience. It will be the bricks-&-mortar store's job to create a stage and a story that involves the consumer in a new reality.

Synergy between all your channels will be, once again, vital if your clicks-&-mortar is to be legible to consumers. You will need a channel integration strategy which clearly states how to conduct communications with your consumers across all media. Every icon you use — your logo, your signage, your colours — will have to be accounted for as part of your well-planned strategy. Why? Because you will be communicating your presence via screens: on the mobile phone's display, on television and PC monitors. Your icons will have to be entirely synonymous with your identity because these will be your chief means of communicating your presence to the icon-literate future consumer.

Immediate Answers

Every product in the offline store will be integrated with the store's online identity, on the web and on the mobile Internet phone (There's more about this angle on m-commerce in Chapter 7.) This will mean that consumers' complex questions will receive answers on the spot. Staff won't fulfil this function as the questions will be too many and too complex for employees to be adequately prepared for. Don't forget that fifty new products find their way into western countries' markets every week. And consumer queries won't just be about price. They'll want to know how much fat there is in the product; where the cheapest price for the item is to be found within a specified area, and so on, ad infinitum. Which leads me to discuss the importance of online data retrieval and networks.

Peer-to-Peer

This topic presages the next chapter. Imagine a retail system that could tell you where you could get a product for the cheapest price in the world. Now imagine you could ask your friends what they thought about the product right there and then, in the display store. All possible, because the future consumer will roll into stores with their PDAs (personal digital assistants) or their mobiles which will be constantly hooked to the Internet. Every time consumers see a product they'll be able to research it to their hearts' content. Already WAP and iMode technology makes permanent mobile Internet access possible so we're well on our way to future shopping.

Electronic networking will be the vehicle for the websters' social networking. They're used to sharing information and the buzzword "P2P", peer-to-peer, describes their interactive communication flow. Shopping of the future will be a matter of research and recommendation as much as impulse. Brands haven't yet begun to build upon user knowledge, but the millions of websters exchanging ideas every second via the Net offers brand-building untapped promotional potential.

Already, Net consumers receive e-mails from companies asking for opinions and information; most chatrooms do the same. Eventually, jaded websters will need to be motivated by some

Peer-to-peer — knowledge shared between users.

form of reward for contributing their knowledge to a brand. The reward will be knowledge, inspiration, ideas or money. Knowledge, shared between users, is the Internet's currency. Peer-to-peer is the exchange of ideas and knowledge between users. The potential for clicks-&-mortars lies in exploiting the leverage they gain from the recommendations of consumers, every online customer being an interactive testimonial source.

Your Store Version 1.1

Your offline store will have to change every day, every hour if possible. The consumer will be visiting your store to be entertained and inspired, not to buy. Already today some of London's hottest clothing stores change their look every week. The future consumer will want a reason to come back to your store. And because the Internet has eradicated the two chief choice drivers, price and selection, the store will be left to offer visitors new and stimulating experiences and sensory gratification. Remember I talked about the five senses in Chapter 8? It will be sensory appeal that differentiates bricks-&-mortar stores from their online partners and competitors.

Easy Navigation and Rapid Communication

First tell me where the vegetables are in your usual grocery store and then where the magazines are. I'll bet your two answers were the vegetables are right where I walk in, and the magazines are just by the checkouts. Am I right? Probably, because 95% of grocery stores stick with a planogram that dictates this layout. It works because customers are familiar with it, and retailers are comfortable with what they know. Clicks-&-mortars will have to translate this layout logic to their other media channels so that webster consumers can find their way around with ease. Even established clicks-&-mortars rarely understand how to integrate and standardise their navigation flow across all channels, online and offline. Easy, logical and consistent navigation will be vital in determining the success of clicks-&-mortar strategies.

Future consumers, being the impatient, demanding websters of today, will probably give retailers thirty seconds' worth of consideration. This will be an offline concession to the real world. They'll give online stores less time to meet their needs, pique their curiosity or attract their interest. The mobile phone display will be given less time again. All a clicks-&-mortar's goodies will have to be declared upfront, with a blast. And the question of whether the goodies attract or bore a consumer shouldn't arise. Data research systems will help target consumers and feed relevant information to them via all media channels accordingly.

Knowledge and Volume

As we've seen, 78% of a parent's shopping decisions are forced, advised or encouraged by their children. Will this be the same case when the websters are parents? Their children too may influence their consumption habits, already characterised by high expectations of service and product performance. Clicks-&-mortars need to be prepared to satisfy those expectations, and the key to preparation will be knowledge and volume.

> *78% of a parent's shopping decisions are influenced by their children.*

Knowledge

In the future, it won't be enough that brands talk *at* consumers. Websters will demand personal attention if their loyalty is to be won. So brands will have to talk with and listen to consumers, learn about their needs and preferences, and respond to them. The same will apply to clicks-&-mortar partners, retailers offering contextualised product demonstrations and e-tailers following up with information and sales service to suit the individual.

Retailing will be treated as a science, with analysts determining consumer habits, trends, purchase patterns and product preferences. Space management, introduced in Europe in the eighties and nineties, was thought by some retailers to be outlandishly analytical. But this was the modest beginning of the "scientification" of offline commerce. The next task will be to develop systems which enable predictions about instore consumer behaviour. Systems which equip retailers with the knowledge of what consumers will buy before the customers know themselves.

A thorough understanding of consumer purchase patterns will be essential. Already, many stores are selling consumer profiling data that outlines purchase patterns to research companies like AC Nielsen. And this is just the beginning. Retail outlets will need built-in mechanisms which can, at any time, come up with information on what particular consumers think, prefer and dislike. This won't be about storing data on huge servers and acting upon it in a year's time. By the end of every week consumer profiles should have prompted revised instore strategies, all of which will have to be communicated with the clicks-&-mortar's other media channels to maintain consistency at the consumer interface. This way, the clicks-&-mortar enterprise will adjust instore strategies to ensure return visitation and prompt sales or will know why a customer is unlikely to repeat their visit. Consumer streams will change hour by hour, because the information flow between the clicks-&-mortar business and the consumer, and between the consumers' communication networks with each other, will affect purchase patterns. If one consumer discovers an attractive offer in one store, ten friends will know about it within minutes, ten more each of those friends' friends will know and ten of the friends of the each of the friends' friends will know within hours. Remember the Love Bug virus which appeared in mid-2000? Consumer communications will operate with similar rapidity.

Volume

This asset belongs chiefly to large retailers and chains. With more than 1500 toy stores in 25 countries, Toys "R" Us and giants like it, can support large volumes of stock. Volume enables the flexibility necessary for quick market responses. Pokémon, for instance, might not be hot by the time you read this. It's hot today. If it takes a month to get distribution of a product up and running, you're likely to end up with a surfeit of lukewarm product on your hands. Toys "R" Us, Gap, Sainsbury's, Tesco, H&M — you can name the retail giants yourself — all have well established supply-demand systems which enable them to respond within a few days to flash-in-the-pan crazes as well as long-held demands. As soon as the *Star Wars* movie hits the screens, the retail giants' shelves answer predicted demand with merchandise. The only way to achieve this distribution speed is by having the means to dispose of volume.

Summary

- We face a future that recognises the desirability of an off- and online balance.

- The pivotal difference between what was and what will be, in the consumer and marketing worlds, resides in one concept: interactivity.

- The computer is influencing children's skills and learning patterns: gross motor skills, such as those used in juggling, are being replaced by a new set of skills including accelerated reaction speeds, advanced understanding of 3D environments, and quicker but superficial comprehension of large amounts of data.

- Importantly for clicks-&-mortar businesses, websters will be the first generation to begin their consumer-lives with online shopping being a natural and expected part of everyday life.

- Today's thirty-one million teenagers spent $141 billion in 1998, up almost $20 billion from 1997 and estimates are that websters will start spending more of that cash online. Forecasts indicate that Webster Net shopping in the States will grow nineteen-fold and reach $1.2 billion by 2002. US kids will account for US$100 million of e-commerce's dollars.

- As the webster market is a lucrative growth sector for online spending and because the Internet is becoming more and more integrated into the family home, parents will need to closely monitor how their children use the Internet. Fortunately, kids are sceptical about what to believe and what not to believe on the Internet. A 1999 Time/CNN study on teenagers, between thirteen and seventeen years of age, showed that only 13% of kids trusted the Internet a "great deal" while 24% didn't trust the Net at all.

- The future of the web lies in social interaction.

- Fifty-five per cent of websters prefer Internet surfing to watching television.

- Websters value privacy and freedom on the Web as they do in real life.

- Forty-three per cent of websters have their own websites and 29% of them intend to start an online business.

- The e-teen personality is underscored by the expectations and responses it has learnt from interactive environments; expectations of immediate satisfaction, of having every query or demand answered without delay. Websters have ultra-high expectations of service and product performance; they have a demanding curiosity that expects answers *now*; and they expect to be entertained and diverted constantly.

- Their responses are born of the skills and weaknesses they've learnt from the interactive environment: they're fast icon readers, trained in the art of recognising branding as well as programming instructions; they're facile Web navigators; they lack patience and creativity.

- The future consumer will need to clearly perceive an added value from visiting the offline store. In the shopping environment of the future, products will be demonstrated in context. Retail stores will need to be inspiring, creative, fun and original to fulfil their role of stimulating purchases.

- When a story starts for a webster, it has to continue. Products isolated from evident application, that don't exhibit their context, won't be relevant to the future consumer. To be visible, products will have to either be the result of a preceding product or lead to a new one.

- But the most important reason why every product will have to be part of a chain reaction is because the familiarity that context creates will foster loyalty. Loyalty is inextricably related to trust, the retailer's and e-tailer's most precious acquisition.

Action Points

Examine the webster types (explorers, visibles, status quos, non-teens and isolaters) and traits (material demands, social networking, lack of creativity, entertainment demands, visual literacy, value demands and brand consciousness). Analyse what type of e-teen customer you're likely to attract with a clicks-&-mortar version of your business and how you will respond to this market segment's needs.

How much is your current revenue dependent on the webster contribution to it? Do you expect your revenue to be affected by webster consumption trends in the future? Examine these webster categories and analyse what type of e-teen customer you're likely to attract with a clicks-&-mortar version of your business:

Explorers are characterised by a high degree of creativity and independence.

Visibles are the most noticeable members of a student population, the "cool" kids.

Status quos display traditional values of moderation and pride in achievement. Mainstream acceptance is important to them.

Non-teens are most unlike the typical teenager, usually because of their lack of social skills, indifference to teen culture and style and/or their intense interest in academic pursuits.

Isolators are alienated from both their peers and adults by their disruptive or dysfunctional behaviour and antisocial psychologically.

In a clicks-&-mortar partnership, how well do you think your business will respond to one or more of these webster traits? How will you achieve this response?

Websters *want* and they want *now* Research shows that 78% of parents accede to their children's demands when shopping.

Websters network E-teens and e-kids conduct much of their social interaction via their mobile phones or PCs.

Websters lack creativity Kids' patience and imaginative control has decreased with the availability of quick-response interactivity and "pre-programmed fantasy" toys.

Websters need entertainment Websters crave and demand diversion and entertainment, and need to comprehend products as part of a context that is meaningful to them.

Websters are icon readers Being used to responding to visual prompts on the PC screen and mobile display, websters' icon-literacy fosters superficial comprehension and a preference for short messages.

Websters want added value Websters are keenly aware of their consumer rights and have high expectations of product performance. They also require ever-changing stimulation and entertainment.

Websters choose brands Websters are highly brand conscious and brands dominate their product choices.

So now you're analysing your clicks-&-mortar's relevance to the webster market. One way to ensure that your concept will always be up-to-date and able to respond to the rapidly changing world of e-teen consumer demands is to consider acting as an infomediary. So, read on. Turn to Chapter 13 and see how this leadership concept might change your clicks-&-mortar vision.

Chapter 13

The Infomediary
Revolution

E-commerce is growing exponentially, and e-tailing sites are mushrooming around the globe. The consumer is faced with an infinite array of choices and, in the process, is becoming confused by it all. One outcome of this proliferation is the growing need for shopping assistance tools: infomediaries.

As more e-commerce sites appear on the Internet, the need for tools to help consumers navigate their way through the maze of choices is growing.

You might think online auction sites are the answer to this shopping dilemma. The auction at least defines market price according to consumer demand. But the fact that more than 50 new auction sites appear daily on the Net makes it tough for most of these sites to generate the traffic and, consequently, the auction activity needed to ensure attractive offers. Because the race to capture consumers is spread among so many competitors, there's not enough interest on every site to stimulate the market and establish price. Moreover, with over than 20,000 auction sites available on the Net, comparing price and assessing each site's selection and range have become baffling tasks for the individual consumer.

From One-to-Many to One-to-One

While auction sites have been garnering attention, a range of new online shopping concepts has quietly been born. The emergence of the "infomediary" indicates consumer confusion with the plethora of choices now available on the Net, and it signals that auction sites are not necessarily a means of making shopping on the Net easier. Infomediaries are shopping agents that assist with personal shopping. They are tools that virtually and continually roam aisles and rifle through racks, looking for items to fit the individual shopper's tastes, needs and budget.

The need for infomediary tools that roam the Internet looking for items to fit the individual shopper's tastes, needs and budget, indicates consumer confusion with the array of choice on the Net.

The Dawn of the Infomediary

The term "infomediary" was coined in 1998 to describe an independent third party which acts as a buffer between the Internet and the consumer. The infomediary comes to know the individual over time, and customises Internet data according to their consumer interests and behaviours. The infomediary also arranges data in relevant one to one formats and, at some point, is able to react on behalf of its clients by purchasing products, searching information and selecting data.

The infomediary has evolved as a tool for helping create an online relationship between the portals (or brands) and the consumer. The term has been seized upon enthusiastically, and so has the concept. Infomediaries are thought to be the answer to ameliorating consumer problems of mainly selection with the Net. Infomediaries provide consumers with tools to help them compare data and thereby select the sites that suit them best, isolate products they're after, and so on. There are also infomediaries that can help consumers protect their privacy.

Infomediaries to Internet users act as agents do to movie stars. They are with them twenty-four hours a day; they know exactly what their users prefer and what they dislike; they accept offers on their users' behalf; they respond on behalf of their clients; and can act as proxies when their users aren't available. So far only bits and pieces of the concept have emerged: we have yet to see a true infomediary in operation.

> *Infomediaries customise Internet data for individuals whose consumer interests and behaviours it comes to know over time.*

How Our Shopping Experience Will Change

I want to give you an insight into how shopping is likely to be within a few years. Let me take you on an infomediary shopping journey.

First of all, forget about surfing the Internet. Surfing as we know it today will change dramatically, and it's possible that the current incarnation of the Internet will become obsolete. Why? Because the infomediary, in various forms, will help the consumer to cut away information clutter and focus on relevant material. And the Internet, as a communication, information sharing and consumer tool, will be joined by tens of new media channels: everything from the mobile phone to the microwave, including the refrigerator and stationery cupboard, will be online, and thus remove Net surfing from the position of centrality it has in our lives today.

Surfing will be reincarnated as searching, and infomediaries will assume this responsibility. The Internet already consists of more than three billion pages and expectations are that it will grow to more than ten billion pages by 2002. Given this exponential growth, humans will be unable to satisfactorily find what they're after simply by surfing. Their agents, the infomediaries, will constantly keep an eye on what's relevant for their "masters".

In response, the type of information we see on the Internet today will alter over time. It will become easier to read, understand and navigate. But it's also likely that a second Internet layer will appear, one which works with emerging online channels like the mobile Internet, household hardware and whitegoods, television and the infomediaries. This "second Internet" won't be useful unless it's connected to a device which can translate the data into action. For example, the fridge might receive data on grocery specials from the second Internet, contribute its own data about your shopping needs, send your shopping list to the supermarket and prompt delivery of your foodstuffs.

A New Search Dimension

Searching, as we exercise it today, will also change. Typing in a keyword and receiving 100,000 or more link suggestions won't work. How could we possibly sit and check every link the keyword search suggests?

Search directory companies like BT LookSmart (www.btlooksmart.com) have taken searching to its next stage or progress by employing real people specialised in all sorts of disciplines. They surf the Net, and by applying quality-assessment criteria they select useful sites to fit a range of product categories. The third search development will be one in which the search result is no longer dependent on keywords but on individual consumer profiles.

Let's imagine that you key in "insurance" as your search criteria. Instead of showing you a list of the 100 best (as assessed by established criteria) insurance websites available on the Net, the system will recognise your profile from previous visits to all sorts of sites. If you've bought a car online the system will suggest, as the first link, an automobile insurance company specialising in the type of car you purchased. As the system becomes more sophisticated it will be able to take into account your geographic position as a search criterion. When you use your mobile phone to access the Internet, it will feed your exact position into the search criteria you have entered. If you key "flowers" into your phone, rather than offering a list of flower stores in a dotcom domain category, the system will point out the two florists closest to you.

Removing Buyer Barriers

One of the chief barriers preventing people's conversion to Internet shopping is the lack of trust they feel in the system: the unfamiliar dotcom business, untried products, the inability to actually see, feel, touch, taste and smell a real sample, and the fact that they have to launch their credit card number into this unknown territory. But apart from the insecurities cyberspace instils in some consumers, there's another major obstacle to the widespread adoption of Internet consumerism: the user's inability to find what he or she is looking for. The arrival of the infomediary will help remove this barrier.

Infomediaries will supply their clients with data that's not only relevant to them but which has their permission to be presented to them. The "virtual shopping list" will, therefore, become a household fact. It will be based on the consumer's previous shopping patterns rather than being composed by the consumer before each virtual shopping expedition. The system will already know that last week the householder purchased cereal, milk, ice-cream and Pepsi. Each of these products will have its own purchase cycle, based on the consumer's history and known to the system. This data will collude to calculate likely grocery and personal needs, compose a list for the consumer's onscreen perusal, and when commanded, order the goods and their delivery from the online supermarket.

Already supermarket databases can predict, with about 90% accuracy, the FMCG products consumers will purchase every week. Some virtual shops today offer free delivery of a standing order if the customer only changes two or less items on their shopping list.

Clicks-&-Mortars and Data Synergy

So what has this to do with clicks-&-mortars? A lot! Here's why. The virtual shopping list is the link. As consumers become more time-poor they have a greater need for time-saving aids. This makes the role of a shopping assistant a welcome one. An infomediary, or let's call it a virtual shopping list, can know its user's shopping habits, needs and preferences.

The technology is likely to affect every facet of our shopping behaviour and the changes will put question marks on the future role of the retailer. And this is where clicks-&-mortars step in. The online/offline setup builds a bridge between traditional shopping behaviour and cyberspace from whence consumer profiling data will come. Retailers, being part of a clicks-&-mortar future won't escape the inevitable changes this bridge will demand. Nor should they wish to. They will no longer be exclusively in the goods-selling business. They will move into the media and research business. Really, they will be selling space in the consumer's brain. Let me explain.

Retailers: From Sales Vehicles to Media Players

The whole game will be about getting as close to the consumer's decision-making processes as possible. The closer a retailer and e-tailer get to this process the more influence they can exert upon it. In the good old days, television advertising had to create an impression that lasted in the consumer's mind for at least eighteen hours. Because of the advertising overload, with so much information being placed in front of consumers, the retention rate has shortened. So advertising oppor-

Proximity to the consumer's decision-making processes allows retailers and e-tailers to exert more influence on them.

tunities are no longer simply defined by media choice. Timing has a value of its own.

As a result, it is those minutes before the consumer makes up their mind and selects products from the shelves that have become valuable windows. This, combined with the retailer's ability to actually see what products sell, why and when, makes this window even more interesting and relevant. In control of this data, the retailer is potentially the most effective brand promoter in the future of e-commerce. So, retailers are likely to become media players: they will sell those windows, the space in the consumer's brain in the minutes before purchase, with decision-making and product selection. This space could earn the retailer more revenue than it earns from selling the products.

All this ties into the ability to predict the consumer's behaviour before, during and after the purchase takes place. If a retailer has monitored a consumer's purchase of Gillette shaving cream tens of times, the modelling process is easy, and the hit rate high. By "hit rate" I mean successful prediction: the ability to predict what a customer wants and ensure that the customer acts according to the prediction. Profiling and modelling will make purchases predictable. Let's say I usually purchase Gillette razor blades. What if the day before I need to restock my shaving gear I received a message from my supermarket (or from Wilkinson Sword — if the company has purchased this space on my list) making me a special offer on Wilkinson Sword instead. Buy two for the price of one, say. I would then have to weigh up whether the delivery charge I would have to pay on my groceries would be outweighed by the saving I would make on the razors. (A virtual shopping principle will be that the less changes a consumer makes to their regular shopping list, the easier it is for supermarkets to predict purchase volumes months in advance and achieve discounts from suppliers and manufacturers. These discounts will be passed on to customers as a reward for not altering their orders.)

So how is it that the retailer will be entering the media business? Do you think Wilkinson Sword would be getting the advantages of promotion via countless personalised virtual shopping lists for free? Of course not. What do you reckon the price for being promoted through the supermarket's most valuable link with the consumer might be? I can tell you now, and I'm sure you'll have rightly presumed, that the fee would be enormous because the conversion rate is likely to be higher than ever.

Retailer Data Mining

But wait! There's more. If I decide to purchase the recommended products, I confirm that the purchase suggestion the supermarket made was correct. But if I don't respond to such offers my silence also adds valuable information to the database. When Amazon.com sends you product recommendations, they're based on your previous purchase habits. Yet many people complain that the information isn't spot on. Some people even say that they don't reply back because it's never correct. But think about this. Not replying is the same as confirming that they were wrong, all relevant information for Amazon.com's data modelling.

Amazon.com has in the past surveyed the books people were buying and asked consumers if they'd be interested in being told of their chosen author's next book release. Let's take this survey fact one hypothetical step further. Imagine that Amazon.com asked its users what type of Stephen King book they would next like to read. Based on the feedback they would then be able to conclude that x-thousand preferred a book about such-and-such a topic with this-and-that storyline. Amazon.com's next question would be whether respondents would be prepared to purchase the hypothetical book if it were to be published. Amazon.com would be able to contact Stephen King's publisher to say that they had presold x-thousand copies of a Stephen King book possibly titled *The Such-and-Such of This-and-That*. What would Stephen King's publisher do? Turn down the offer? Or ask Stephen King to start writing?

The key to predictive modelling and product development is in the clicks-&-mortar relationship. Co-operative online/offline retailers will have a major advantage over purely online or offline setups: the synergy of data sharing.

Loyalty Programs

Many retailers have established loyalty programs as a means of getting to know each customer that visits the bricks-&-mortar store. Customers belonging to the loyalty program earn points as rewards for purchases in the store and its affiliates. Such schemes generate volumes of data. Every single item purchased by every single consumer is recorded. The resultant databases are potential gold mines. But how often is their potential realised?

Australia's largest retailer, Coles Myer, established a concept in 1994 named FlyBuys™. The purpose of the program was to give consumers points as rewards for purchasing within affiliated stores, and also to develop profiles of consumers' shopping behaviour. Since its launch, the program has since been hugely successful. It has attracted 2.1 million members — 15% of Australia's population. Interestingly, FlyBuys™ has never leveraged upon the huge amount of knowledge they have accumulated about their customers. Its customer contacts are still via mass communication with no attempt at any one to one contact. Coles Myer is not unique in this lack of data use. Most retailers running loyalty programs struggle with data mining, and their valuable databases remain untapped. That's as ineffective as orchestrating a direct marketing campaign and not sending out the letters. It's imperative that you use the data you gather by transforming it into relevant statistics and using it to analyse consumer purchasing patterns.

Tesco, a supermarket chain in the UK has managed to get this far (see also case study in Chapter 1). In fact the company has won several awards several for its outstanding loyalty program which is recognised as one of the most advanced in the world. But it did take Tesco more than ten years to establish this well-regarded and useful program.

Ensure that the same type of data is collected online as well as offline
Integrate your two systems to create an all-channel profile of each customer. Few retailers have reached this integrated and sophisticated level of database construction. More usually, the online database and the offline database struggle to work together because either the systems talk different languages or because they are simply capturing different types of data.

Transform data into a means of communicating one to one with your customer Only a handful of companies in the world have achieved this, which makes the value of the achievement that much greater. Let me tell you about one of them.

Outside Phoenix, Arizona is a low-rise building surrounded by lawns and a chain-link fence. The building's like an iceberg with most of its bulk existing underground. It's under Phoenix airport's flight path, so the building was designed to withstand the direct impact of a 747 crash. The chain-link fence is meant to thwart assault by a speeding car. Though should a tank get through the fence, the lawns would give way, plunging the trespassing vehicle into a concrete-lined trench. The company within is protecting a super-sophisticated database. This database is so advanced that it allows near one to one communication with customers.

The company is American Express and its defences should tell you something about how valuable its database is. Its system enables the company to send out customised letters with unique finesse, to as few as six people at a time. The letters are generated automatically thanks to Amex's years of well-integrated customer profiling data.

The capacity for one to one marketing and predictive modelling should be prime goal among the clicks-&-mortar's priorities.

Predictive Modelling
We don't yet have a model for a predictive virtual shopping list. Several retailers are developing versions of these, but many claim to be at least six months to a year away from launching them. Virtual shopping lists are one outcome of the transformation of consumer purchase data into predictive

models. Predictive modelling is central to enabling your system to use history to predict what product choices consumers will make in the future, and to inform consumers about them before they know themselves. Barnes

> *Predictive modelling saves the consumer time and the clicks-&-mortar money.*

& Noble is the only clicks-&-mortar book retailer that's achieved workable predictive modelling. Amazon.com, as a pure-play, has been doing it for years.

Affinity grouping In August, 1999, Amazon.com introduced a service called "Purchase Circles". The feature was designed to find the ten hottest products in 3,000 different cities, universities and various public and private workplaces. For example, one month the bestselling book among Walt Disney Company employees was *Dancing Corndogs in the Night: Reawakening Your Creative Spirit.* Amazon.com came up with the result by cross-indexing the bestselling items with buyers' postal codes and e-mail addresses.

The "affinity-grouping" technology was created by PlanetAll, which Amazon.com purchased in 1998. For some people, it was a chilling reminder of how much data Amazon.com has on the purchasing habits of its fourteen million customers.

Visit **DualBook.com/cbb/ch13/VirtualShoppingList** and I'll tell you about the most recent virtual shopping list developments.

Supply-on-Demand Systems

By integrating captured consumer data with suppliers' backend infrastructure, some manufacturers and retailers have developed really successful supply-on-demand systems. These systems allow both parties to update each other constantly on stock levels, potential demands and order flow. For example, in 1995 Toys "R" Us introduced a system that was totally integrated with LEGO's ordering system. So when LEGO stock was low in any of the Toys "R" Us stores, suitable LEGO orders were generated.

Drugstore.com, in partnership with Rite Aid (see case study in Chapter 5), has developed a fully integrated system which follows the order flow electronically and ensures that all orders placed online are immediately transferred to the stores, and if necessary, to the manufacturer. They are one of the few enterprises to have integrated the system on a clicks-&-mortar basis.

A survey of twenty-five manufacturers and twenty retailers carried out by Forrester Research in 2000, showed that 23% of retailers used the Intranet to connect with the manufacturer and 35% used EDI (one of the world's largest electronic data research companies). However, 52% of retailers expect to be using Intranet by 2002 to connect with their manufacturers. Even though not much customer data sharing occurs between manufacturers and retailers, up to 17% of retailers expect to be sharing inventory management and 16% expect to be sharing customer service by 2002.

Model 13.1: *What percentage of retailers do manufacturers connect with using these methods?*

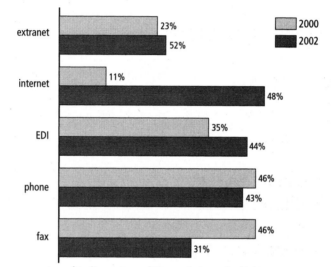

Average percentage of trading partners of 23 manufacturers (multiple responses accepted)

Source: The Manufacturer-Retailer Link, *Forrester Research, 2000*

If clicks-&-mortars also manage to integrate their consumer profiling data with manufacturers' production programs they can take advantage of new product developments and new trend predictions, making the most of fleeting trends and product-chain purchase reactions. This concept is explained under **Presentation and Context** in Chapter 12. As I write, no clicks-&-mortar retailer has achieved this level of data integration. I would expect, though, that we'll see one or two early examples of totally integrated systems by 2002.

Model 13.2: *What Processes Do Manufacturers Share With Retailers over the Net?*

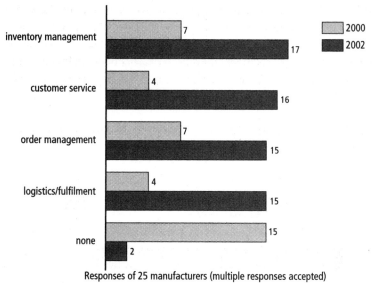

Responses of 25 manufacturers (multiple responses accepted)

Source: The Manufacturer-Retailer Link, *Forrester Research, 2000*

Visit **DualBook.com/cbb/ch13/DataSystem**
for the latest on fully integrated data system developments.

Where are the Clicks-&-Mortar Infomediaries?

Always-online shopping browsers that float onscreen while shoppers surf from e-tailer to e-tailer, like Entrypoint.com, NeoPlanet, and RUSure, may represent the first generation of infomediaries. These e-commerce shopping guides do all the things we'd expect of them as independent third parties: they track consumer habits and negotiate prices on behalf of the shopper, compare products and brands.

The real benefit of these shopping agents is that, because they roam the Net comprehensively and investigate consumer criteria thoroughly, they're able to recommend solutions to consumers that they themselves may never have come up with alone. These personal shopping tools establish the consumer's brand loyalty by demonstrating an understanding of the consumers for whom they work. And this is a factor that promises to influence the shopper more strongly than even price or selection.

The data an infomediary gathers creates both a solid platform for customisation and a negotiating tool. As a negotiator, the infomediary can gain discounts for consumers by leveraging on the bank of information it has about them. PrivaSeek.com is one of the better-known services. It will not only buy your next flight to LA, but will also know what airline class you prefer to travel, what hotel you normally use, the name of your favourite restaurant, and will pre-order your duty-free items before you even ask. This is an outcome of predictive modelling, a technology that will become key in all Internet-based communication.

Predictive modelling saves the consumer time and the clicks-&-mortar money. It also opens the door for advertisers to target messages. The Australian site Freeonline.com.au, for example, offers free Internet access and advanced infomediary services. Access is free as long as users allow the infomediary to monitor their behaviour.

Take the case of someone spending a lot of time on BMW's site. The system will automatically capture consumer data and inform BMW about potential customers, their interests and geographic location. BMW will then customise individual ads for those users. These messages won't appear as e-mails, but as ads on the screen. If users show interest in them, their identity will be made available to BMW.

Concepts like Freeonline.com.au and PrivaSeek.com will not only change advertising on the Net, but will force portals to offer much more than stock quotes and horoscopes. They will become infomediaries, gigantic databases, the purpose of which will be to collect and use consumer data and achieve one to one communication between brands and consumers.

Little wonder Excite and Yahoo! have acquired some of the world's most respected data-mining companies over the last six months. Attempts have been tested since 1998, but so far no clicks-&-mortar retailer has established itself as an infomediary between consumers and brands.

Optimising Information

As I discussed in Chapter 12, the future retailer will be a demonstration centre, a recreational facility and a data-gathering house employing analysts to constantly evaluate data and make actionable observations on consumer trends and needs. Both the online and offline clicks-&-mortar partners will have joint dominion over massive consumer databases which will demonstrate how to manage five key optimisation areas:

1. Consumer spending across all channels.
2. Consumer return-visit rate.
3. Selling accumulated data.
4. Value of the channel's real estate.
5. Selling real estate.

Optimise consumer spending across all channels If a television show doesn't attract as many viewers as expected it's taken off the air, immediately and with no ceremony. Some shows have only lasted for one episode but station executives know they've missed the mark. They're able to react this decisively and quickly because they constantly monitor viewer statistics and measure and compare how well viewers are receiving shows.

The future retailer will have to be able to monitor reception and respond similarly. Most retailers haven't yet developed channel strategies to optimise revenue across all channels. This optimisation is achieved by having each channel perform the role it's most suited to, without replicating, disrupting or cannibalising the roles of parallel channels. Some channels perform better for some products than others, and clicks-&-mortars need to understand their products and consumers thoroughly to direct their media avenues optimally. The mobile Internet, for example, is ideally suited for impulse FMCG purchases. The Internet channel suits products that attract consumer research. And the retail store suits products that consumers need to assess using all five senses.

Optimise consumers' return-visit rates Products will need to relate to product chain reactions: purchasing one product should automatically activate the consumer's purchase of another. Selecting a cereal, for example, should trigger a sale of milk. But besides this concept, the purchase of one product should necessitate a return visit to the store to acquire the next product in the chain. The gradual acquisition of a cutlery set, for example, or a dinner set, would require return visits to complete the set.

This optimisation function will also need to ensure that the consumer is spending their time in the best way when visiting each channel. If, for example, a consumer spends a lot of time purchasing repeat prescription medications from the offline store, the system should be alert to the situation and suggest that the consumer purchase the same product online. This encourages the consumer's return visits and optimises them by promising to save the customer time while, crucially, saving the retailer money.

Optimise the value of accumulated data by selling it Nobody knows customer flow better than the retailer, especially the retailer with data-capturing systems in place that allow minute by minute monitoring. You could say that research companies like AC Nielsen and Forrester Research are familiar with trends through their wealth of market research experience, but most consultancy data is sourced from panels of individuals gathered for the exercise. Only in a few countries is data sourced directly from the store by research companies. This data will be an important revenue source for clicks-&-mortars. Currently, such knowledge is more or less neglected or given out free of charge.

Optimise the value of channel real estate The mobile phone's display, the website inventory and the shelves in bricks-&-mortar stores all constitute property. Like consumer data, this real estate constitutes a revenue source for clicks-&-mortar players. In the past, instore POS materials were sometimes outlawed, as they were in the UK. Elsewhere, retailers charged brands money to have signage in their stores. Remember, almost 80% of worldwide marketing spending goes on below-the-line promotions (direct mail, events, competitions, etc., as opposed to above-the-line promotions like television, radio and print advertising). But in the future, POS materials will assume a range of forms. Every promotional element, from online coupons, direct e-mails, banner ads, listing fees and digital shelf displays will have a value and attract fees for using them. The value will be dependent on the level of consumer traffic in the given channel.

Sell real estate and products at the highest possible price The previous CEO of the Coca-Cola Company said that, in future, a Coke would be priced according to the temperature of the day. On a cold day, the price would go down. On a hot day, the price would go up. Theoretically, every product could have a variable price based on the time of the year or any other factor that could influence or discourage sales. Demand-controlled price will make the clicks-&-mortar environment a dynamic one across all channels.

Summary

- The infomediary is an independent third party that acts as a buffer between the Internet and the consumer. It customises Internet data for individuals whose consumer interests and behaviours the infomediary comes to know over time.
- As more e-commerce sites appear on the Internet, the need for tools to help consumers navigate their way through the maze of choices grows.
- The emergence of "infomediary" tools that roam the Net looking for items to fit the individual shopper's tastes, needs and budget, indicates consumer confusion with the plethora of choices now available on the Net.
- Surfing will be reincarnated as searching and the responsibility for this will be assumed by infomediaries. In response, information on the Internet will become easier to read, understand and navigate.

- Virtual shopping lists will be based on the consumer's historical shopping patterns rather than being composed by the consumer before each virtual shopping trip.
- The closer a retailer and e-tailer get to the consumer's decision-making processes the more influence they can exert upon them.
- The minutes before a consumer makes up their mind and selects a products from the shelf has become a valuable window. This, combined with the retailer's ability to actually see what products sell, why and when, makes this window even more interesting and relevant.
- Retailers are likely to become media players: they will sell those windows, the space in the consumer's brain occupied, in the minutes before purchase, with decision-making and product selection. This space could earn the retailer more revenue than from selling the products.
- All this ties into the ability to predict the consumer's behaviour before, during and after the purchase takes place.
- The key to predictive modelling and product development is in the clicks-&-mortar relationship. Co-operative online/offline retailers will have a major advantage over purely online or offline setups: the synergy of data sharing.
- Many retailers have established loyalty programs as a means of getting to know every customer that visits the bricks-&-mortar store.
- The resultant databases are potential, but currently, unresourced gold mines.
- Virtual shopping lists are one outcome of the transformation of consumer purchase data into predictive models.
- If clicks-&-mortars integrate their consumer profiling data with manufacturers' production programs they can take advantage of product developments and trend predictions, making the most of fleeting fashions and product-chain purchase reactions.
- The portals of today will probably not exist a year from now, thanks to the appearance of infomediary-based one to one communication.
- Predictive modelling saves the consumer time and the click-&-mortar money. It also opens the door for advertisers to target messages.

Action points

Do you believe the role of the infomediary will affect your business? If your answer is yes, let me drive you through a couple of scenarios.

List the downsides your business represents, according to your consumer. For example, does the consumer find shopping in your store or on your site tedious? What would you do if your consumer consider transferring patronage from your concept to the competitor's? What would you do to encourage the consumer to return?

Could an infomediary ameliorate any of these downsides in the customer's eyes? Nominate them.

Would you consider adding the infomediary role to your online business mix? Knowing that such a development takes time and patience, list five objectives you would expect to achieve by operating an infomediary program.

Turn your objectives into action points by identifying deliverables, responsibilities and deadlines.

Compare your existing data-collection processes with the data collection you would need to make Step 3 and Step 4 improvements realities. Now, extend your vision and create a new list of the data would you dream about having access to five years from now.

Chapter 14

The 10 Critical Success Factors

Creating a clicks-&-mortar partnership is highly complex, not only because the initiative requires command of emerging technologies, but also because it merges two disparate retail environments, polarised by culture, technology and method. After interviewing hundreds of dotcoms, bricks-&-mortars and clicks-&-mortars, I've honed down the factors that are most frequently cited by all parties as being crucial to clicks-&-mortar success. The result is a list of ten Critical Success Factors (CSFs).

Before looking at the ten CSFs, let's review four important steps in preparing for a clicks-&-mortar strategy's development. They deal with choosing the ideal clicks or mortar partner. In theory you only have one shot at this. Once the partner has been carefully chosen, there's no backing out.

1. **Determine what type of partnership would best suit your business's overall objectives.**
   Typically, a clicks-&-mortar partnership is based on one of these four categories:
   - A pure marketing relationship in which both parties support joint marketing exercises.
   - An infrastructure partnership in which infrastructure and distribution channels are shared and co-ordinated.
   - A product-development partnership in which product-development resources are pooled in a joint initiative.
   - A service-support partnership in which the clicks and the mortar of customers package solutions and services which are complementary to them.

   A partnership must fulfil at least one of the above four roles if it is to gain value for both parties and their customers.

2. **Evaluate the proposed partnership's potential synergy by assessing brand match, philosophy and value parallels, fulfilment capabilities, marketing objectives, human resources management, and so on.**
   Positive synergy is achieved when total value of the clicks-&-mortar businesses in partnership is greater than the value of each partner separately. Synergy should be achieved in all operational areas and its progress monitored and measured. For example, monitor developments in customer satisfaction, production and distribution efficiencies, the point of the proposed partner's differentiation in the marketplace.

3. **Determine the length of time you expect the partnership to live.**
   Some partnerships are planned to last forever, especially when they are motivated by joint distribution benefits. Others are temporary partnerships, only effective during a marketing campaign period. Lifespan depends on the objectives that occasioned the marriage and its subsequent success.

4. **Measure the partnership's progress towards operating synergy by defining deliverables, responsibilities and deadlines.**
   How will you know if the partnership is a success if you don't measure progress? Setting up expectations and milestones at the outset is essential

to the venture's success. Well-controlled and logical monitoring that keeps an eye on objectives and the clicks-&-mortar's progress towards their achievement maintains workplace morale, underlines purpose and keeps the organisation on track.

To ensure you're on the right track with your clicks-&-mortar strategy, check your situation, and that of your proposed partner, against the ten CSFs below.

Ten Critical Success Factors

1. Positive Synergy

A clicks-&-mortar partnership must achieve added value for both parties. Added value is attained through synergy in all operations. If the website is merely an extension of the store, or if the store is just an extension of the website, synergy has not been achieved. Synergy, the complementary union and operation of all joint effort, begins with a clear and shared business purpose and results in added value for both the consumer and the business partners: cost savings, increased infrastructural efficiencies, improved fulfilment capabilities, effective marketing initiatives, improved data-capturing and data-mining techniques, and so on. If such goals are not achievable, the clicks-&-mortar strategy should not be executed.

2. One to one Dialogue

A healthy clicks-&-mortar strategy should be reflected in both parties' increasingly close relationships with consumers. The end goal should be effective dialogue with the consumer that is so well-advised by joint data resources that it's conducted on a one to one basis.

3. New Revenue Channels

In the future, retailers will command new revenue streams from consumer profiling data — a new commodity. Manufacturers will pay premium rates for relevant consumer data that illuminates information on purchasing patterns, product selection and choice motivators. Such valuable information, monitored and gathered by the retailer, will be sought by brands wishing to embark upon one to one marketing strategies via the at-home Net and mobile Internet. The mobile Internet will enable brand exposure at the very minute a consumer makes a purchasing choice.

4. Optimum Brand Channel Strategies

The question is not fundamentally about whether a business should move on- or offline. It's about analysing brand, product and customer needs, and determining the channel which serves all three best and most profitably.

5. Constant Customer Consultation

There's no such thing as a standard customer. Consumer habits and preferences, tolerances and needs change every minute, so your clicks-&-mortar strategy needs to be flexible enough to accommodate frequent changes in consumer demand and behaviour. Survey your consumer group regularly to keep pace with its changing personality and expectations. And ensure your strategy responds accordingly.

6. Explicit Added Value

Consumers, especially the maturing Webster generation, are educated and cynical. They have high expectations of products and service and demand that these are met. The clicks-&-mortar must offer the consumer tangible value gains (better prices, more efficient service, larger selection, etc.) and ensure that every minute the consumer spends instore or online is optimised.

7. Cross-Channel Staff Co-operation

The clicks-&-mortar will fail if it gives the consumer the impression that its online channel doesn't co-operate with its online channel and vice versa. Value-adding synergy must be apparent in universal staff understanding of company objectives, values and operational systems and facilities.

8. User Power and Control

Consumers should never feel trapped into a purchase, a transaction channel or any relationship with your business. Foster a principle of consumer primacy in all communications with customers and staff.

9. Customer Contact Through All the Senses

The online channel is confined to communicating with the customer's eye and ear, so optimise the website's visual and aural message delivery. The retail outlet can communicate with all five senses and must do so with the objective of stimulating online purchases. Your promotional strategy will fail if one channel uses its capacities at the expense of the other.

10. The Brand is the Primary Tool

In a clicks-&-mortar partnership, as in any retail venture, it's vital to foster the healthy growth of your brand's image and reputation. Brand loyalty is just a short hop away from customer trust. Trust = brand. Without trust the brand can't survive online and will fade offline. Focused brand-building on the Internet is a prerequisite for creating solid clicks-&-mortar presence.

Chapter 15

E-tailing in the Year 2010

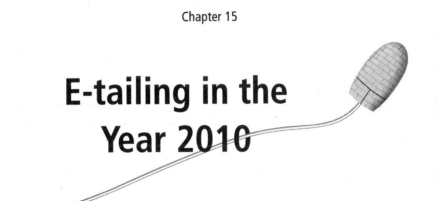

E-tailers and retailers are set to become real estate agents monitoring, valuing and optimising every square centimetre of Net space, every minute of Net time, and every second consumers spend in the store. The most valuable promotional real estate will be in the consumers' minds — in the few minutes before they make purchase decisions.

The consumer's point of greatest vulnerability, or receptiveness to suggestion exists as a small window. E-tailers and retailers will find ways to sell this space to brands. The retail store will be just one of a multitude of shopping channels, but it will be a consumer laboratory where consumer habits are tested and observed on a minute-by-minute basis. The bricks-&-mortar store will also be a demonstration centre, an environment where consumers can experience products with every one of their senses. The retail store will also be a place of entertainment where products are demonstrated in context to make their application to the consumer absolutely plain. Stores will change their entertainments often, concentrating on offering customers a multisensory recreational experience, redolent with reasons as to why consumers should visit the store.

One to One Marketing

It's amazing, isn't it? The World Wide Web as we know it today was born less than ten years ago. Would you have been able to predict the Internet's rise and development as a global information, commercial and social tool? Probably not! And nor would I.

Prediction is still a difficult pastime for me and forecasting what might happen for clicks-&-mortars, retailers, e-tailers, the Internet and the consumer a decade from now is no exception. But I do enjoy contemplating the matter, so I asked Martha Rogers and Don Peppers, authors of the groundbreaking book, *The One to One Future,* and founders of the leading management consulting firm, Peppers and Rogers Group, for their view of e-tailing in the year 2010.

2010 Predictions

By Don Peppers and Martha Rogers, Ph.D.

Within just a few years, it is likely that you will be able to count the number of times per day you are offline more easily than you can count the number of times a day you are online. You will surf the web more or less constantly, and not just from your personal computer, but from your cell phone or pager, your television, wrist watch, automobile, treadmill, or CD player. More devices will be connected to the Web than people, including refrigerators, soda machines, medical instruments, die cutters, thermostats, and so forth.

The company you work for will order its office equipment and supplies over the Web; it will schedule deliveries from suppliers over the web; and it will invoice customers, pay vendors, communicate with employees, customers, agents, channel partners, and others via the Web. Your company's website will increasingly become the company, maintaining automated relationships not just with customers, but with suppliers, lawyers, accountants, strategic-alliance partners, employees, contractors and perhaps even competitors.

At home, you will use smart refrigerators to note used items and create shopping lists for your next order. Stores will send you pre-populated email-shopping lists that include suggestions and leave room for comments. Once ordered, items will be delivered to a three-temperature delivery unit at your home or a designated pickup point, whether it be your office, day care, or service station, which also receives your postal and FedEx packages, dry cleaning and film processing. Some stores will even charge admission to partake in the overall experience of shopping in its traditional form.

By 2010, look for more integration across direct-to-consumer channels, as well as between Consumer Direct and bricks-&-mortar stores, throughout the purchasing process. Successful companies will leverage synergies at every point of contact with the customer. The most successful companies will be those that go a step beyond, using the interactivity Consumer Direct offers to cultivate Learning Relationships with their best customers so they can better meet, and even exceed, individual customer needs.

There will still be many other competitive tools for meeting with and selling to customers — tools such as call centers, retail outlets, automated sales forces, and so forth — but every single customer-interfacing technology will have to be integrated into a company's Web site in order to be effective at all.

We now know what the one to one future will look like. It is no longer a question of "if" this will happen, but "when." In just a few years, operating a genuinely customer-oriented company and Web site will not be a futuristic vision or a technological luxury, but a competitive necessity. Will you be ready?

www.1to1.com

Throughout this volume I've alluded to one to one marketing. We probably won't see a retailing evolution as momentous as this within the next century. Retailing couldn't become more intimate with the consumer than on a one to one basis! So, whatever happens in the consumer world over the next century is likely to be directed by the one to one principle. The only other change will be that we get better and better at it.

One to one is far from new. In the nineteenth century Japanese pharmacists installed medicine cabinets in most Japanese homes. The cabinets were monitored by the pharmacist who would make a weekly visit to check on the medical stock, herbs and potions, and replenish or replace if necessary. Unlike a hotel minibar, the contents of the cabinet changed over the years, according to the household's changing needs. Each cabinet would, naturally, alter reflecting the various maladies and seasonal illnesses. Some households' cabinets would consist mainly of vitamins; others had treatments for heart disease. Can you imagine what a wealth of knowledge pharmacists in Japan have inherited about their customers' families? Today's pharmacist in Japan has more than 100 years of observation to draw from. Now the same system could be conveniently reinvented, using the one to one principle which clicks-&-mortar shopping is taking us towards.

One to one in Action

Libra, a feminine hygiene brand, launched a revolutionary website back in 1997 which, in just over three years, became one of the most popular websites ever for girls in Australia and New Zealand. Why the popularity? Not because it carried articles about pop stars or images of the latest in fashion. It didn't. Not because it had fancy product updates or sex advice. It didn't. But the site was and still is popular because it offers a couple of very one to one-driven activities.

When you visit the site for the first time you have to type in a couple of details about yourself. The site then offers you access to the "sealed" section, a section ostensibly only for girls, though Mölnlycke statistics show that more than 5% of the visitors are men. In this section the girls are invited to type in the date of their previous period and of the period before that. Libra then sends an email two days before their next period is due reminding them about its imminent arrival.

The site also offers a "Dear Diary" facility. Here the girls can record their secrets, be reminded of their boyfriend's birthday, have a place to record homework due dates and other important details. All this information they can then exchange with their best friends.

Hundreds of thousands of Australian girls use the Libra web services creating an outstanding relationship between them and the brand. All Libra's tests show that girls determine what feminine protection brand they want to use at the age of fourteen, and by the time they turn twenty-four, their choice firmly remains with Libra. The triumphant result indicates that very few of the girls move to another brand. The site's target audience is girls from twelve to twenty-three years — a rather broad target group which led Libra to develop not one website but five websites in one. When becoming a member of the site you have to type in your birth date to get access to the horoscope. This simple data creates the foundation for the content direction. The younger audience is addressed in a mother-to-daughter tone, whereas the twenty-three-year-olds are spoken to as girlfriend to girlfriend. The content, tone-of-voice, and depth of sexual information varies from site to site.

Though the site was launched in 1997, it is characterised by the one to one focus we'll see more and more of in the future: the ability to talk directly to people as individuals, in fact so directly that primary criteria like income and geographic location not only determine the special offers and information sent, but they also govern the dialogue, the emotional slant and the tone — all of which varies from person to person.

The One to One Shopping Experience

One to one will become the guiding principle of every aspect of retailing and it will be the key factor in the changes we're likely to see. A one to one shopping experience will make the consumer feel in the centre before, during and after shopping. Remember, one to one wasn't achievable without a stupendous budget before now. The Internet and automated databases have made the technique possible, a technique that is already changing brand-building and marketing.

Before Shopping

When consumers explore offers on WebTV or the Net, the wireless device will listen and gather information about their preferences. The interactive fridge, which is already available, is an advanced device recording everything that's stored in it, everything that's used from it, use-by dates on each product, and it even monitor how much of each opened item remains. The garbage bin will scan its contents to capture other penetrating behavioural information.

All this information will be fed to the wireless Internet device that consumers will carry and which will act as a bridge between home and store. So, while traditional marketing tools will dominate the pre-shopping phase, shoppers' preferences will have been mapped and communicated by the wireless device. It will communicate individuals' consumption information while primary data (like addresses, contact numbers) will be provided by the telephone company that handles the mobile Internet phone. The store is likely to know more about consumers' shopping needs than they do themselves. It will know what products they're out of and need to purchase again, what they purchased on their last visit but didn't like, what products they're considering purchasing (based on attention given to their exposure on television and on information requests), and what products they can afford to buy and which ones they probably can't.

You might wonder what the added value is in you visiting the store. Why should you go at all? Considering that 80% of our weekly grocery shopping consists of repeat, or usual, purchases everything is predicted and prepared. This sort of shopping could be handled by the virtual shopping list. The goal for advertisers will be to get their product onto your virtual shopping list, because once there, it will nearly guarantee a purchase. A major revenue stream for future retailers will be selling this advertising space.

Precision marketing One to one marketing, with a clear focus on quality and message delivery to target consumers, will be of pivotal importance in the clicks-&-mortar future. Retailers will become knowledge centres, supplying manufacturers with consumer behaviour, preferences and trends data. They will broaden their revenue sources from being primarily focused on over-the-counter-sales to knowledge sales and access-to-consumer sales.

The supermarket is the last delivery mechanism in the consumer food chain, and is therefore closest to consumers' decision processes. So, it's a distinct possibility that the retailer's richest revenue stream will come from media sales: inclusion on virtual shopping lists and access to consumers during their decision-making moments will be the most highly valued. Data on consumer behaviour and preferences in relation to product categories and brands will also be a retailer revenue source.

During Shopping

Two shopping influences will emerge as you embark on each shopping experience. Brands and retailers will have been competing for inclusion on that virtual shopping list which predicts up to 80% of your purchases. And the 20% that remains unspecified, which is subject to your own response to the shopping experience, is the second area of influence brands will target.

Eighty per cent Clicks-&-mortar retailers will compete to manage your virtual shopping list. Marketers will use familiar points of differentiation to exact your patronage: price, service and return policy, freshness and delivery costs. Retailers might also promote their hit rates, the accuracy with which they predict your needs. Their advertising might claim a 98% hit rate, offer free delivery, save you planning your own shopping and offer discounts for not altering the items on the virtual shopping list. Hit rates highly valued by many customers, as will return policies. For example, if an incorrect product is delivered will the consumer be allowed to keep the product free of charge, or will it be replaced with the correct item?

Twenty per cent This is where brands have the freedom to capture new customers. The during-shopping experience exposes customers to impulse-driven selections. As discussed in Chapter 8, retailers will create a multi-sensory shopping environment with product demonstrations, contextual displays and opportunities for consumers to see, hear, taste, feel and smell.

A portion of the 20% (and perhaps of the 80%) will be fulfilled by purchases made through online auctions. It's likely shelf prices won't be fixed but will vary according to what day it is, the time of day, the weather, the campaigns running at the particular time, price wars, etc. And the consumer will be able to use the online auction to compare prices between shops. Retailers will make a practice of auctioning some products just to attract new customers.

The shopping experience Retail outlets will become entertainment centres, theme parks for shoes, cars, and so on. Their existences will be determined by the number of visitors they attract, the number of repeat visits those consumers make, and the length of time they spend there. Bricks-&-mortar stores will be exhibition halls with many demonstrations going on simultaneously. The demonstrations will be aimed at harnessing the consumer's 20% of product selection, the impulse-driven portion, for the brands concerned. Like any trade exhibition, the exhibitors will have to pay a premium price for representation. The retailer's firm focus will be on their base business, the 80% which will take place outside the store, from the consumer's home via the virtual shopping list. The aim will be to constantly improve the hit rate and promote repeat purchases.

Offline/online co-dependency The gap between offline and online retailing will disappear with the growth of clicks-&-mortar as the retailing norm. Clicks-&-mortars won't be able to afford any gaps as these will hinder that valuable information flow. Pure-plays will have to team up with real world retailers or have some sort of bricks-&-mortar presence to demonstrate new products and to stand a chance of becoming part of the 80% portion of the consumer's repeat shopping choices. Equally, retailers won't survive without an online presence. Without it they will be cutting themselves from 80% of potential product sales revenue.

After Shopping

Product purchases will trigger offers. Brands will offer consumers a 10% discount on the product in return for accepting follow-up brand information. This strategy will enable brands to follow and predict the consumer's behaviour and it will parallel the store's loyalty program. Together the two strategies will be aiming to secure return visits from consumers and to upsell or cross-sell product categories, thus optimising the consumer contact by achieving maximum sales per dialogue, per minute, per square metre, per every infrastructural investment the clicks-&-mortar makes.

To avoid being solely dependent on the supermarket for consumer access, brands will run parallel marketing programs with other brands in an effort to secure their place on your virtual shopping list. They'll also try to become independent of the supermarket by capturing their own consumer data so that manufacturers can predict needs and prompt sales.

The clicks-&-mortar supermarket will be focused on moving the power over consumer choice from brands to the retailer which could see the value of the brand fall and the manufacturer's role in price setting dissolve. Retail prices will vary according to demand. If every consumer chooses brand X, the price of brand Y will fall to attract customers. Purchase choices will activate responses from competing brands. They'll become more visible on television and WebTV, presenting targeted consumers with tailored commercials. The days of one commercial for all viewers will be over.

Retail's ultimate goal is and will be to maximise repeat purchases. Apart from the revenue gain, repeat purchases offer the retailer the benefit of being able to predict consumer choices more easily. The greater the predictive accuracy, the better the clicks-&-mortar's product delivery and hit rate will become. Ultimately, consumer loyalty will be rewarded by the retailer's ability to predict purchase patterns and increase the virtual shopping list's hit rate.

All clicks-&-mortar communication channels (broadcast and print media, WebTV, the mobile phone, interactive household goods, and so on) will merge into one information pipeline capturing and diagnosing consumer data. Each channel will be interactive and capable of conducting one to one communication with consumers. Monologues won't satisfy webster consumers. Dialogue will be fundamental to this interactive-trained generation and their presumption of informed personal attention will demand responsive and intelligent brand-building and product communication. Information technology has revolutionised our marketing orientation, which can no longer be governed by the principles of passive media reception. Interactive media is leading brand-building and marketing towards the one to one goal. It will be a matter of months before the first results of interactive marketing strategies and one to one communications become apparent. Test trials have been going on for some time in Massachusetts, USA and in Helsinki, Finland. But are we, as consumers, ready for it?

Are We Ready For One to One?

Resolving privacy issues will be critical to the realisation of any part of the interactive marketing vision. And existing legislation concerning the individual's privacy varies around the world. The Internet's global penetration and embrace being both its value and threat, will be at the centre of complicated local, national and international debates. Until now, every nation has been built upon unique and well-guarded identities forged through discrete experiences of shared and singular histories. How will the Internet be used in balancing global interaction with the maintenance of multitudinously various cultural identities and perceptions? Marketing and brand-building are part of civilisation's commercial and social development, and like all contributors to it, marketing's evolution in response to technological change will influence change in human cultures.

All human evolution is gradual, and cultural change cannot be forced without causing trauma and damage. The ideas are with us, and like social developments throughout history, so is the vision. But the technology has led the vision; it's already available and so is the know-how to handle it. Human reticence will control the pace of growth towards the interactive vision. The question is, are we as consumers prepared to enter the one to one world?

Visit **DualBook.com/cbb/ch15/TheFuture**
and check out the latest views on what the future of
e-tailing might look like.

A final word . . .

Before you put this book on the shelf one question might be – when has my clicks & mortar strategy succeeded? This final page is to help you answer that question. The guidelines below are a simple way for you to ensure that your business will always have the right focus to be the best player on the field.

BenchMarketing

Success in retail or e-tail is in most cases a reflection of how strong your focus on your core expertise has been. As stated throughout the book, a clicks-&-mortar strategy is successful when retailers and e-tailers keep their focus on what they are good at and also team up with partners outside their field of expertise. It goes without saying that successful retailing is much more than selling products in a store. It is everything from excellent supply chain management, branding, communication, navigation and people management. That your business survives is a reflection that all these elements are handled well. On the other hand, I would be surprised if your business is the best in all areas required to run a successful business. Enter BenchMarketing.

Who is the best out there?

Regardless of whether you are a bookstore, hi-fi store, pharmacy or car dealer, the importance of not just comparing your business with the category leader within your field is imperative. Here is why. The ability to communicate and build a world-recognised brand is really a separate discipline – Virgin's Richard Branson has managed to handle this with excellence. But just as important as marketing is the infrastructure of your store, the navigation outside and inside your store, placement of products on shelves, customer service and guidance, the price and quality of products, the selection, the cleanliness of your store and so on. Though your competitor might, overall, be the best within your category, I am sure they are not the best within each of these specialised fields.

Ask yourself who is the best within each of the 10 to 15 categories that form the critical success criteria for your store concept, then run through the BenchMarketing process. Avis might be the best at guiding its customers to its offices, so your questions should be: "What can I learn from them in the process of attracting customers to my store?" Disney might be the best at navigating customers through the park – anything to learn here? Toys "R" Us might excel at optimising space management in stores, Marriott Hotels could well be the best at handling a high number of customers checking out.

Becoming a leader within your field is not necessarily a comparison of your business with the category leader. Success may well depend upon the ability to learn and adapt knowledge from any successful businesss, regardless of the category they belong to or field they play in.

As people say in Scandinavia – you will never become a leader by following one leader's track in the snow.

Index to Case Studies